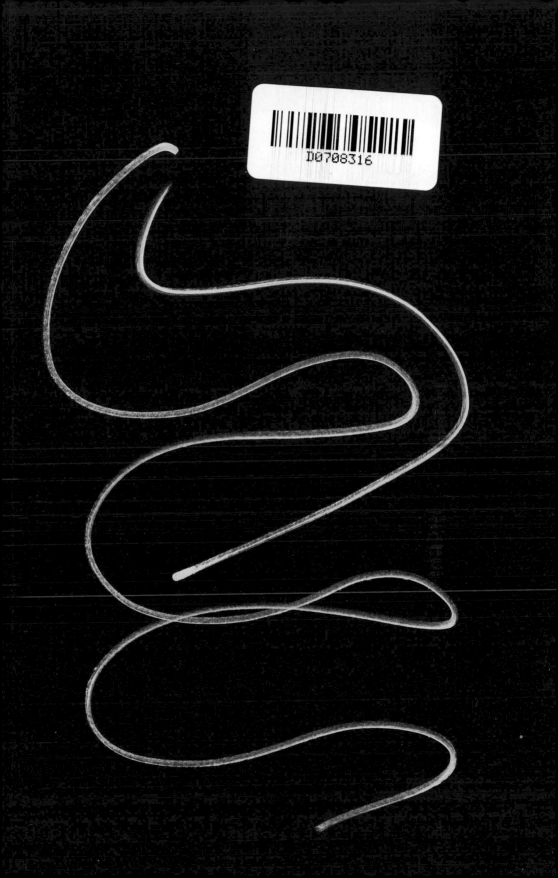

REEFER MEN

Also by Tony Thompson

Gangland Britain
Gangs

REEFER MEN

THE RISE AND FALL OF A
BILLIONAIRE DRUGS RING

TONY THOMPSON

HODDER &
STOUGHTON

Copyright © 2007 by Tony Thompson
First published in Great Britain in 2007 by Hodder & Stoughton
A division of Hodder Headline

The right of Tony Thompson to be identified as the Author
of the Work has been asserted by him in accordance with the
Copyright, Designs and Patents Act 1988.

A Hodder & Stoughton Book

2

A CIP catalogue record for this title is available from the British Library

Hardback ISBN 978 0 340 89933 5
Trade Paperback ISBN 978 0 340 89934 2

Typeset in Sabon by Hewer Text UK Ltd, Edinburgh

Printed and bound by Mackays of Chatham Ltd, Chatham, Kent

Hodder Headline's policy is to use papers that are natural,
renewable and recyclable products and made from wood grown
in sustainable forests. The logging and manufacturing
processes are expected to conform to the environmental
regulations of the country of origin.

Hodder & Stoughton Ltd
A division of Hodder Headline
338 Euston Road
London NW1 3BH

For Harriet

'He smokes a reefer, he gets high.
Then he flies to the sky.
That funny, funny, funny reefer man.'
Cab Calloway, 'Reefer Man'

'I can smoke anything . . . I even smoke that tied stick.'
'Tied stick?'
'That stuff that's tied to a stick.'
'Oh, Thai stick.'
Cheech and Chong, *Up in Smoke*

CONTENTS

CONTENTS

PROLOGUE
June 1988

All they had to do was sit back and wait.

It had taken months of planning, millions of dollars of invest-ment and the combined efforts of more than three hundred people from five different countries to pull it off, but the drugs were finally on their way.

In a quiet corner of a plush Bangkok restaurant the man behind the massive shipment, an eternal hippy named Brian Daniels, nursed a drink and contemplated his next move.

In little more than a decade 'The Ring' – a loose-knit collective of British, American and Australian entrepreneurs that Daniels had established – had smuggled more than $1 billion worth of marijuana into the United States and beyond. The business now operated on such a vast scale that just one shipment was enough to lower the price of pot along the entire West Coast of America.

Daniels had arrived in South East Asia at a time when the main drug associated with the region was opium. Marijuana was indigenous, particularly in the north-east of Thailand where the dried leaves were used as a seasoning in curries, but few locals smoked the weed and it barely figured in the illicit export trade at all.

Daniels soon changed all that. He forged alliances with the warlords who held sway over the remote regions where the drugs could be grown, helped to introduce new seed stocks and state-of-the-art agricultural techniques to boost production and quality. Within the space of a few years he found himself at the head of an enterprise that offered all the profit of the opium trade with only a fraction of the risk. What started out as little more than a group of college dropouts looking for cheap dope to peddle to

1

their friends had evolved into one of the most sophisticated and profitable drug rings on the planet.

Organised as a series of independent cells, each receiving their drugs from Daniels, the leadership of The Ring was composed of adrenaline junkies – amongst them helicopter pilots, rally drivers, powerboat racers, deep-sea salvage experts and members of the Army's elite special forces – whose methods were as slick as they were successful.

They chartered planes to fly over their smuggling routes to warn of nearby coastguard patrols. They used a network of informers and moles to feed false information to government agents, sending them off on outrageous wild goose chases. They even hired market research consultants to study the techniques used by unsuccessful gangs and ensure they would not make the same mistakes.

Over the years Daniels and other key members of The Ring had become multi-millionaires many times over and built up lifestyles to match. They owned sprawling estates in the heart of the English countryside, massive ranches teeming with wild horses in the Old West, and swish houses and apartment complexes in cities such as London, Paris, Hong Kong and New York. They owned whole fleets of luxury sports cars and had chauffeur-driven limousines and private jets on permanent standby. One bought an incredible yacht that didn't just have a helicopter landing-pad: it had its own helicopter.

The drugs kept getting through and the money kept piling up. Even the smugglers themselves were astonished at the seemingly endless demand for more and more marijuana.

'I don't even know who the fuck smokes all this shit,' said Thomas Sherrett, an Oregon-based importer and distributor, as he casually handed over $6 million in cash to two Mafioso money collectors sent by his main supplier. 'I figure they got like a few thousand people locked in rooms that have joints going day and night. I've been doing this for twenty-two years – who the fuck would smoke all that pot?'

Over the years the members of The Ring had enjoyed a run of

extraordinarily good fortune, but now the stakes were getting higher. Scotland Yard, the FBI, US Customs and the Drug Enforcement Administration were all closing in on their operations.

Several members had already been arrested and some had secretly testified before various grand juries. Others were believed to have become informants, and were suspected of turning up at crucial meetings while wearing wires or allowing incriminating phone calls to be recorded. Several major shipments had been intercepted. The gang's own informants did their best to keep them one step ahead but everyone was getting increasingly paranoid. No one knew who could be trusted.

Some of the cells, such as the one run by brothers Chris and Bill Shaffer, had shut down all together. In 1987 the pair, admired throughout the drug underworld for their smuggling skills, had successfully landed 42 tons of marijuana in a single operation. What made this particular venture unique is that it had taken place right under the noses of the DEA, who had been tipped off about the importation and were keeping the gang under close surveillance at the time. The brothers were now laying low in London, living a life of luxury with the $60 million they had made in the space of just two years.

Another cell working with Daniels was the one run by long-time smuggler Dennis Ingham. That had briefly run into problems when Ingham himself had been arrested while planning a new importation, but others in his gang had busted him out of prison to ensure the smuggle went ahead.

Then there was the cell led by Briton, Michael Forwell. Knowing that the good luck he had experienced up until then could not possibly last, he decided on a more elaborate plan.

He and his team would, they decided, smuggle one final shipment. It was to be so vast and so profitable that the key members of his organisation would be able to maintain their glitzy lifestyles indefinitely without ever having to resort to crime again.

Brian Daniels had long specialised in supplying multi-ton loads, usually organising three or four boatloads each year, but this one was special. At 72 tons it was the largest single shipment The Ring had ever attempted. The wholesale value of the load was close to $300 million. The street value was in excess of $1 billion.

To put that into context: during the whole of 2004 the *total* amount of cannabis seized by HM Customs and Excise in the UK – the country with the highest levels of cannabis use in Europe – was 58 tons.

The cannabis had originated in the Nakhom Penn region of Thailand, up against the border with Laos. The specialist brand, known as 'Thai stick', was widely acknowledged to be some of the most powerful dope money could buy and, as a premium product, commanded a premium price. In the summer of 1988, Thai sticks sold for up to $3,000 per pound compared to just $150 per pound for top-grade Mexican marijuana.

After harvesting, the marijuana was loaded on to trucks and driven through the Thai badlands to the border with Vietnam. There, around a hundred soldiers from the Vietnamese army transferred the bales of drugs to military vehicles and drove them along Route 9 to a nearby port where a ship was waiting to take the load to its final destination – the north-west coast of America.

The ship was the *Encounter Bay*, an 800-ton, 187-foot ocean going, oil rig supply vessel. She had been bought by Forwell two years earlier for $3 million and a further million had been spent fitting her out for her new role as a drug carrier. The bridge was filled with the latest electronics and state-of-the-art radar systems, the antennae hidden inside innocent-looking masts. The fuel tanks had been expanded to carry more than 500 tons of diesel and a desalination plant had been added to provide fresh water. It all meant the *Encounter Bay* could cross the Pacific at full speed without stopping and, if necessary, remain at sea for months at a time.

The marijuana took up so much space that it would not fit in the massive steel containers that had been welded to the vast ship's deck. Extra space was found between the containers, and a false deck was constructed from plywood so that any aircraft flying over the boat would not immediately become suspicious.

It took two full days to load the 8,250 bales of cannabis – each the size of a standard suitcase and weighing in at 60 pounds – and two further days for the crew to recover from the exertion. Then, on 3 June 1988, the *Encounter Bay* set off on its three-week journey across the ocean.

All the bases had been covered; every element of the trip, the offload and the distribution had been worked out in advance right down to the smallest detail. Every possible precaution had been taken and a dozen contingency plans were in place. The buyers were waiting and the gang knew the drugs on the boat would be converted to hard cash within days of arriving on dry land. Rich as they were, they were soon set to become considerably richer.

All they had to do was sit back and wait.

PART ONE

1
LOOMINGS

September 1969

He sat on the edge of the kerb at the corner of 2nd and St Marks, shirtless and shoeless, the soles of his feet flat in the gutter, his skinny arms resting limply in his lap. Weeks of neglect had turned his hair and beard into a bushy black mane and you could tell from his eyes that he had spent most of the day crying.

'No weed in a month!' he sighed. 'I guess I might as well accept that athletics scholarship to Notre Dame and study business economics after all.'

This forlorn young hippy first appeared in a cartoon titled 'The legendary dope famine of '69', published in an underground newspaper in September that same year. By that time everyone was ready to see the funny side of the situation, but just a few short weeks earlier, the chronic shortage of marijuana across America had been no laughing matter.

Supplies had all but dried up in several major cities and the price of what little was left had risen to an all-time high, while the quality had fallen to an all-time low.

'There's just not any available,' a New York dealer nicknamed Porky Pig sobbed to the Associated Press after three fruitless trips to the West Coast in search of the elusive weed. 'If I had a bunch of grass I could take it to New York or Miami and make a million dollars!'

The seeds of the shortage had been sown months earlier when the usual heavy spring rains that fall across central Mexico – the source of around 80 per cent of all the marijuana smoked in the US at the time – failed to appear. By the end of May the crop had been ruined, drying out to little more than matchwood. In

11

Sinaloa, one of the main growing regions, the local police chief took advantage of the situation and ordered his men to set fire to around fifty acres of fields containing the few remaining viable plants.

For the growers, already considerably out of pocket, this proved to be the final straw. Before the day had ended, the police chief had been shot dead.

The response of the Mexican government was immediate. Martial law was declared and the army flooded into Sinaloa carrying out house-to-house searches in a bid to track down those responsible. All cars heading for the American border were forced to pass through heavily guarded roadblocks, and search-and-destroy squads travelled deep into the countryside to torch every marijuana crop they could find. Within the space of a few days, more than one million plants had been destroyed.

Prior to the crackdown, grass had been flowing through the US–Mexico border like water flowing through a burst dam. But once the leak was well and truly plugged, it was only a matter of time before supplies began to dwindle down to nothing.

It could not have come at a worse time. In the weeks leading up to the shortage, the popularity of pot had grown beyond all expectations. In July the film *Easy Rider* had been released to massive commercial success and critical acclaim. Featuring dozens of scenes in which its stars Peter Fonda and Dennis Hopper smoked pot, and fuelled by rumours that the actors had been getting stoned for real, the film helped to popularise marijuana almost as much as it popularised motorcycling.

The fast-growing anti-Vietnam movement had adopted marijuana as one of its sacred tenets and use by well-to-do middle-class college students was also soaring.

At the Woodstock festival in August 1969, an estimated 90 per cent of the 400,000 attendees smoked marijuana over the course of the event. The drug was rapidly making inroads into

mainstream society to the point that even those considered otherwise 'straight' had begun using and selling it.

This soaring demand, combined with the sudden shortage, meant
that the few dealers lucky enough to have stock in reserve found
themselves making serious money. Selling marijuana became
something more than just a way to get your own dope for free
or 'stick it to the man'; it became a way of making a living.

A few chancers tried to jump on the bandwagon, selling alfalfa,
oregano and even lawn grass as the real thing, but for those with
access to the genuine article, profits were high and the risks were
low.

For one student, the son of a wealthy ranch owner, the situation
seemed to represent nothing less than a golden business opportunity.
'The way I see it,' twenty-one-year-old Ciro Mancuso told his
friends that summer, 'is that anyone with a bit of sense who can
get hold of some pot is going to be in a position to get real rich,
real fast.'

Mexican grass may have been off the menu but for those willing
to put in a little effort, there was an abundant source of marijuana
far closer to hand.

During the Second World War the US government urged
farmers throughout the Midwest, from Kansas and Nebraska to
Ohio and Indiana, to sew the botanical equivalent of marijuana's
first cousin – hemp – with a promise that, in return, both they
and their sons would be exempted from military service.

Just five years earlier the plant had been labelled 'the assassin
of youth' and all cultivation had been banned. But the war in
the Pacific meant vast quantities of hemp were needed to replace
supplies of cheap foreign fibres that had been cut off by the
Japanese.

An inspirational film, *Hemp for Victory*, showed how the
plant could be used to make rope to rig battleships, fire hose,
thread for army boots and parachute webbing – all essential for
the war effort. Special permits were issued, millions of free seeds

were handed out and soon America's 'Corn Belt' was thick with ten-foot high hemp plants.

Once the war ended the farmers switched back to corn and other grains, but the 'wild marijuana' continued to spread. Some called it 'loco weed' because it made farm animals that nibbled on it giddy, even though the plants contained barely one-tenth the amount of the active ingredient, delta-9-THC, found in Mexican marijuana.

Local pot dealers used it mainly as filler, but once imports of the good stuff started to dry up many users decided that, in this hour of great need, bad grass was better than no grass at all.

Unlike the hard-to-find Mexican marijuana, the domestic variety was plentiful. That summer Kansas alone had some 52,000 acres growing wild and the university town of Lawrence soon became a Mecca for eager potheads. The local hippy hang-outs – the Gaslight Tavern and the Rock Chalk Café – even sold hand-drawn maps giving directions to the prime sites down by the banks of the Kaw river, alongside politically active fare like 'fascist pig burgers' at thirty-five cents a pop. But the maps were hardly necessary – college campuses along the East and West coasts buzzed with whispered tales of the fact that, so abundant was the marijuana, all you had to do was stick your arm out of the window as you drove through town and you would come away with a handful.

One July weekend, lured by the promise of easy money, Ciro Mancuso and his college room-mate Brian Degen loaded up a car with sacks and machetes and set off on the forty-eight-hour drive to Kansas.

The pair were party-loving students at the Paradise College, an unremarkable liberal arts school on the south shore of Lake Tahoe. Classmates remember them as the kind of guys who were so laid back they were practically horizontal. Mancuso in particular was friendly and outgoing, but although he had bags of charisma and a strong personality, he kept his distance and was never part of the 'in' crowd.

Exceptionally bright and quick to learn, Mancuso excelled at anything he put his mind to. During the summer he played defensive halfback for the Patterson Tigers, in the winter he joined the wrestling team while in the spring he worked the running track. But skiing was by far his favourite pastime.

He and Degen had met after initially enrolling on a course at the University of Reno but transferred to Paradise at the end of their first year on skiing scholarships. The move suited them, as their achievements on the slopes had long overshadowed their achievements in the classroom and Paradise College was just minutes from at least three ski resorts.

The pair had smoked and traded small amounts of dope for kicks since their school days and bonded over their equally desperate desire to find an escape from small town life. And now, for the first time, they had stumbled across it.

In Kansas, under cover of darkness, they hacked down plants until their backs ached and their palms were red raw. Back at Lake Tahoe they cured the stems by placing them inside pillow cases which in turn were placed inside dryers at the college launderette. One- and five-dollar bags were then weighed out and, as an added touch, wrapped in pages torn from Mexican newspapers. The dope sold like hotcakes.

That first trip was so successful that Mancuso and Degen spent the next few weekends driving up to Kansas and Nebraska for more supplies.

They were not the only ones. Police officers in the Midwest were initially puzzled at what seemed to be a vast increase in the number of birdwatchers that summer. When they decided to investigate, they realised that this new breed of ornithologist invariably failed to bring binoculars, had long hair and usually drove vans with flowers and peace signs painted on the side.

Across the Corn Belt, arrests for illegal harvesting of marijuana more than tripled that summer, with the vast majority of those caught coming from out of state. A single sheriff in Cloud

County, Kansas bagged forty-three suspects in the space of a few weeks, all but three of them from California. Every night shift, if things got a little too quiet, he and his deputies would head down to the river and almost always return with at least a couple of collars.

It was only a matter of time before Mancuso and Degen's luck ran out and on 8 August they were arrested in Kansas and charged with attempting to illegally possess marijuana. They spent a couple of nights in jail but the money they had made from their previous drug runs was more than enough to pay the $1,000 they were fined before being sent back to California.

Some might have taken such an arrest as a sign that it was time to get out of the trade, but Mancuso was already hooked. He and Degen would not return to Kansas, but it had nothing to do with the fear of being caught again. The drug runs had been profitable, but the work had been slow, tedious and physically exhausting. Selling marijuana was, they decided, the way forward. All they needed now was to find a way to make it even more lucrative.

By the middle of the summer the weather had achieved something that tens of billions of dollars spent on the war against drugs had failed to do: reduce the marijuana traffic across the Mexican border to a trickle.

Six months into his first term, President Richard Nixon spied an opportunity to strike a decisive blow against the trade. A loser in the 1960 election that saw John F. Kennedy take the White House, Nixon had won through this time round thanks to millions of votes from the so-called 'silent majority' – blue-collar Americans deeply opposed to hippy counter-culture, anti-war demonstrators and, in particular, marijuana smokers.

At 2.30 p.m. Pacific Daylight Time on Sunday 21 September, Nixon launched Operation Intercept. More than two thousand customs agents were moved down to the American side of the border with Mexico and given orders to stop the marijuana.

Timed to coincide with the September harvest, Nixon's plan was to hit the trade hard at a time when supplies were already running extremely thin.

Within an hour of the operation's launch, traffic at the main border posts was backed up for more than two and a half miles. By the end of the afternoon the tailbacks stretched out for six miles.

The chaos continued in the days that followed. In theory every vehicle was supposed to be subjected to a three-minute inspection. In reality not all vehicles were searched, many of those that were received only a cursory glance, and the odds of being caught had shifted enough to ensure that few smugglers were willing to risk the trip.

Supplies of freshly harvested marijuana began to pile up in the stash houses on the south side of the border and the price, already high, began to rise higher still.

After the Kansas debacle, Mancuso and Degen had begun looking for new and innovative ways to stay in the marijuana business. As Operation Intercept began to bite, the pair quickly realised that the increased retail value of their chosen product meant that a method previously deemed too costly and impractical had suddenly become feasible. Rather than taking a chance by driving through the border, they would simply fly over it.

It was a possibility the Nixon administration had already considered. As part of the crackdown, the Federal Aviation Authority had installed mobile radar equipment on trucks positioned at strategic points along the border, while the air force stationed a fleet of intercept planes nearby. Within days of the blockade, blips of light moving south to north appeared on the screens, but by the time the interceptors had been scrambled, the blips had already vanished.

Mancuso, Degen and dozens of other smugglers had realised that small planes were able to dip between the mountain ranges and canyon corridors that made up much of the border, and thus travel underneath the radar blanket.

Each flight required nerves of steel. In Mexico the landing strips were heavily disguised to prevent them being spotted from the air by the military. In many cases, the sole difference between a patch of treacherous rough ground and an official landing strip was that, on at least one occasion, someone had managed to land there. By the same token, the only difference between a landing strip and a crash site was that the same aircraft had subsequently managed to take off.

The journey back was little better, with the planes flying low and navigating through the potentially deadly mountain peaks by moonlight before landing in the desert where trucks would meet them to carry away their precious cargo.

Within days of the crackdown customs agents estimated that at least ten planes a night were crossing the border, and admitted there was virtually nothing they could do about it. 'They are developing their own air force,' noted one official, 'and it's getting bigger and bigger.'

After just two weeks, Operation Intercept was abandoned amid growing protests from employers fed up of workers arriving late, and from legitimate businesses and traders on both sides of the border who had experienced a 70 per cent drop in sales. But the new techniques devised by the smugglers soon became the norm.

Having fast discovered the profitability of their new enterprise Mancuso and Degen dropped out of college, joined forces with a team of 'crossroaders' – professional casino cheats – and began using a variety of small aircraft to smuggle marijuana. Over the next two years the pair helped to organise more than fifty flights that brought in a total of 35,000 pounds of dope.

Selling at around $225 per pound, the gross profits amounted to almost $8 million. It was a small fortune but Mancuso and Degen received only a modest share due to the large number of others involved, the high cost of running the planes and the money spent hiring the trucks and drivers.

It was clear to Mancuso that the only way he would ever be able to keep more of the money for himself was if he found a way to cut out the middlemen.

It was time to head south.

Fluent in Spanish ever since his schooldays, Ciro Mancuso took his profits from the airborne smuggling operation and bought a run-down ranch near Guadalajara. After a few essential renovations the ranch became Mancuso's permanent home and he and Brian Degen began contacting local growers and suppliers before launching themselves on to the market as marijuana brokers.

Each month tons of the drug would arrive at the ranch for processing and buyers from America and beyond would visit to select the goods they wanted to purchase. The customers would then choose their own way of getting the drugs across the border or, for an additional fee, have Mancuso make arrangements on their behalf.

The pair bought a caravan and had it fitted with a cleverly concealed secret compartment where large amounts of marijuana could be stored. This could then be towed back and forth across the border to get the drugs into California.

The drugs were so well concealed they were virtually undetectable but as an extra precaution, the mobile home was always towed by pick-up trucks driven by late middle-aged men or couples – far less likely to arouse suspicion from border guards than young men like Mancuso and Degen.

Within weeks hundreds of pounds of marijuana had made its way north, but the scale of the operation soon attracted the attention of the local authorities who were still under pressure from the US government to help stem the tide of pot flowing across the border. Even tucked away in the boondocks of Mexico, the combination of a luxury lifestyle with no visible form of employment made Mancuso stand out like a sore thumb.

In March 1972, while Mancuso was in the middle of negotiating a price with a group of American buyers, Mexican police raided the ranch, arresting him and nine others, including four key customers. Brian Degan, running his end of the operation from back in Lake Tahoe, missed the swoop. After a swift search the Federales seized more than two tons of marijuana from the property as well as a plane.

Transferred to prison that same day, Mancuso refused to allow what he saw as a relatively minor setback to have any effect on his fast-growing smuggling empire.

Mexican prisons in the early seventies were notorious for being run by guards willing to turn a blind eye to almost anything, just so long as they were properly compensated. Mancuso started out in a bare, filthy cell but was quickly upgraded to a beautifully decorated 'suite' where he had his choice of meals, regular female companions, a guitar and a host of other creature comforts.

All inmates were required to carry out some form of work and Mancuso was no exception. He set up a furniture factory in the prison with the intention of creating cut-price products for the American market.

It was a front of course. Each item the factory produced featured a specially made secret compartment, and after leaving the prison the goods were taken to a nearby warehouse run by junior members of Mancuso's gang. There the compartments would be filled with marijuana. The furniture was then shipped up to California or Nevada where Degen would extract the drugs and sell them on.

Smuggling operations with the caravan also continued while Mancuso was in prison. In October 1972 the gang's regular driver, Harry McKeown, towed the vehicle across the border and made his way up to San José where the drugs were to be dropped off.

No sooner had McKeown arrived at the rendezvous and spotted his contact than dozens of police officers swooped down and arrested them both.

'They knew all about the trip we made,' McKeown later recalled. 'He told me all the officers had come up from Los

Angeles and had been following me all day.' McKeown and his contact were taken to jail, certain that, like Mancuso, they would now be spending a long spell behind bars. But to McKeown's surprise it was not to be.

'The next morning, ten o'clock or so, they took me down, took me to the desk, gave me my things and said "get out", so I left. The other guy was nowhere to be seen and they didn't say anything about anything. I went back to Reno and got my lawyer to call the police station and they said "well, the truck and caravan is sitting right here in the parking lot, get it out". So I flew back.'

The caravan was in tatters, having been torn apart by the police officers looking for the concealed drugs. All the wall and roof panels had been pulled off, the floorboards had been ripped up, the cushions had been slashed open and each and every interior fixing had been removed or smashed. The search had been comprehensive and the officers had even brought in sniffer dogs to ensure every last nook and cranny was explored.

'I can't even begin to describe all the damage done to this thing,' says McKeown. 'This was a disaster. I took it to a repair place and the guy had an estimate of like $4,000-plus to get it fixed. He was amazed. He couldn't understand what possibly could have happened to it.'

McKeown drove the wreck back to Reno and left it parked on his driveway. It sat there for three or four days before a couple of Mancuso's men came over to assess the damage for themselves.

Their faces, initially grim, soon burst into broad, radiant smiles as both they and McKeown realised the almost unbelievable truth: 'It was still loaded.'

2
SCHOOL OF POT

Mancuso and Degen were not the only marijuana smugglers expanding their operations in Mexico that year. In the affluent Californian island community of Coronado, just twelve miles north of the border, a dynamic group of high school swimming champions turned drug traffickers were looking to do the same.

Marijuana smoking had been rife at Coronado High School for as long as anyone could remember. By the mid-sixties the problem had become so acute that the Federal Government launched a controversial pilot project in an effort to help students kick the habit.

Under the 'no bust' policy, teachers would not report those caught using the drug to the police but, instead, would talk to them about its negative effects.

Such discretion was welcomed by the wider community – Coronado is the site of two naval bases and many of the school's students were the sons and daughters of prominent members of the armed forces – but it did little, if anything, to discourage drug use.

In the early seventies, one of the most successful dealers on the island was Lance Weber. A tall, muscular and permanently tanned surfing addict, Weber had graduated from Coronado High and joined the navy, training as an elite SEAL commando. At the end of his commitment, he went to college but soon quit when the marijuana smuggling ring he had put together with two friends began to blossom.

The technique he used to import drugs was daring, dangerous and, in the words of one investigator, 'not just under the radar, but completely off the screen.'

Every few weeks he and his friends would cross the border and visit the Mexican city of Tijuana, a magnet for underage drinkers and a popular destination for day trippers. There, the Coronado boys would find a source and buy up to twenty-five pounds of marijuana at a time.

Waiting until nightfall, the trio would then head to one of the many rocky coves just south of the border checkpoint, place the drugs inside a watertight dive bag and secure it with a length of rope. Weber would then don a wetsuit, tie the loose end of the rope around his waist and slip into the dark, murky waters to swim his way to America.

It was a high-risk undertaking. For much of the year the night-time waters of the Pacific are easily cold enough to induce hypothermia, and during the summer sharks come close to shore in search of food. Each year dozens of illegal immigrants attempting the exact same swim are swept out to sea by powerful currents, never to be heard from again. And as if that wasn't enough, the Tijuana River, which hits the sea just north of the border, teems with potentially deadly pollution.

But Weber was an exceptionally strong swimmer and utterly fearless – a legacy of his time in the navy. He would head west until the streetlights of Interstate 5 were just tiny pinpricks of colour and then head north, following the coastline until, out of sight of border patrol agents and the occasional coastguard cruiser, he would come ashore at a pre-arranged spot a few miles north of the checkpoint. After several hours in the water, Weber would emerge exhausted and dehydrated, but elated to have once more brought in drugs right under the noses of the authorities.

The marijuana that Weber and his friends swam up the coast sold easily, particularly to students at the school, and the frequency of the trips increased as demand soared. Soon, Weber alone could not carry sufficient quantities of dope and was joined in the water by his friends. But while one man swimming alone can easily go unnoticed, three swimming together may not. In early 1971 the trio were spotted by a customs patrol boat. Weber, the best swimmer of the three, managed to escape out into the ocean only to be arrested later as he returned home. He was sentenced to six months in jail.

In his absence two other drug-dealing students of Coronado High rose to prominence. Edward Otero, known as Eddie to his friends, was a blond-haired, barrel-chested athlete whose party trick involved tearing the three-inch thick San Diego phone directory in half with his bare hands. Easy-going with a sunny disposition and warm smile, Otero was the son of school employees and a leading member of the swim team.

He dealt dope alongside his close friend and fellow swim team member Paul Acree, a man with a gift of the gab so advanced he could easily have sold ice to the Eskimos. The pair had started out smuggling small amounts of pot from Tijuana in their underwear, graduating to hiding slightly larger amounts in the hubcaps of their cars and occasionally hiring mechanics to conceal the drugs inside the spare tyre.

They had also tried the swimming method, eventually making enough of a profit to invest in a small, high-speed Zodiac inflatable boat, the kind used by the US Navy's commando squads.

On Lance Weber's release from jail in early 1972 he was immediately approached by Paul Acree who offered him $1,000 to pilot the newly acquired Zodiac up from Mexico, along with 100 pounds of grass. 'Eddie and I were still in college and we had been doing some smuggling,' Acree recalled. 'Lance had just gotten out of jail and we knew he had also been involved in smuggling too, that he knew how to pilot a boat. So we kind of got together, the three of us, and formed a partnership, agreeing to split all the profits equally.'

The Zodiac proved to be a huge success. Not only were the Coronado boys able to carry at least four times more dope on each trip, but also the boat was so fast that, even if Weber was spotted by the coast guard, he could easily outrun them. On more than one occasion, Weber could not resist giving a finger to their heavily armed but slow-moving cutters and frigates as he sped past, out of range, out of reach and, to all intents and purposes, out of danger.

An unexpected side effect of Operation Intercept and the great dope famine was a significant shift in consumer attitudes towards grass. Up until that time, pot was simply whatever was available and people smoked whatever they could get their hands on. But the boom in sales of domestic marijuana during the summer of '69 had highlighted just how bad the bad stuff could be, and in the months that followed smokers quickly became far more discerning, often asking their dealers to specify exactly which varieties of weed they had in stock.

Branding became everything. Regular Mexican was OK, but Acapulco Gold was far better. Further south, a Colombian strain known as Santa Maria was fast gaining popularity, while out to the west Hawaii's 'Maui-wowie' brand generated high praise and near-religious devotion from its users. Veterans returning from the war in Vietnam were known to be bringing back a particularly potent form of pot that was harder to come by than rocking-horse shit but reputed to be the best weed money could buy.

The famine also significantly boosted imports of hashish – a preparation made chiefly from the resin-rich hairs of the cannabis plant – which until then had been relatively unknown outside the Middle East. In 1967 just 70 pounds of hashish had been seized on its way into the US. By the end of 1969 the figure had reached 623 pounds and there were at least eleven Americans in prison in Lebanon on trafficking charges, an upward trend that would show no sign of slowing in the years that followed.

The new strains of marijuana set new standards for consumers across America and beyond, and it became increasingly difficult for dealers to get away with selling an inferior product.

This soon became a problem for the Coronado boys. Lance Weber and his swim team buddies were ready and willing to expand their operation further still but they were having trouble getting hold of the better strains of marijuana because, unlike Mancuso and Degen, none of them spoke any Spanish.

In Mexico in the early seventies it was theoretically possible to buy top-grade pot for as little as $1 per pound, but the students always ended up paying a lot more, sometimes as much as $40 per pound. It was the wrong time to be losing out.

Both prices and demand had remained high and, with law enforcement far more concerned about the rising use of heroin and focusing all its efforts in that direction, the chances of being caught were extremely low.

The drug's increasing popularity among the mainstream was starting to catch the attention of politicians, some of whom were advocating its possible legalisation or decriminalisation.

A bona fide trade in marijuana seemed only a few years away at most and it became clear that those who managed to get involved right from the start would be able to do very nicely out of it. All across California and beyond brand new dealers were cropping up like mushrooms after a rainstorm, some of them threatening the Coronado patch, offering a better quality product and stealing away the gang's profits.

If Lance, Paul and Eddie were ever going to move into the big time and survive in the drug business, they were going to have to get some help.

They found it close to home.

From the moment he arrived in southern California, screeching through the school gates in his bright red Corvette convertible, Louis Villar was an instant hit among staff and students alike.

Every bit as stylish and flashy as his car, Villar favoured sharply creased trousers and beautifully cut jackets, dressing like a cross between a pop star and a secret service agent. His thick, dark hair was always neatly slicked back and he often taught class while wearing his Ray-Bans sunglasses.

Born in Havana in 1938, he at first seemed destined to live the modest life of a Cuban peasant until the sudden death of his father prompted his mother to flee to America. Within a few short years he had transformed into a smart-mouthed, streetwise teenager growing up in a tough New York neighbourhood.

Cocky and arrogant, the young Louis was forever getting himself into trouble and refused to take anything seriously, but just as his teachers were getting ready to write him off as a lost cause, he suddenly evolved into a hard-working student and impressive athlete, winning a place at New York State University and graduating with a degree in education.

From there Villar enrolled as a law student at Syracuse University but dropped out after a year and a half when a dream of a job landed in his lap. Once again he left his old life behind, headed west and became a Spanish teacher at Coronado High School.

Despite being fifteen years older than his pupils and picking up the nickname 'Pops', Villar easily bridged the gap between teacher and student, becoming someone they could trust and talk to about their problems.

After class he would hang around the grounds to play basketball with the after-school crowd and it wasn't long before his athletic prowess attracted attention. Soon, as well as teaching Spanish, Villar was coaching the water polo and swimming teams.

Fiercely competitive and hugely ambitious, Villar put his teams through lengthy and arduous training routines, constantly pushing them to work harder and achieve more. At times he could be aggressive to the point of fanaticism: failure was not an option and rival athletes were seen as an enemy who had to be defeated at all costs.

It worked. The school's cabinets were soon bulging with trophies and each new victory would be celebrated with a private party at Villar's home where, despite his guests being underage, he would allow the youngsters to get drunk, just so long as there were no lessons the following day.

Villar took advantage of his special bond with the students when he agreed to become one of the first teachers to take part in the controversial 'no-bust' anti-drug counselling initiative. He held a series of encounter groups where pupils were encouraged to talk openly about their use of marijuana – by far the most popular drug among students.

The thinking behind the programme was that the teachers would help steer the pupils away from drugs, but in Villar's case, the more he learned about the world of the pot smoker, the more attracted to it he became.

For those around him, the changes seemed to come quickly. First Louis sold his once-beloved Corvette and bought himself a VW combi van, the official transportation of the counter-culture movement. He began to dress more casually, to wear beads, to grow his hair long and to let his sideburns creep down his face until they eventually joined into a full beard.

Villar began spending an increasing amount of his time at the beach, learning to surf and giving impromptu lectures to anyone willing to listen to his views on Eastern philosophy, mysticism and the evils of materialism. By now he was smoking marijuana on a daily basis and spending less and less time at Coronado High. It was only a matter of time before he and the school parted ways.

In the space of a year he had turned his back on all the things that had previously been important to him. Teaching had once been a great adventure, something he strived to give his all to. But now the fire that once burned in his belly had been extinguished and there was no way to reignite it.

He had fallen in love with a homecoming princess and cheerleader called Katherine Stocker, one of the most popular girls at the school. She embraced the man her one-time teacher had become and the pair married and moved to Los Angeles. There, Villar embarked on a new life as a boat builder and dreamed of one day exploring the world.

But the dream quickly turned sour when the reality of completing such a complex construction project proved too demanding for Villar's new-found sense of liberation and freedom from the rat race. Katherine got fed up and left, and Villar returned to Coronado, eventually setting himself up as a house painter.

And it was while he was perched on some scaffolding, painting the front of a clapperboard beach home, that Paul Acree and Lance Weber suddenly appeared.

'Hey Lou, come on down here, I want to talk to you,' said Acree.

Villar looked down at the pair and scowled. 'Get lost guys, can't you see I'm busy.'

'I mean it Lou, come on down here,' Acree insisted. 'I wanna give you the chance to make some easy money.'

Villar hesitated for just a moment, then climbed down. Acree's proposal was a simple one. Would he accompany them to Tijuana and help secure a decent price for a load of marijuana they planned to import? There was $50 in it for him.

Villar smiled at Acree and Weber, looking from one to the other and back again. 'Sure,' he said at last. 'Why not.'

On that first trip to Tijuana, Villar slipped into his new role with ease. Taken to a bar and introduced to the gang's source, a shady character known simply as 'Joe the Mexican', Villar established that the Coronado boys were being significantly overcharged for a substandard product. He not only negotiated a satisfactory reduction in the price but also a substantial hike in the quality. Everyone went home happy, even Joe the Mexican who, at last able to communicate properly with his eager young buyers, treated them with new-found respect.

A few days later, Villar was called upon to translate again and this time asked Weber if he could invest a modest amount of his own money – $100 – into the shipment. Weber agreed and, shortly after the smuggle had been completed, returned Villar's original $100 with an additional $50 on top. Villar handed the money right back, asking that it be invested in the next shipment.

Right from the start the former schoolteacher had proved to be a far greater asset to the gang than the boys had anticipated.

He had saved them money, boosted their profits and greatly simplified the business of acquiring marijuana. Not only that, but the same motivational and organisational skills Villar had displayed while coaching the swim team to victory were now returning with a vengeance. Enthusiastic, ambitious and a natural leader, it was clear that he could help the gang reach their full potential.

Weber, Otero and Acree had a quick conference and instantly reached a unanimous decision – they would invite Villar to join them as a full partner and split all future profits four ways.

Within a month they were importing pot two or three times a week, rapidly moving from 50-pound to 100-pound loads, and Villar had abandoned his house-painting business entirely. Each of the four had a clearly defined role: Villar was in charge of procurement of the marijuana and negotiations over price, Acree was the salesman responsible for distribution back in the States, Otero was appointed 'beachmaster' and organised the offloading of the drugs boats, while Weber was mechanic and pilot.

Soon Villar had boosted profits further still, negotiating a fresh deal with Joe the Mexican that allowed the gang to buy at a discount if they paid cash up front in advance of the harvest. For every 100-pound load, the gang was now making a clear profit of $5,000. With no shortage of demand – most of the drugs were sold wholesale to a beachside restaurant owner in Del Mar – Villar suggested they pool their resources and move up to 500-pound loads.

The others were happy to let Villar take control of the group's finances. Villar decided it was sensible to pay out equal shares to all while retaining a fifth share to pay for equipment and other sundry expenses. These monies were used to purchase additional Zodiac boats, rigs and motors, which quickly became necessary as the size and frequency of the loads increased. The loads soon became so large that managing the offload became too big a job for Otero alone. It was clear that the gang needed more hands.

Villar turned to the only source of willing and available labour that he knew: his former students and swim team members. They were approached and offered thousands of dollars to take part in offload operations, which involved standing on freezing beaches in the middle of the night to form human chains that rapidly shifted bales of marijuana from the Zodiacs to waiting trucks. Villar, seemingly possessed by the spirit of a doped-up Fagin, began referring to all those involved in the operation as 'my boys'.

Business was booming and soon there was so much money in the kitty that the gang realised they were able to buy an ocean going vessel, a former fishing boat, to replace the inflatable crafts that had previously served them so well. It was a riskier proposition – the boat would be slower and more easily spotted – but the potential rewards ought to more than compensate them for the added danger of getting caught. For the first time, they would be able to smuggle marijuana by the ton. They were ready to hit the big time.

The preparations for each importation now began weeks, sometimes months, in advance, with members of the gang arranging to rent at least four separate properties. First would be the 'beach house', a base for the fifteen or so members of the offload crew.

To reassure the members of the beach crew that they would not be abandoned in the event of a catastrophe, the gang agreed to cover the cost of any legal fees they might incur. They also promised to look after their families and loved ones while they were incarcerated, just so long as they didn't snitch.

Those who agreed to the terms would be contacted by Villar a few hours before they were needed with a simple coded message: 'Hey, do you want to go to a barbeque?'

The beach house would be at most a few hundred yards from the offload site but the 'stash house' would usually be several miles away. This was the place where the drugs would be weighed, graded and repackaged before being sent out for sale.

Somewhere between the two would be an 'equipment house'; usually a large barn where all the gear needed for the offload would be stored in order to keep it out of sight for as long as possible. By now the gang had an impressive inventory of gear including Zodiac boats, Maravia rafts, generator trucks, conveyor belts, power winches and a selection of four-wheel drive vehicles.

Finally the gang needed a 'communications house'. Here a large, high-power antenna would be concealed in nearby trees and a cable run into the house containing the gang's ship-to-shore radio. This would be tuned to a pre-selected channel agreed with the captain of the ship carrying the drugs, who would call in when he was in position.

Profits for each importation now ran into the hundreds of thousands of dollars and the potential seemed almost endless.

There was just one cloud on the horizon.

While the rest of the gang were spending their new-found wealth on the traditional pursuits of fast cars and fancy homes, founder member Acree had chosen to spend his on increasing amounts of heroin for his personal use. As his addiction grew he became increasingly erratic and unreliable. Although had been instrumental in bringing the gang together and he personally had recruited both Weber and Villar, his partners decided the only thing they could do was to buy him out.

Although hundreds of thousands of dollars were now floating around the company coffers, they offered Acree just $8,000 dollars for his share of the business, along with an agreement that he would continue to receive regular supplies of marijuana to sell on to his vast network of customers.

Having gotten rid of the deadweight, Villar announced his intention to introduce an even more streamlined and professional business methodology to the enterprise. They should, he suggested, act as though they were running a small corporation. He had even come up with a name for their organisation that the others eagerly agreed to adopt.

The Coronado Company had been born.

3
BANGKOK BOUND

After just over a year in prison, Ciro Mancuso returned to his ranch in Guadalajara to find that the Federales who had raided it had somehow failed to uncover the full extent of the renovations he had made to the property.

Several rooms in the main building had been given false walls that he had used to conceal vast amounts of drugs. Despite an extensive search by dozens of officers, more than two tons of marijuana remained behind these panels.

But while the drugs were safe, Mexico itself was anything but, and Mancuso soon packed his bags and headed back to Lake Tahoe. While he had been locked away, an increasing number of marijuana suppliers had switched to heroin, which was proving more profitable. By 1974 Mexican interests controlled two-thirds of the US heroin market.

Those dealers that had stuck with pot were facing increased competition from each other and from Colombian dealers who were fast moving into the trade. Violence, once a rarity, was now becoming commonplace and the once-congenial atmosphere in which deals had taken place was a thing of the past.

Members of the Coronado Company experienced this new, darker mood first-hand when Louis Villar decided to cut out the middleman and deal directly with Joe the Mexican's suppliers for their biggest load to date – 12 tons.

When the new supplier arrived to meet Villar and the others he was accompanied by ten heavily armed bodyguards.

It was a chilling sign of the times. Rip-offs were becoming increasingly common, but not the kind of rip-offs that the mostly docile American hippies had been used to. Everyone had stories about being burned, deals where you came away with a lower grade of dope or got home to discover half the weight was made up of packaging rather than product. Deals like those were seen to be part of the territory, but the new rip-offs didn't just cost money, they cost lives.

Around the time the Coronado Company were entering negotiations for their 12 tons, a teenage smuggler, a Mexican-American by the name of David Ortiz, had a lucky escape.

Ortiz had started out dealing lids – ounces of marijuana – in high school and had spent ninety days in prison after being caught at a checkpoint in a fully loaded car. Through a contact in Mexico he met a pilot named Loren Smith and the two men arranged to fly a load of dope up from a town called Guerro.

David was also supposed to fly down to act as ground crew and oversee the loading but he had to pull out at the last minute. Desperate to find someone he could trust, he persuaded his close friend Glen to take his place. The flight down to Mexico went smoothly and Smith managed to land the plane on the makeshift strip in the middle of the jungle, but the pair never made it home.

Exactly what happened has never been fully established but it is known that the plane took off again with both Smith and Glen on board, but with no marijuana. Shortly after take-off, the plane crashed into the ocean killing both men instantly.

It was an early example of what would become an increasingly common scam among Mexican merchants. A crucial element of all the deals involving aircraft was that, as well as supplying marijuana, the growers would have to procure aviation fuel to top up the plane's tanks for the return journey.

It didn't take long for the less scrupulous drug cartel bosses to work out that withholding the drugs and replacing half the kerosene with diesel or water would make the plane stall and crash soon after take off. The Mexicans would get to keep both the money and the drugs and the buyers would be left in the dark. Dozens of drug planes had crashed after being overloaded and they would simply assume they had been hit by bad luck.

Ortiz only found out his friend's fate because Glen's father flew down to Mexico and spent months diving in the ocean until he found the empty plane and identified his son's body still in the cockpit.

Ortiz was left deeply shaken by the loss of his friend and tried to quit the drug business altogether. He stayed out for a while but then was all but forced back in by his younger brother, Brian.

When David had been selling, Brian had been one of his biggest customers. Once David stopped, Brian had been forced to go elsewhere but had been repeatedly burned in deals and even had threats made against his life. Fearful for his brother's welfare, David decided his only option was to return to dealing in order to keep his brother safe.

Mexico was out of the question. One possible alternative was Morocco, an annual Mecca for thousands of hippies, surfers and backpackers, and firmly established throughout the counter-culture underground as a good place to buy top-quality hash. But just as he started putting out feelers, Ortiz came across a new source of supply that put both the Central American and North African products to shame. The natives were friendly and completely in tune with the hippy ideal, the prices were low and the quality of the pot was better than anything he could have ever imagined.

Best of all, the trade was being pioneered by a group of individuals that no one in law enforcement, not even the eager agents of the Drug Enforcement Administration, had the slightest interest in seeing inside a courtroom.

From the moment they arrived in Vietnam, the leaders of the American military found they were fighting a war on two fronts. The first involved the action against the Vietcong, the second an ongoing series of battles to keep the troops from getting high.

Marijuana had been a small yet integral part of Vietnamese culture long before the arrival of the Americans, but as soon as the first trickle of soldiers began to arrive during the 1963 advisory period, entrepreneurial farmers realised they had a lucrative new cash crop on their hands. By 1966, there were twenty-nine fixed stalls selling marijuana in Saigon alone. The drug could be bought loose or in the form of ready-made cigarettes delivered in neat, cellophane-wrapped packs of twenty.

Recreational drugs were frowned upon in the field because of the risk of enemy contact, but back at the fire support bases it was another story. Attacks here were infrequent and many young draftees took full advantage of every opportunity to relax.

At first Army officials were willing to turn a blind eye – alcohol abuse was, after all, a far greater concern – but with so many journalists embedded with the troops, reports of the fast-growing problem soon found their way back home.

Newsreel footage shot at Fire Support Base Ares from the summer of 1969 shows Vito, a twenty-year-old draftee squadron leader, demonstrating a technique called 'shotgunning'. The stem of a pipe loaded with marijuana was inserted into the chamber of an empty shotgun, and air was blown through the bowl. The members of Vito's squad then took it in turns to suck in the concentrated smoke from the end of the barrels. 'You get really stoned,' explained one miserable soldier, 'and then, who cares about this war.'

In April 1970 nineteen-year-old Specialist 4 Peter Lemon of Company E was serving as an assistant machine-gunner at Fire Support Base Illingworth in Tay Ninh province when the base came under heavy attack by more than 400 Vietcong. Despite being hopelessly outnumbered, Lemon took on the waves of enemy soldiers first with his machine gun until it jammed and then with his rifle until that too malfunctioned.

The attackers began to focus on his position and Lemon was wounded by a hand grenade. Despite this he used his only remaining armaments – his own hand grenades – to kill all but one of those pursuing him. He then chased after the last enemy soldier and killed him with his bare hands.

Lemon moved back to his foxhole where he picked up a more seriously wounded colleague and carried him to an aid station. Returning to his foxhole, a mortar shell exploded, vaporising the man next to him. Lemon was wounded a second time but ignored the hail of bullets and grenades and took up his fighting position. He then realised the area was in danger of being overrun and once more took on the enemy with hand grenades and hand-to-hand combat, eventually managing to drive them back. Finding a working machine gun, Lemon stood out in the open and fired on the enemy until he passed out from loss of blood. When he came to at the aid station, he refused treatment until his more seriously wounded comrades had been evacuated.

Lemon was awarded the highest possible military award, the Congressional Medal of Honour, and it was only after he had received it that he revealed that he had been as high as a kite throughout the whole ordeal.

'It was the only time I ever went into combat stoned,' he told CBS evening news a few months later. 'You get really alert when you're stoned because you have to be. We were all partying the night before. We weren't expecting any action because we were in a support group. All the guys were [pot] heads. We'd sit around smoking grass and getting stoned and talking about when we'd get to go home.'

He was not alone. In one study of 1,064 soldiers, 67 per cent admitted smoking marijuana in the previous month.

No longer able to simply ignore the problem, the army set about trying to wipe it out. Education campaigns and compulsory lectures were introduced to highlight the dangers of the evil weed; helicopters and fixed-wing aircraft were diverted from other duties to fly out in search of marijuana fields; sniffer dogs were introduced to search billets and property.

Soldiers caught with even a small amount of marijuana faced court martial and, at the height of the eradication campaign, arrests for possession were running at a thousand per week. As a direct result of the campaign, many soldiers switched to heroin and by the end of the war one in five would be addicted to the white powder.

But by the time the marijuana crackdown was introduced, soldiers weren't just smoking the stuff; they were bringing it back with them. Some was simply posted home using the military's own mail system; larger amounts were being brought back hidden among the personal belongings of returning soldiers.

Authorities on the West Coast noticed that huge amounts of South East Asian marijuana flooded the market hours after the docking of each homebound troopship. There were even rumours that some marijuana was shipped back inside sealed HR boxes – the large aluminium chests used to hold unidentified human remains – but prosecutions were rare. No one wanted to face the political repercussions that would follow the large-scale prosecution of veterans freshly returned from an increasingly unpopular war.

The marijuana coming out of Vietnam was good but that which came out of neighbouring Thailand, where many of the troops were sent for their R&R, was even better.

Not only did Thai marijuana look unique – the premium buds and leaves were skewered on stems or tied to thin bamboo reeds using animal hair – but it was also considerably more potent than anything else available at the time. Two or three puffs of Thai would produce the same effect as smoking an entire joint of Mexican and the high the drug produced was smoother and longer lasting.

Thai marijuana was so good that many believed the effects could not be attributed to THC alone. The story was that the real reason for the stick design was that it allowed the buds to be dipped in opium-infused water. No definitive answer about whether this actually happened has ever been produced but the rumours helped spread the popularity of the new brand as increasing numbers of sticks found their way to America and beyond.

Profits were huge and overheads were low: $75 worth of Thai sticks purchased in Bangkok sold for more than $4,000 on the streets of San Francisco. Smuggling became so rife among certain members of the United States Marine Corps that many suggested the initials USMC actually stood for Uncle Sam's Marijuana Club.

In April 1974 the DEA issued its first public warning about potential imports of Thai sticks, following a modest bust in Hawaii, but the unintentionally enthusiastic tone they used served only to boost demand for the new product. Thai marijuana was, an unnamed official noted, at least three times more potent than the regular stuff and anyone smoking a joint made of it would invariably 'go on one hell of a trip . . . could stay up for a couple of days.' And although the price was considerably higher than the regular stuff, the official pointed out that this was justified as Thai sticks were effectively 'the Cuban cigar of the marijuana world'.

That summer, David Ortiz became one of the first major dealers to tap into the potential of this new product, obtaining regular supplies from a Bangkok-based soldier who used military post to mail home packages of up to 20 pounds at a time.

As Ortiz's imports found their way across California, demand for the potent new strain rocketed and canny dealers began exploring ways of obtaining supplies of their own.

By pure coincidence, Paradise College, where Mancuso and Degen had studied, had been taking part in an ongoing cultural exchange programme and Mancuso had played host to a young man from Thailand a couple of years earlier. It took only a few phone calls for a source to be arranged. Mancuso and Degen then purchased a brand new Air Stream caravan, complete with a custom-made secret compartment, and despatched it on the lengthy voyage to Bangkok.

Once there the vehicle was met by Sunthorn Kraithamjitkul, a local businessman also known as 'Thai Tony'. The owner of a Bangkok automobile dealership, Sunthorn also had extensive contacts among the dope growers and was thus able to secure the highest quality product for the lowest possible price.

The caravan, driven by Harry McKeown's brother, Joe, spent

several weeks on an extended sightseeing vacation before returning to Bangkok where 1,200 pounds of Thai sticks were concealed inside. It was then shipped to Canada where Joe collected it and drove it down through British Colombia back into California.

Back at Lake Tahoe, the drugs fetched around $1,500 per pound – at least four times more than Mexican pot could have generated.

Eager to present a legitimate front, Mancuso invested the money into the small construction company he had launched when he returned to Lake Tahoe. Contractors soon began to develop suspicions that some of his funds were being sourced from outside the traditional banking system – one noted that Ciro always paid his bills in cash and that the money often smelled as if it had been dug up out of a hole in the ground – but no one complained too loudly.

The construction company was the real deal and all the projects it embarked upon were genuine, but Mancuso had no intention of going straight. He had found the perfect product and the perfect way to disguise his income. All he needed to do now was find a way to get hold of a great deal more.

Back in Thailand, Mancuso's supplier, Sunthorn Kraithamjitkul, eager to exploit growing demand for his country's finest export, was in the process of signing up another young American as a customer.

Robert Lahodney was a keen sailor who, after graduating high school, had spent his time travelling around the world on the *Pai Nui*, a small yacht belonging to his father, before ending up in Thailand for several weeks. Lahodney was yet another former member of the Coronado High swim team and his best friend was none other than Eddie Otero.

Returning to Coronado, Lahodney was eager to tell Otero and the rest of the company of his discovery. 'You guys can make the same money from two tons of Thai sticks as you'd make from twenty tons of Mexican pot, and it will only cost you a tenth as much up front!'

Otero and Weber were eager to switch to the safer, more lucrative source but Villar resisted. Despite concerns about violence and safety, the Coronado Company's importation of 12 tons of Mexican marijuana had gone without a hitch and had been closely followed by an equally successful consignment of 15 tons.

They were making plenty of money and had managed to keep the risks to a minimum. Why change a system that was working so well? In truth, Villar's reasons for objecting were far more selfish. He had been brought into the enterprise purely because of his ability to speak Spanish and this remained the cornerstone of his role. If the gang stopped using Spanish-speaking suppliers, he feared they might no longer need him.

But with his being the only dissenting voice, he was out-voted and arrangements were made to transfer money to Kraithamjitkul in Thailand to pay for the upcoming shipment.

Lahodney was not a member of the Coronado Company so the profits would not be shared equally. Instead he would effectively hire the company to perform the offload and hand over a third of the drugs as their payment.

In December 1976 the *Pai Nui* and its precious cargo sailed into a small natural harbour just south of San Francisco. This time around, instead of using the Zodiac boats and rafts, Weber had come up with a brainwave and bought a DUKW, an amphibious military vehicle capable of reaching 10 knots on water and 50 mph on land. The name is pure coincidence. DUKW is a US Army acronym, with the D meaning the vehicle was first introduced in 1942, the U standing for 'Utility', K referring to all-wheel-drive and the W designating twin rear axles. The vehicles have always been affectionately referred to as 'Ducks'.

Instead of bringing the drugs in by boat and then loading them onto the truck, Weber took the Duck out to the *Pai Nui* and tied up alongside her while the drugs were transferred. The Duck then returned to shore, drove straight up the beach, onto the main road and made its way to the stash house. It all worked perfectly, significantly reducing the time the drugs spent on the beach – the most vulnerable part of any offload operation.

Even with their small share of the load, the Coronado partners still made more than $150,000 each and it was clear that Thai marijuana was the way to go. The Company offered Lahodney the chance to become a full partner, in return for a one-off payment of $85,000. It was a token gesture, nothing more. By then each of the partners had each made more than $1 million from their smuggling activities. Now, thanks to the switch from Mexican to Thai, they were set to make many millions more.

4
SEA WEED

Just as Robert Lahodney was shaking hands on the deal that made him part of the Coronado Company, Thai Tony's other major customer, Ciro Mancuso, was waiting nervously for his first seaborne shipment of marijuana to arrive.

The venture had started life late the previous year when a dark-haired man in his mid-thirties walked into the office of New Mark Yacht Sales in Newport Beach, San Francisco and introduced himself as Joe Evans.

Speaking with a slight European accent, Evans explained that he was the head agent for Carib Cruise Ltd, a leisure-boating company based in the British West Indies, and was looking to buy a boat the company could offer out on a charter basis. After browsing through New Mark's catalogue, one boat in particular caught his eye: a sixteen-year-old cruising ketch named *Drifter* with an asking price of $125,000.

Built by a prestigious West Coast company, the *Drifter* featured a distinctive design and many state-of-the-art features. She carried a LORAN-A navigational system, a 600-foot recording fathometer, a Decca radar with a range of 48 miles, a weather facsimilator that took short wave inputs and printed out weather maps, a 600 watt ship-to-shore single side band radio with a range of 2000 miles, an automatic pilot and three compass systems: electric, magnetic and gyro.

Evans immediately made an offer of $93,000 which the broker accepted. Evans then opened the attaché case he had been carrying and counted out $8,500 in $100 dollar bills as the deposit, promising the balance would be paid in the next few days.

In reality Evans was Jurgen Aherns, also known as 'Joe the

German', a Singapore-based engineer who Mancuso had appointed chief liaison between him and the sources of supply in Thailand. As well as helping to acquire a suitable smuggling vessel, Aherns would also be in charge of organising a foreign crew to load the drugs and would take care of all the logistical arrangements for that end of the operation.

On 14 January 1977 the *Drifter* was hoisted on to the deck of the transport ship *Montana* which then set off for Singapore. The ocean-freight charges amounted to more than $24,000 but Mancuso considered this a worthwhile investment because it would dramatically reduce the amount of time it would take the *Drifter* to reach Thailand.

Three men were hired to sail the boat back with its cargo. Marcus Zybach, a Swiss engraver turned smuggler, was captain and Richard Tegner, a cabinet maker who had helped build the secret compartments in Mancuso's caravans, was appointed mechanic and handyman. The last position was filled by a carpenter friend of Tegner's. The trio were given $5,000 in advance and airline tickets to Singapore. Zybach, as captain, had been promised a fee of $125,000. Tegner would receive $100,000 while his friend would take away around $75,000.

In all the trip would set Mancuso back around $500,000, not including the cost of the drugs, but this was only a tenth of what he expected to make in return.

In Thailand Aherns met the crew and supervised the transfer of the dope. The drugs were packaged into neat 2-pound bricks, each containing 480 Thai sticks and each wrapped with heavy-weight plastic intended to keep out the sea air and prevent the drugs from going mouldy before their arrival in the States.

There were so many packages that they would not all fit in the boat's hold and finding somewhere to put the remainder initially posed something of a problem. They had to be out of sight and someplace where they were unlikely to be splashed by high waves, but not where the additional weight might unbalance the boat. In the end, Zybach settled on the smallest room in the house. The packages filled the boat's only lavatory from floor to ceiling, rending it unusable. When it was time to go the trio would have to revert to tradition, drop their pants and do their business over the side.

In early April 1977, with the loading finally finished, the *Drifter* set sail for San Francisco, tacking north-east as she followed the Japanese current towards the Aleutian Islands in the northern Pacific Ocean.

The crew whiled away the hours listening to cassette tapes of the hit albums of the day: Jimmy Buffett's *Changes in Latitudes, Changes in Attitudes* featuring the artist's breakthrough track, 'Margaritaville'; Steely Dan's *Katy Lied,* and the recently released *Best of Eric Clapton.*

Near the Aleutians, the *Drifter* was buffeted with icy waves and a wind-chill factor uncomfortably close to zero. All three men began to regret the decision to stuff the toilet with pot. Going over the side was bad enough but exposing their nether regions to artic temperature was out of the question. In a desperate bid to reduce the need to venture out, the trio stopped eating for several days.

Two weeks later, the crew had moved south and reached the warmer waters of the tropics, only to immediately run aground on a reef. It should have been only a minor setback – the *Drifter* carried equipment allowing the men to fix a line and winch them-selves into deeper water – but while they were setting up the line, the trio heard a noise that made the blood in their veins run ice cold.

It was the sound of a large, low-flying aircraft approaching from the west. They watched with growing horror as the military surveillance plane began circling them, clearly observing them closely.

Tegner turned to Zybach, swallowing hard and fighting back repeated waves of terror and nausea: 'We're fucked man. Totally fucked.' The trio did their best to continue winching themselves free of the reef but there seemed little point. Instead they watched the horizon, convinced that at any moment a customs cutter or navy cruiser would come steaming towards them, ready to board and place them all under arrest. With the plane above, they couldn't even ditch the drugs overboard into the ocean without being spotted. It was, they concluded, all over.

After ten minutes of circling, the airplane made one extremely low pass and dropped a small, watertight package close to the *Drifter*. The crew dragged it on board and, with trembling fingers, unzipped it.

The first thing they found was a printed sheet. An arrest warrant? Advance notice that they were about to be boarded? Instructions to remain where they were and await the arrival of the navy?

Zybach unfolded the piece of paper and read it out loud: 'Your vessel has been photographed from above using the military's latest, state-of-the-art airborne surveillance technology. If you would like a souvenir copy of this photograph, please quote the reference number at the top of this page and send a cheque or money order for five dollars to . . .'

On the back of the order form, someone had scrawled: 'Are you OK?' while the rest of the package contained some fresh fruit and a copy of the latest issue of *Playboy* magazine.

The three men calmed themselves, went out on deck and waved up at the sky, giving thumbs up and 'A-OK' signs. The plane broke off and headed east, never to be seen again.

On 2 June 1977, after ninety rigorous days at sea covering the 7,500 miles from Thailand, the *Drifter* slipped underneath the majestic Golden Gate Bridge. It stopped first at Tiburon so the crew could come ashore and inform Mancuso of their arrival.

Filthy and exhausted, the three men were tying up when a coastguard patrol boat passed slowly by, just a few feet away. Tegner started hyperventilating, convinced he was about to have a heart attack. But the officer at the rail of the patrol boat merely waved and shouted hello.

Tegner's stress levels continued to rise. Mancuso informed the trio that the offload crew who had been standing by had been unable to wait any longer and had moved on. It would take him at least three days to put together another one.

The idea of spending three days around San Francisco bay with $5 million worth of marijuana on board was even closer to a living hell than the trip they had already made, but the crew had no choice.

Finally, on 5 June, the *Drifter* pushed upwards to a remote area near the mouth of the Petaluma River in San Pablo Bay where, under cover of darkness, the cargo was transferred to inflatable boats.

Despite the difficulties, the drugs had arrived without a hitch. Zybach and the carpenter left the boat, leaving Tegner and another man to sail it across the bay to where Mancuso wanted the boat placed into dry-dock for repairs.

On the way to Richmond, the *Drifter* was spotted by a local police boat known as the *Blue Knight*. The boat looked like it had been through hell but Tegner, confident and cocky as hell now that the drugs had gone, insisted they had simply been cruising around the bay. Suspicious, the officers escorted the boat into the port where it was boarded immediately by customs officers.

Again Tegner was asked where he had been.

'Tiburon,' he replied.

'And where before that,' asked Customs Officer Thomas Tinger.

'Nowhere,' said Tegner. 'We're bringing the boat over to have it repaired.'

'Mind if we take a look around,' asked Tinger.

'Sure, go right ahead,' came the reply.

What Tegner did not know was that during the voyage, the carpenter had decided to dip into the main cargo and removed some drugs as his own personal stash, only to forget all about it. As the customs officers swarmed the boat, they soon found the 28 pounds of Thai sticks hidden under the floorboards below deck. Tegner was arrested and taken to Richmond police station.

Told that if he cooperated and named names he would be released, Tegner broke down almost immediately. In a frequently tearful all-night confession he told the officers he had only agreed to take part in the venture because he wanted the money to start his own business.

Once Tegner started talking, he found it hard to stop. In an ideal world he would not have known anything about the men behind the venture but Mancuso had made the mistake of having someone on the crew who knew him only too well.

Tegner named Mancuso, he named Zybach and he named Degen and Aherns. He told the officers every last detail of the operation and when he had finally finished, the police kept their promise, releasing him on $50,000 bail.

When Mancuso heard that the *Drifter* had been seized and that Tegner had been arrested he knew there was only one man who could save him – his lawyer, Patrick Hallinan.

A rising star in legal circles throughout California, Patrick was the son of legendary attorney Vincent Hallinan, a man who had been captivating courtrooms since the thirties and become a universally recognised lawyer and political figure, even running for President.

But Patrick Hallinan was not content to live in his father's shadow and had quickly made headlines of his own, showing he was prepared to go that extra mile in order to protect his clients' rights. Early in his career, Patrick had got into a shouting match with a judge while attempting to present evidence in a traffic case and had ended up on a contempt charge. Given the choice of paying a $100 fine or spending five days in jail, Hallinan chose jail.

Mancuso had first hired Hallinan two years earlier after finding himself in a tight spot. He had travelled to Half Moon Bay, a coastal town just south of San Francisco, to visit his old friend Michael McCreary, who ran a beachside surf shop by day and helped to distribute marijuana by night.

The pair met up, swapped a few stories and then decided to share some cocaine while sitting in McCreary's car. By an unfortunate coincidence, the day Mancuso chose to visit was also the day that agents from the Drug Enforcement Agency, who had been keeping an eye on McCreary for several weeks, decided to make their move.

The agents were interested only in McCreary but Mancuso panicked. Moments earlier he had been snorting from a bundle of cocaine that was now sitting on the seat beside him. Anxious not to be caught with the drugs, he picked up the package and tossed it out of the open window into some nearby bushes. But the agents spotted him, recovered the drugs and took both he and McCreary into custody.

More marijuana – much of it belonging to Mancuso – was found at McCreary's house along with a quantity of cocaine. The two men had both been on the wrong side of the law before but, for Mancuso, this was the first time he was facing a serious felony charge and potentially looking at a long spell inside.

He knew a few lawyers back in Lake Tahoe but the case demanded someone with local knowledge. Mancuso had more than enough stashed away to buy himself the best defence that moncy could buy and after asking around, one name and one name alone kept cropping up: Patrick Hallinan.

The more Mancuso heard about Hallinan the more he wanted him and so he was thrilled when the lawyer agreed to take on his case. Frighteningly intelligent, articulate and deeply persuasive, Hallinan soon worked his magic.

According to Mancuso, the young lawyer took McCreary to one side and began his pitch. If the police hadn't been looking for McCreary, then the drugs would never have been found. So naturally it followed that if the police hadn't been looking for McCreary, Mancuso would never have been arrested. 'So,' Hallinan had explained softly, 'it doesn't really matter who the drugs belonged to, the point is that if you hadn't have been with McCreary, they would never have been found.'

By the end of the meeting McCreary had agreed to say the drugs, even those that belonged to Mancuso, were his responsibility. McCreary went to jail; Mancuso was sent for a one-hour session with a drug counsellor. To say that Hallinan's new client was impressed would be a massive understatement.

Now, thanks to Tegner's loose lips, Mancuso was in trouble again and knew that Hallinan was his only hope. He pleaded with his lawyer to somehow make the problem go away and even hinted that he would be willing to pay Tegner hundreds of thousands of dollars to 'vanish' for a year or two. Hallinan told his client that he would do what he could.

Within weeks, Tegner had somehow had a change of heart and told the police he wanted to withdraw the statements he had previously made. When the officers explained that this was not possible Tegner vanished for several months, eventually turning up in a hippy commune in Oregon.

Despite significant circumstantial evidence linking him to the *Drifter*, Mancuso was never even questioned and was once again more than pleased with the way Hallinan had protected him from prosecution. But this time he had learned his lesson.

Despite having made millions of dollars and having the potential to make millions more, Mancuso told Hallinan that he had decided to quit while he was ahead and retire from the marijuana business.

'He'd had a narrow escape,' says Hallinan, 'and felt it was just too dangerous to carry on. He told me he was getting out of drugs and would instead focus on running his own construction company, which was becoming increasingly successful in its own right. And as far as I was concerned, that's just what he did.'

5
BAD COMPANY

The weeks that followed the successful importation of their first shipment of Thai marijuana should have been blissful for Louis Villar and his boys. Instead, the first cracks in the Coronado Company's corporate façade began to appear.

Soon after Lahodney joined the organisation Lance Weber proposed that the company merge with another group of California marijuana smugglers he had come to know. By combining their resources and manpower, Weber explained, they would soon be able to dominate the market.

Villar and Otero were sceptical, although they agreed to at least meet with others and talk it through. But as they made their way to the venue they suddenly realised they were being followed and that the hotel bar they were heading for had already been staked out by DEA agents. They aborted the meeting and returned home, shaken.

At an angry meeting the following day a furious Villar accused Weber of being reckless, failing to take the proper precautions and attracting too much heat. The biggest criticism was that Weber had remained friendly with Paul Acree, the founder member of the company who had been expelled a few years earlier. There were vague rumours floating around the marijuana circuit that Acree had begun cooperating with law enforcement and both Villar and Otero were terrified that Weber might now do the same.

What no one in the Coronado Company realised at the time was that, in revenge for being kicked out of the gang, Acree was busy telling anyone who would listen everything he knew about its operations.

In January 1977 he had appeared as a witness before a grand jury in San Diego to help kick-start a probe by local law enforcement agents into the group's activities.

For federal prosecutors, a grand jury represents one of the most powerful weapons they have in their crime-fighting arsenal. Rather than deciding if someone is guilty or innocent, grand juries listen to evidence and then vote on whether or not someone should be charged. The evidence they hear is presented by one side alone: the prosecution. As no one has been charged yet, there is no need for the defence to be represented. In fact, when witnesses are called to give evidence, they are not allowed to have their lawyers with them in the grand jury room, even if they themselves are the target of the investigation.

Everything about a grand jury – from the names of the people being investigated to the evidence they hear – is cloaked in absolute secrecy to prevent witnesses from being tampered with and to decrease the chances of those being investigated fleeing before they can be arrested. The indictments they issue are kept under wraps until a judge rules they can be made public.

The greatest power of the grand jury comes from the prosecutor's ability to call absolutely anyone as a witness and compel them to give evidence. If a witness refuses to appear or answer questions, they can be charged with contempt. If a witness lies, they can be prosecuted for perjury.

Although the Fifth Amendment of the United States' constitution protects the individual against self-incrimination, grand juries can grant witnesses immunity, virtually forcing them to testify and implicate everyone they ever worked with.

Such witnesses are caught in a classic catch-22 dilemma: if they hold back on evidence to try to protect friends, their stories may not match with those of other witnesses, in which case they face a potential perjury charge. But Acree didn't need to be compelled to testify; his expulsion from the gang he had helped set up still rankled, and so he was more than happy to appear on the witness stand.

Through his continuing friendship with Weber, Paul Acree knew not only about the smuggling that had taken place up until the time he had been kicked out but also all the importations that had taken place since. Asked by the grand jury if it was correct to describe the activities of the Coronado Company as an ongoing conspiracy running between the years of 1971 and 1976, Acree had smiled. 'Yes. In fact it is still going on now, you know.'

Although they could only speculate about a possible grand jury investigation, the Coronado Company took the discovery that they had been under surveillance as a major wake-up call; a sign that they had to smarten up their act.

Louis Villar, Robert Lahodny and Eddie Otero promptly moved away from the Coronado area and began living under an assortment of false names while planning their next shipment.

Although Villar and his ex-wife, former cheerleader Katherine Stocker, were no longer together, the former teacher had maintained a close friendship with her brother Fred, who had spent some time travelling and surfing around North Africa and the Middle East.

Eager to recapture his status within the group, Villar opposed the idea of sending another boat to Thailand right away and suggested that instead they turn their hand to importing several tons of hash from Morocco.

Stocker was despatched to Tangier to make the negotiations to buy ten tons of the product but after a few weeks telephoned to say he had been unable to find a supplier after all. Weber and Otero flew out to join him and while they also struggled, they eventually made arrangements to buy tons of kif, much of it low grade and therefore worth considerably less than the company would have liked.

Only a portion of the money was paid up front – the remainder was to be paid once the drugs had been sold. But the Moroccan sellers were nervous about such an arrangement and insisted on being given some kind of guarantee.

'You mean, want something for security? OK. What?' asked Otero.

The leader of the Moroccan gang stroked his chin then pointed at Fred Stocker.

'Him. We take him as security. He stays with us. When you pay the money, we let him go.' Fred swallowed hard. The whole deal had been his idea and it was clear that this was the only way to ensure it went ahead. He had no choice but to remain behind.

With the deal done the company's tuna boat set sail for the North African coast and David Vaughn, one of Villar's former students who had taken over the role of 'beachmaster', was despatched across the country to find a suitable offload site. This time around there was no question of bringing the drugs into California, partly because the area had become too hot but also because the East Coast was far closer to Europe.

After a brief search, Vaughn settled on the small town of Machias in northern Maine, close to the Canadian border. A sparsely settled two-dock fishing village with a fog-bound cove and a population of just 1,400, it seemed to be the perfect place to do business.

Vaughn rented a house on a cliff and brought over a small advance party that installed a huge clandestine winch in the garage overlooking the beach. There was no road up from the shore and the cliff was too steep for any other vehicle to simply drive away. Instead the gang planned to use the winch to lower the trucks down to the beach, load them with the drugs and then winch them up, ready to be driven off.

It turned out to be a textbook importation. It was only when it came to selling the actual drugs that the company ran into problems. The main buyer, who had been lined up in advance, balked at the poor quality of the drugs and decided not to buy after all. The company were forced to drop the price in order to get rid of the product.

It wasn't a complete disaster – the total profits were still in excess of $2 million but this was far, far less than they had expected and everyone ended up taking a massive pay cut. The tuna-boat captain was particularly upset. Promised a cool million dollars for his role, he ended up receiving less than half of that amount.

The lower selling price also caused difficulties with the Moroccan suppliers, who insisted on receiving the agreed amount. By the time the situation was finally resolved, Fred Stocker, who had been chained in a bare, windowless room in a bamboo hut while being kept as security, had been away for months. When he was finally released, he had gone completely insane.

The company needed a scapegoat for all the problems the Moroccan venture had encountered and Weber, still under a dark cloud because of the incident with the DEA, seemed to fit the bill perfectly. Villar, Otero and new partner Lahodny held an emergency company meeting and made the decision to kick Weber out.

Furious, Weber at first refused to leave, but then Otero claimed that he had somehow obtained tapes of Weber talking to Acree that proved he had been cooperating with narcotics agents. Although Weber had done no such thing, he had indeed spoken to Acree and began to get increasingly paranoid about just what he might have said, even though Otero never offered any proof that the tapes even existed. With his partners becoming increasingly irrational and paranoid, Weber decided that it was in his own best interests to quit as quickly as possible.

'I sincerely believed that Villar and Otero might consider killing me in order to prevent my testifying against them or providing information which might lead to their arrests,' Weber recalled. 'In those years I remember that Otero frequently wore a shoulder holster with a 9 mm automatic pistol. I remember him wearing the gun in the holster sometimes when he was just driving around town and we were not working on a "scam".

'I also remember Villar telling me and Otero that he would follow the example of a Mexican Mafiosi named Pepe if he had to eliminate people who were stealing from the company or providing information to the cops. Villa said that Pepe had told him he had eliminated several people who he had caught with their fingers in the pot by taking them on a one-way plane ride. Pepe said he took the people in an airplane up to about 20,000 feet over the mountains of Baja California and then threw them out. I remember Otero saying he would do basically the same thing but that he'd use a boat instead.'

Weber eventually agreed to accept a 'retirement' package of $400,000, although he received only $250,000. In return, he agreed not to testify against the others or assist the authorities in any way.

But it was already too late. In December 1977, while skiing in Colorado, Louis Villar got a call from David Vaughn. 'We've been indicted,' Vaughn said solemnly. 'They just unsealed it today.'

The San Diego grand jury had finished its investigation and handed up a seven-count indictment naming twenty-five members of the Coronado Company in a massive drug smuggling conspiracy.

Within days dozens of arrests were made, mostly of the low-ranking members of the offload crews who had worked at most two or three days for the company during the previous couple of years. Villar, Otero, Weber and Lahodney – all named in the indictment – were already living under the radar but now they were officially fugitives from justice.

As was the case with Ciro Mancuso, the first person that the members of the Coronado Company turned to in times of crisis was their lawyer.

A few months earlier Villar had retained Phil DeMassa, a brilliant young San Diego attorney who was fast earning a reputation as someone brave enough to take on the government whenever necessary, smart enough to win even the most difficult, seemingly hopeless cases and happy to represent any clients – just so long as they were able to pay his fees.

While Patrick Hallinan did drug cases as and when they came along, DeMassa was a leading light among a select group of West Coast lawyers who actually sought out dealers as clients.

DeMassa chose to make the law his profession for one reason and one reason alone: he wanted to make a lot of money. And soon after he qualified, he realised that in order to achieve his goals he would need to do two things. The first was to be willing to work hard; the second was to restrict himself to clients who were able to pay his hefty fees.

In those early days of the war on drugs, money laundering was not yet a crime. Attorneys regularly received their fees in cash and were under no legal or ethical obligation to withdraw their services, even if they suspected the money had been generated directly from illegal activities.

Instead of cash, some lawyers received their fees in land, boats, cars, paintings, jewellery and even silver bars – all of which was perfectly moral and legal. It was, by all accounts, a great time to be a lawyer.

Initially DeMassa spent his time dealing with the company's business interests – there were properties to be bought, corporations to be chartered and tax shelters to arrange – but once the indictments were issued, DeMassa began to tackle the gang's legal problems too.

A few weeks later, Villar met with DeMassa at the Mark Hopkins Hotel in San Francisco to decide how best to proceed.

Although Villar was a wanted man, DeMassa was under no obligation to turn him in or even report on his whereabouts, just so long as he did nothing to assist Villar's life on the run. Lending money, allowing Villar to use his car, offering him a place to spend the night or even paying for lunch – to do any of those things would have left DeMassa open to a potential charge of harbouring a fugitive.

The two men soon got down to business. DeMassa had so far arranged for more than a dozen clients to plead guilty and agree to fully cooperate with the government's investigation of the Coronado Company by providing information about the group's structure and management. In exchange, all the arrested men had been granted bail and those without previous convictions had been promised they would not have to spend any time in jail.

In reality the notion of absolute cooperation was something

of a sham. The men had agreed to say the absolute minimum necessary to convince the government that they were indeed doing their bit. The hope was that in two or three years time, when the excitement surrounding the case had died down, things might have cooled and the leaders would be able to give themselves up without threat of heavy sentences.

'Hell, by the time you guys are ready to come in they might even have legalised pot,' DeMassa told Villar.

The next topic on the agenda concerned DeMassa's fees. After the indictments he had been given a retainer of $300,000. Some of the money had been used to hire other lawyers to represent defendants whose cases were being tried in other jurisdictions; some covered the cost of drafting and redrafting endless motions in support of others and a large chunk had been spent on hiring a leading private detective, Jack Palladino, to probe into the government's case and interview potential defence witnesses.

In DeMassa's experience, all but the simplest cases usually required the services of a competent investigator to ensure that important facts were not overlooked. As Villar balked over the demand for more cash, DeMassa explained that the best private detectives on the market could quite literally make or break cases, and Jack Palladino was simply the best there was.

The son of Sicilian immigrants, Palladino had grown up in Boston. After gaining a law degree, he had been drawn into the world of investigation after finding work with a legendary private eye called Hal Lipset, an electronic surveillance expert famous for once hiding a bug in a martini olive. The Gene Hackman character in the 1974 Francis Ford Coppola movie, *The Conversation*, had been loosely based on Lipset and his antics.

DeMassa pointed out to Villar that, while he was still a fugitive, it was key to have someone like Palladino on the defence team who could root out what was happening with the government's case, uncover what information Acree was giving to investigators and interview potential witnesses to the grand jury to find out what they were likely to say.

As DeMassa explained the calibre of the defence he was helping to build up he made it clear that much of the credit for keeping so many people out of jail was down to the work that Palladino had done. He also made it clear that every last cent of the initial $300,000 was now gone. If DeMassa was going to carry on representing the Coronado Company, he was going to need some more cash.

For the first time in many, many years, money had become something of an issue. On top of all the legal fees the partners of the Coronado Company had some very expensive lifestyles to maintain.

Villar and Otero had both bought homes in the exclusive Santa Barbara suburb of Montecido, home to dozens of celebrities and multi-millionaires from the oil industry. Lahodney had bought himself a ranch-style residence complete with seven polo ponies and employed two full-time grooms to care for them.

Villar, living under a variety of aliases including Richard Bentley and Richard Sheldon, had up to eighteen classic sports cars in his collection and employed a full-time mechanic to maintain them. His fleet included seven Mercedes, three Ferraris – one of them an extremely rare Ferrari Dino – and a mint condition 1965 AC Cobra.

Villar also owned an original Salvador Dali, appropriately titled *Smugglers Cove* worth more than $1 million, massive amounts of jewellery, and a fine wine collection worth tens of thousands of dollars.

After meeting with DeMassa, Villar flew back to Santa Barbara and met with Otero and Lahodney to discuss their next move. The partners quickly reached an obvious conclusion: if they were to maintain their luxury lifestyles and meet their lawyers' bills there was no choice, they were going to have to go back to work.

Having easily survived the fallout from the Morocco debacle, Villar was finally ready to accept that his position with the Coronado Company was totally secure and no longer dependent on his language skills. It was clear to all three partners that the best money-making opportunity came from the high returns and low initial costs that were part and parcel of dealing Thai marijuana. They unanimously agreed that, from that point on, they would focus their attentions on that one product.

But just as they were poised to begin planning a trip to Bangkok, the dangers associated with smuggling drugs from Thailand suddenly shot off the scale.

6
DEADLY VOYAGE

In early April 1978, James Clark and Lance McNamara set sail from California to Thailand on a mission to collect as much marijuana as they could carry and bring it back home. The pair easily made it to Thailand, loaded up with Thai sticks and set off on the return journey. They were never seen again.

By the end of that summer at least six other yachtsmen from Britain, America, Australia and New Zealand had vanished just off the coast of Thailand. Although only Clark and McNamara are believed to have been smuggling dope, the disappearances worried other traffickers who started to wonder if the risks now outweighed the benefits.

Pirates were known to haunt the waters off the Thai coast and potential smugglers would also have to pass dangerously close to Vietnam and Cambodia, both of whom patrolled the area with heavily armed gunboats.

Clark, thirty-five and originally from Minnesota and McNamara, twenty-six, a native of New York, had met in California. By the mid-seventies they were well ensconced in the counter-culture movement and were avid fans of the Thai marijuana that sold periodically at a premium in the haunts around Santa Barbara beach.

Excited by the prospect of a great adventure and of becoming millionaires overnight, they had built their own 40-foot yacht, the *Mary K*, and set off on a whim. Although they were aware that an element of danger was involved – both men carried guns for their own protection – they could never have imagined the sheer terror that awaited them.

The Khmer Rouge infamously arrested and eventually executed

anyone classed as an 'enemy' of the regime. Such enemies included anyone with a formal education, anyone wearing glasses, anyone who failed to produce the required quota of rice and, of course, anyone with connections to foreign governments.

A key detention centre was at the Tuol Sleng high school which the Khmer Rouge had turned into a prison known as S-21. Prisoners were kept in tiny cells and forbidden to even turn over without permission. They were tortured every day: they were forced to drink water from the sewers, had the bones in their fingers broken and their toenails pulled out with pliers. If this failed to produce the required results, they were repeatedly given electric shocks.

Sometimes it took days, sometimes months, but everybody confessed in the end. Of the 20,000 or so detained at S-21 during the three years of its operation, just seven survived.

When the Vietnamese Army liberated the prison, pictures of all the missing yachtsmen were found in the files and the truth behind their mysterious disappearances could finally be pieced together.

It transpired that Clark and McNamara had been on their way back home, crossing the Gulf of Thailand, when they spotted a fast motorboat on an intercept course. Assuming that the motorboat belonged to pirates, they set full sail and tried to outrun their pursuers. While McNamara desperately tried to maintain full speed, Clark took out his revolver and began shooting. When he ran out of ammunition he picked up his friend's pearl-handled Colt .45 instead.

But this was no pirate ship; it was a Khmer Rouge patrol boat looking out for Vietnamese naval craft. The *Mary K* had unwittingly strayed into Cambodian waters. The patrol boat opened fire with a 50-calibre machine gun, scoring a direct hit on the *Mary K*'s hull.

The pair were blindfolded, hauled ashore, thrown into the back of a truck and taken to S-21 where eyewitnesses saw them being dragged across the courtyard by the bushy beards they had both grown during their trip.

'I knew from experience that if they were only tortured they wouldn't say anything,' the prison's director, Kaing Khek Leu said later of the Western hostages. 'So torture had to be accompanied by psychological tactics. I told them they would be released if they talked. This was a lie, but it worked.'

The increasingly paranoid Khmer Rouge regime was under the impression that Cambodia had been infiltrated by countless foreign agents and would accept no other explanation for the presence of any outsider. The notion that the two men were simply trying to get rich quick by smuggling drugs from neighbouring Thailand back to America was seen a nothing more than a pathetic cover story. After a month of carrot-and-stick games accompanied by a starvation diet, chronic sleep deprivation and daily electric shocks, Clark was finally ready to tell the 'truth' about his trip.

'My name is James William Clark. I am thirty-five years old,' he wrote, going on to describe his California childhood, his studies at the University of California at Santa Barbara and even the two years he spent in prison at the end of the sixties for refusing the draft.

He told of meeting a CIA contact at the Raffles Hotel in Singapore and being recruited as a spy. 'He wanted me to photograph essentially the central and southern parts of Cambodia. I was to photograph fishing boats and war boats, notice their speed, how they were painted, and what they were made of (wood, steel, cement, etc.), whether or not they were doing military practice (manoeuvres) three or more at once, whether they had radio antennae.

'The key country to watch in South East Asia is Cambodia, the most successful communist country,' Clark continued. 'Cambodia seemed to be getting stronger every year. The US thinks that if Cambodia becomes strong enough, it will invade Thailand and turn it to communism. After Thailand, it would be easy to make Malaysia communist and then Singapore would be threatened.'

The confession states that he was taking photographs of an island at the moment he was captured. 'This finishes my Cambodian job, and with that we have taken only twelve pictures. For this mission . . . my pay is about $700,000 and Lance's about $400,000. As to Cambodia, the CIA will keep on bringing its agents of all kinds to spy upon it.

'The CIA has men all over South East Asia to keep up with the political events there. Even though I was caught, there will be someone else to do the job. The CIA must know what is happening.'

The confession is signed and dated 23 May 1978 and carries Clark's inky thumbprint.

No confession belonging to McNamara was ever found and it therefore seems likely that he died from injuries sustained during the gun battle or while being tortured.

The CIA, in line with its standard policy, will not confirm or deny whether Clark was an agent, but the ludicrous nature of his and other similar confessions obtained at the time, combined with the use of torture, makes it highly unlikely that any of the Westerners caught up in the genocide were anything other than innocent victims of a murderous regime.

Once the confessions had been obtained the prisoners were no longer of use to the Khmer Rouge. Clark would have been taken to a patch of waste ground just outside Phnom Penh called Cheong Ek but better known as 'the killing fields'. Blinfolded, he would have been made to kneel down at the edge of a pit and then hit on the back of the head with the metal axle from an oxen cart. His throat would then be cut to make sure they were dead.

Most victims were simply buried, but foreign prisoners like Clark were then placed inside tyres and burned and their bones smashed into powder, with the intention of destroying all evidence that they ever even existed.

With Thailand out of the picture during the summer of 1978, the Coronado Company had no choice but to look for a source elsewhere.

In September, Eddie Otero was despatched to Singapore where he promptly purchased a new fishing boat called the *Tusker* for $190,000, hired a crew and arranged for the boat to collect 5 tons of hashish from Pakistan.

A dozen members of the offload team were despatched to the offload site in Machias Bay to wait for the *Tusker*'s arrival. Knowing that trying to blend in among such a small population would prove almost impossible, the gang members opted to live like recluses. That turned out to be a huge mistake.

The locals didn't have any problem with strangers in general, only with those strangers who failed to go drinking in the local bars, nod hello to other customers in the post office and chat to staff in the general store. It was a crystal clear sign they were up to no good. One later noted: 'These people didn't understand a darn thing about how to fit into the scenery of a small town in Maine. They were stupid.'

Concerned residents reported their suspicions to the police who, suspecting a smuggling operation was underway, called in the DEA. Undercover agents flocked to the town but quickly ran into the same problem as the men they were trying to keep watch on: they stood out like sore thumbs.

A few days before the marijuana was due to arrive, members of the beach crew spotted the agents and fled the town. The *Tusker* was still out of radio range so there was no way to warn the crew they were heading straight into a trap. In desperation, Otero was sent to South Africa where he chartered an aircraft to fly grid patterns over the ocean to try to find the ship. It was nowhere to be seen.

In fact the *Tusker* had made such good time it arrived at the bay ahead of schedule, right into the arms of the coastguard. But when agents boarded the vessel to carry out a search, they thought they had made a terrible mistake – there were no drugs on board.

Confused and frustrated, the coastguard captain ordered the *Tusker* to follow his vessel into port where a more thorough search could take place. It was an opportunity the *Tusker*'s captain planned to take full advantage of. The initial search had failed to find the five tons of hash because the drugs had been placed in a compartment hidden behind a thick sheet of ice.

During the trip to shore, the *Tusker* positioned itself directly behind the coastguard vessel. The crew smashed the ice covering the hold and began dumping the marijuana bales off the stern of the ship.

The position of the two ships meant the coastguard had no idea what was going on. For a short while the crew truly believed they had managed to get away with it, but as they pulled into the harbour, they saw dozens of bales of marijuana bobbing up and down on the waves and following them in. The drugs may have been off the ship, but the DEA had all the evidence they needed to make their case, and several low-ranking members of the Company were jailed.

In total, Villar, Otero and Lahodney lost more than $600,000. They knew only one way to recoup their losses – they had to arrange another shipment. And this time, in order to minimise their costs and maximise their profits, it had to be from Thailand.

The following June, with the Khmer Rouge out of business, the Coronado Company arranged to import two and a half tons of Thai marijuana into Bear Harbour in California. The area chosen for the offload was close to a popular camping spot so, in order to clear the area, a company employee wearing a fake park ranger uniform was sent out to warn campers of a rabies outbreak and order them to move away.

From there on it was a textbook operation with the drugs being sold on a few days later. Villar, Otero and Lahodney were each $400,000 richer and the Coronado Company was back in business.

7
FEAR OF FLYING

The success of Bear Harbour didn't just renew the confidence of the Coronado Company, it also spurred them on to carry out their most audacious operation to date. Not only would they be bringing in 6 tons of Thai weed but, thanks to beachmaster David Vaughn, they would be pioneering a revolutionary new technique which promised to minimise the risk of law enforcement interception and drastically cut the offload time.

Vaughn had proposed that, rather than using boats, the company should use helicopters to get the drugs from the mother ship to the shore. Through Lahodney, Vaughn had met Hugo Butz, a pilot in the army reserve who knew a pilot, navigator and mechanic all based at Fort Lewis, Washington who would do the job for around $125,000. They would use Huey helicopters from the base itself, booking them out on spurious reasons around the time of the offload.

Vaughn had designed a series of wire cages filled with cargo nets to hold the marijuana. Each featured a large hook that could be used to attach it to the helicopter. By his estimations, the whole consignment would be removed from the boat within five minutes, rather than the usual six or seven hours.

Vaughn also equipped the helicopter crew with a four-stage electronic device that could notify them when the boat was in position and ready for them, identify the direction of the landing spot, identify the landing spot itself and then point the crew to the makeshift refuelling depot the gang had set up for them.

With the offload due to take place at the remote Neah Bay, a cove close to an Indian reservation in the state of Washington, all the gang had to do was acquire a boat to ferry the drugs across the Pacific. Soon they managed to source a freighter – the *John L. Winter*.

The plans continued to progress smoothly but then fate intervened. An accident at a military air show led to a tightening of the rules about who could sign out a helicopter. Before the accident, pilots were allowed to sign on their own behalf. Afterwards, an officer had to countersign all such requests.

It was a minor setback but one that would only add a layer of administration, not cause the project to crumble. Vaughn still believed that helicopters represented the fastest way by far to complete the offload and everyone else in the Coronado Company was in full agreement with him. The cages were placed on the *John L. Winter* as it travelled off to Thailand to pick up its drug load.

An advance team had secured the area several days beforehand, decked out in fake park ranger uniforms and chasing out several campers with the story that the land was privately owned and they were not allowed to stay there.

On 23 August 1980 the ship arrived at Neah Bay but so did a dense fog. The boat crew were upset as they had finished the last of their food and water and were desperate to get the job finished, but the helicopter crew wanted to wait. As well as needing the fog to pass, the crew said that in two days time a more 'friendly' officer would be on duty, one more lax in permitting the signing out of helicopters.

In an effort to pacify the situation Butz, who was in contact with all parties, took out a light plane and made air-drops of food and water to the increasingly nervous boat crew, but it was not enough. The boat crew was threatening to dump the load into the ocean.

David Vaughn called Villar to tell him of the problems and the former teacher immediately flew to Washington on a chartered plane flown by Butz. Garrett, the man who had helped to buy the freighter, also arrived on the scene. Villar decided that the gang had no choice but to abandon the idea of using helicopters.

But time was running out and the boat crew were getting increasingly anxious. There was not enough time to assemble a new offload crew and equipment to carry out the job in the traditional way. Because of the plans to use the helicopter, the size of the beach crew had been dramatically reduced and there simply wasn't enough manpower to go around.

But then Garret had a brainwave. He had spent some time in the area in recent years and had got to know members of the local Native American tribe who lived on the reservation nearby. He recalled that they spent a lot of time fishing and had a small fleet of boats nearby. He was sure they would be willing to lend a hand almost immediately, for the right fee.

For $125,000 the tribe members agreed to help unload the marijuana into their boats. However, their boats were loaded with fishing gear, drastically reducing the amount of room they had on board. Garrett had asked them to remove their equipment but they had feigned a lack of understanding. In reality, removing the gear was a long, complex task and none of the Native Americans were in the mood for it. Even with the money they would be making from helping out with the smuggling venture, they would still need to go fishing the following day and none of them wanted to get up a couple of hours early to get the boats ready.

The first trucks arrived in the early hours, just as the tide was pushing seawater up the river towards a small beach that carries traffic to Sooes Beach, south of Cape Flattery on the ocean side of the peninsula.

The men worked quietly and quickly to unload two 35-foot long inflatable rafts and another rubber craft around 20 feet long. Donning rubber wetsuits they tied the rafts together and attached an outboard motor to the shorter craft in the lead. On the shore opposite, a lookout set up a tripod that held an electronic night-vision scope to watch out for the coastguard, police or innocent members of the public who might stumble across the scene.

As the boats headed off, other members of the crew unloaded

an electric generator, an electric conveyor belt and several long lengths of conveyor track. All the wheels of the track, each the size of a skateboard wheel, had been coated in rubber in order to reduce the noise and muffle the sound. The end of the conveyor track was moved into the river and the men sat down to wait.

Ducking low to provide as small a silhouette as possible, the men came alongside a darkened vessel where a crane was swinging a heavy net down towards the water. The men stacked the 50-pound plastic-wrapped bales of marijuana into the rafts. When all three were loaded to the gunwales, they headed back towards the shore, guided by one-word radio commands from the watchman on the night scope: left, right, left and so on.

The helmsman fought against the receding tide. Water washing down from the river across the sand was much shallower now and each succeeding wave left the beach a little barer. One wave carried the lead boat into the river but the second raft got hung up on the sand as the water receded. The next wave – a rogue, extra large one – pushed both the cargo rafts sideways against the rocky bank. Jumping down, the men fought against the current to get the rafts off the sand and back into the shallow water. The motor was useless now. They could not free the second raft because the third was high and dry.

They had to cut one of the rafts loose. Grabbing a diving knife from a scabbard on his leg, one of the frogmen sawed through the rope connecting the last raft. Another wave came and tipped it sideways into a pool of water at the base of the cliff. A pole of plastic bricks washed overboard and bobbed gently just below the surface of the water like green slabs of ice.

They were getting desperate now. They scrambled around to gather what bricks they could and loaded them onto the remaining rafts. They took them up on the trucks, stacking split pieces of cedar behind the cargo for camouflage.

Squinting in the darkness, the driver of the first truck tried to make out the tracks in the grass as the truck crawled, headlights off, towards the road. Suddenly the truck lurched sideways. The driver fought for control but the vehicle's double rear wheels had slipped over the edge of the bank and the vehicle fell on its side. The men conferred. 'Leave everything, let's get the hell out of here.'

It was noon the following morning before hikers from a nearby campground noticed the small plastic bundles floating in the water. By the time the Makah tribal police and other authorities got there, more than seven hours had passed. The gang had left behind drugs with a wholesale value of more than $50 million. It was the disaster to end all disasters.

The clues they left behind at the offload site were bad enough but Louis Villar's growing arrogance was a far greater problem. Over the previous year Villar had spent a lot of time in Hilton Head where he hired two handymen to build a guest house. He could not resist bragging to the two men about being a drug smuggler and even told them that he had taken their salary of several thousand dollars and invested it into a drug deal. They were lucky men – they were going to be rich and they would not have to even break the law.

There seemed every reason to be confident. Villar spent money like it was going out of fashion. He paid an interior decorator $50,000 in cash for her services – making sure the builders were in earshot – and always had vast quantities of cocaine lying around the house for anyone who fancied a toot.

When the Neah Bay operation failed, Villar decided that he did not want to bear the loss alone. He told the builders: 'It looks like you won't be getting your money for a while. The drugs were lost during the offload. I have personally lost $2 million in this venture.'

There was more trouble on the horizon. In the summer of 1981 Sunthorn Kraithamjitkul, the man who supplied both the Coronado Company and Ciro Mancuso with their marijuana, travelled to California to collect some of the money that was owed to him.

Sunthorn flew to San Diego and met with members of the company, then visited Mancuso and travelled with him to Lake Tahoe, where Sunthorn looked at homes to purchase, decided it was too cold and headed home. He arrived at San Francisco Airport for his return flight and, after checking in, passed several small signs warning international travellers to report cash over $5,000 or face a fine or forfeiture.

At the security checkpoint, an attendant observed peculiar dark masses on his X-ray screen as Sunthorn's suitcase passed through the machine. Within minutes, agents from US Customs and the Drug Enforcement Administration were swarming around him like hornets.

In halting English, Sunthorn told them an odd story. He said he had entered the country with gold – which he had neglected to declare – equal in value to the $831,000 in US currency that he was now carrying.

It was a lapse of judgement. If instead Sunthorn had said that he wanted to declare it, he could have filled out a form, left the money there, and boarded the flight. They couldn't pin on him that he made his money dealing dope.

Sunthorn was immediately jailed and indicted by a federal grand jury for lying to customs. Because some of the money he was carrying belonged to the Coronado Company, Phil DeMassa was hired to act in his defence.

But in Sunthorn's suitcase, agents found the business cards of Ciro Mancuso, his wife Andrea, Brian Degen, and documents relating to the Mancusos' shell corporation in the Cayman Islands. Ciro knew the heat was on.

Mancuso became worried that the contents of Sunthorn's suitcase would prompt a tax probe, which it did. Mancuso gave his lawyer Patrick Hallinan a cash retainer of $100,000 and asked for help in foreclosing on properties that his shell corporation owned in Nevada. Hallinan, still believing his client had left the drug business behind, went to work as quickly and efficiently as he could. Then, secure in his belief that his client's smuggling days were long behind him, Hallinan swung into action and the probe quickly fizzled. Mancuso was so pleased with his lawyer's work that, as a bonus, he handed him the keys to a brand new Mercedes Benz convertible.

DeMassa worked his usual magic and won the case, though Sunthorn was obliged to remain in the country pending the outcome of an appeal by the government.

Later that same year the Coronado Company attempted another importation, this time bringing four tons of Thai marijuana into Bear Harbour, the site of an earlier successful importation. The drugs arrived but only just – the mother ship became disabled soon after starting its journey across the Pacific and had to be towed to Japan.

The company was forced to pay $250,000 for repairs and a further $300,000 to members of the Yakuza, the fearsome Japanese mafia gang, who in exchange ensured that customs officials did not board the ship while it was being fixed.

In November 1981, just a few weeks after the importation, the world of the Coronado Company came crashing down around its ears. Louis Villar left his Santa Barbara home for a drive, only to find the police waiting for him when he returned.

The builders, furious at being short-changed for the work they had done for Villar, had gone to the authorities, who had asked them to continue working but pass back information about Villar's operations.

Simultaneous swoops were made on other members of the gang. The company lawyer, Phil DeMassa, soon heard rumours that Lance Weber had flipped and agreed to become a government witness. Eager to find out if this were true he despatched his top investigator Jack Palladino to find out.

Palladino lured Weber to a hotel room in Reno, Nevada, which he had kitted out with hidden microphones, hoping the founding member of the company would say something that would rule his testimony invalid. But Weber came fully prepared and insisted on conducting the whole 'conversation' using words drawn out on a series of etch-a-sketch pads which had the advantages of being silent and left no permanent record.

Ultimately it made no difference. The government had assembled more than enough evidence to secure its convictions and Villar, Otero and Lahodney found themselves facing long prison sentences and multi-million dollar fines.

At the same time Thai Tony, who was staying with friends in Los Angeles still waiting for his appeal, took ill and died in hospital.

The reign of both the Coronado Company and their main supplier was over, but the market they had helped to create for South East Asian marijuana showed no sign of going away, prompting a fresh generation of entrepreneurs to step in and fill the gap.

As the popularity of the highly potent strain of dope began to grow, increasing numbers of foreign nationals began to flock to Bangkok with the sole intention of getting involved in the trade, either helping to facilitate those travellers looking to buy the drug or to organise their own shipments out of the country.

Some were former members of the military who had stayed behind in the region after the end of the Vietnam War, others were dope-loving travellers who had simply stumbled across this stoners' paradise while making their way around the world; still others were cool-headed businessmen eager to capitalise on the high returns the product had to offer, regardless of its legality. In all cases they had seen the potential of the international market and were eager to grab the opportunity with both hands.

A whole new era of Thai marijuana smuggling was about to begin.

PART TWO

8
THE IN-CROWD

Bangkok, June 1982

To the casual observer there seemed to be little about the Superstar to make it stand out from the other bars in and around Patpong, the heart of Bangkok's red-light district.

A sea of multi-coloured neon, dark wood and polished chrome, the interior of the bar was littered with small silver tables, each surrounded by black leather chairs and sofas. The walls were painted black, too, the lack of colour broken up only by occasional eccentric displays like vintage motorcycles, sports memorabilia and the odd video game machine.

Like all the other bars in the area the Superstar was permanently filled with a mixture of scantily clad women, transvestites and transsexual 'ladyboys' who split their time between dancing on the stage, parading along the catwalk and mingling with the customers. In return for the price of a drink, these 'women' would happily chat, giggle and play the occasional board game. For only a little more they would accompany the customer to a nearby hotel and perform a wide variety of sexual services.

Less sleazy than most – the nearby Supergirls and Superpussy both featured 'ping-pong shows' where women performed the local party trick of inserting objects into their vaginas, then using their muscle contractions to shoot them out across the room – the Superstar was a magnet for those seeking other forms of entertainment. During the regular 'movie club' slot bootleg copies of films, many of which had yet to be released in the cinema let alone on video, would be shown on a large screen. There was also a comprehensive menu offering Thai staples like green curry with rice alongside international favourites like fish and chips, burgers and nachos.

A hit from the moment it opened its doors, the bar appealed to locals and *farang* (Thai for 'foreigners') in equal measure, attracting a clientele from all walks of life. Yet for many, the bar's most compelling attraction was one that was never advertised. Unbeknown to the vast majority of those drinking there, the Superstar was the home of Bangkok's most exclusive club. To become a member you needed just one qualification: you had to be involved in the marijuana trade.

On any given night, the corners of the bar would be packed full of dozens of American and European traffickers as well as local suppliers, negotiating prices, working out delivery schedules, hiring boat captains, arranging cash transfers and examining samples, all relatively openly.

The traffickers had come to Bangkok in pursuit of the vast fortunes to be made from selling the very best marijuana in the world, exploiting the growing demand created by the likes of the Coronado Company and Ciro Mancuso. By the early eighties, the Superstar was virtually synonymous with the entire Thai marijuana trade. The bar's owners were hardly in a position to object. American Robert Lietzman and British-born Michael Forwell were both accomplished smugglers in their own right, and it was as a direct result of their legendary antics that the Superstar became so attractive to their fellow traffickers.

It was the perfect place to do business. Although the DEA had dozens of agents stationed in Bangkok who visited the Superstar from time to time, no one considered them to be much of a threat. For one thing, everyone knew what they looked like, making them easy to avoid. For another, the agents were far more concerned with the trade in heroin coming out of Thailand, Burma and Laos – the so-called Golden Triangle.

After one of the Bangkok agents accidentally shot himself dead with his own gun, many of the smugglers began to believe that the DEA was a far bigger danger to themselves than to anyone else.

The smugglers who met up at the Superstar were as unlikely a band of brothers as there has ever been, ranging from helicopter pilots and former members of the army's special forces to college dropouts and spoilt brats living off their trusts funds. But chief among them was an ageing hippie by the name of Brian Daniels.

A solid six-footer whose once-long hair had begun to recede prematurely, earning him the nickname 'baldy', Daniels had been born in New York but had grown up in California where he had discovered the joys of living life among a Bohemian beach-based community.

A failed marriage while still at college led to him dropping out and heading off into the big wide world in a bid to 'find himself'. He spent eight years hitch-hiking his way across Europe, Asia and the Middle East before finally settling down in Bangkok in 1976 at the age of thirty.

A long-time fan of the holy herb, Daniels not only refused to believe that the sixties had ever ended but lived in the vain hope that they would one day make a comeback. Until they did, Daniels felt compelled to share the spirit of the times, in the form of Thai sticks, as widely as possible.

A confident sailor, Daniels' first ventures were as part of a small, loose-knit collective of smugglers that included Robert Lietzman, the man who would later go on to open the Superstar. He and Daniels loaded up small boats with freshly harvested marijuana and then made their way south to Australia. The Ring also included Briton, Timothy Milner and Phil Christensen, a Vietnam veteran who had been stationed in Bangkok during the war, became fluent in Thai and decided to stay on.

Although they were all friends together, exactly who did what and when within the smuggling ring varied according to who was able to source drugs, pay the farmers and find buyers. When Lietzman began to spend increasing amounts of time in Australia, Daniels began working more closely with Milner. Together they devised a scheme that dramatically reduced their travelling time. Rather than heading all the way to Sydney, they would take their drugs and bury them on Bernier, a remote island off the coast of Western Australia. Milner's contact, Ray Cessna, would travel to the island and collect the drugs, allowing Daniels and Milner to head back to Bangkok far sooner.

At the same time Daniels also began working with Phil Christensen to target the lucrative American market. In 1977 the pair arranged to buy some helicopter engines, filled the gaps between the components with 50 pounds of Thai sticks and then had them flown by air freight to San Francisco where Daniels's brother removed the drugs and sold them on.

The following year Daniels and Christensen increased the size of their load to 200 pounds, concealing the drugs in a consignment of plywood. It was Daniels' first big score and generated a profit of around $200,000.

As Daniels and the other members of The Ring became increasingly successful, so they began to amass increasing amounts of cash and needed a way to launder it. The solution was provided by Timothy Milner who, while investing his own earnings in a Hong Kong-based finance house, had become particularly friendly with an American broker named Bruce Aitken; friendly enough to admit that the money he was investing came from the drug business.

Unfazed by the revelation, Aitken calmly offered to launder Milner's cash, first moving it around the world's money markets and then ultimately into offshore accounts and tax havens, for a modest commission. So efficient was Aitken that he was soon performing a similar service for Daniels and Lietzman. Within a year Aitken had quit his job and set up his own company, First Financial Services Ltd, which was based in Hong Kong. His workload consisted almost entirely of moving money for marijuana traffickers.

But just when things seemed to be going from strength to strength, Lietzman got caught up in a sting operation set up by the police in Sydney. Needing to get out of Australia fast while avoiding the usual customs and immigration channels, he was fortunate enough to run into a freewheeling spirit named Michael Forwell.

The son of an RAF fighter ace who had fought with distinction during the Second World War, Forwell had been born in Buckinghamshire and educated at the exclusive Gordonstoun private school in Scotland, previously attended by Prince Charles and other members of the Royal Family.

As a teenager he divided his time between Britain, Australia and Singapore where his family had significant business interests. At the age of twenty-one he inherited a million pounds from his grandfather. Rather than using the money to start his own business as his family hoped, Michael bought himself a yacht and set off sailing around the world, determined to do as little as possible.

Tall and tanned with a mop of tussled hair dyed blond by the sun, and a warm smile, Forwell ensured he enjoyed his wealth and freedom to the full and took every opportunity to rebel. When he met Lietzman and heard of his dilemma, he didn't hesitate. Forwell allowed him to hide in the hold of his yacht and smuggled him back to Thailand.

Once they were back in Bangkok the friendship blossomed further and Lietzman soon introduced Forwell to the world of international drug trafficking. It turned out to be a formidable pairing. Lietzman's ability to procure cut-price marijuana and Forwell's flair for finding innovative ways of concealing the drugs proved the perfect recipe for success.

But just as Lietzman was getting back on track, another member of The Ring, Timothy Milner, stumbled. He was arrested in Sydney in 1979 in possession of 300 pounds of marijuana with a street value of $1.5 million while attempting to make a delivery to Ray Cessna.

The arrest and loss of the drugs was bad enough but Milner managed to make matters far worse by paying $50,000 to a series of allegedly crooked officials, including a police commissioner, a chief magistrate and a leading solicitor, to bribe himself out of trouble.

Initially facing around ten years, Milner was released after just a few months in prison while Cessna was not jailed at all. The subsequent outcry from the so-called 'Cessna-Milner' affair dominated the Australian press for months and cast an uncomfortable spotlight on the smuggling activities of Daniels and the others back in Bangkok.

Once the worst of the media storm had blown over, Daniels used his new-found wealth to invest in a ruby-mining company to start his own gemstone business, but his real ambition lay in rising to prominence within the marijuana trade.

Such was the demand for Thai sticks back in America that the profits available to smugglers were equal to and often higher than those that could be made from trafficking opium. At the same time the penalties were far, far lower. And with 18 million regular marijuana users in the USA compared to around 500,000 heroin addicts, the market potential was far greater. You didn't need a degree in mathematics or economics to work out where the real profits were being made.

Whenever he had a free evening, Daniels hung out with the rest of the expat crowd at the Superstar and listened eagerly to the numerous stories of the successes and failures of smuggling ventures that were being recounted.

Although the various groups that were involved in smuggling were technically competitors, the general feeling was that there was more than enough dope to go around and that they would all benefit by pooling information on how to avoid law enforcement and maximising their profits.

So when a notorious smuggler and logistics expert named Bruce Perlowin arrived in Bangkok, everyone was keen to hear exactly what he had to say.

Perlowin had started out selling nickel bags of weed in Miami in the late-sixties before moving on to ounces and then pounds. By the mid-seventies South Florida was becoming an increasingly dangerous place to operate. The influx of cocaine that marked the start of the days of *Miami Vice* was turning from a trickle to a tide, so Perlowin decided to check out the more mellow environs of California.

Like Brian Daniels, Perlowin's ultimate ambition was quite simply to run one of the largest marijuana smuggling operations in the world, and to do that he needed information. 'I needed to know where the coastguard, the DEA and the customs people were, where their weak spots were, what mistakes other dealers had made, so I could avoid them.'

To this end Perlowin hired a research firm in Berkeley, telling them he was a movie producer making a film about drug dealing. The firm agreed to analyse every major drug bust that had taken place in the area for the previous ten years.

The study contained a mass of useful information that was rapidly devoured by the regulars at the Superstar, the centre of Bangkok's smuggling underworld. Most of all it showed that the weakest link in smuggling operations is the vulnerability of the entry point into the United States.

It represented the dawn of a new, professional approach to smuggling that had not previously existed within the Bangkok underworld. In the past many of those involved in the trade had wanted to smuggle marijuana simply because they believed the plant should be legal and wanted to share its joys and benefits. If they made some money on the side that was all well and good but hippy ideals came first. As the trade developed, the hippies were replaced by a new breed of smugglers who were in it purely for the money and saw the whole thing as a business. And as with any business, you need to stack the odds in your favour in order to survive in the marketplace.

Night after night huge debates raged about offloading tactics used by the likes of the Coronado Company, the problems that surfaced within the organisation when the main partners got too greedy and the dangers of taking money from investors who were not fully aware of the risks involved.

The more that Brian Daniels listened to the likes of Perlowin and others, the more he learned. He learned about the different techniques the smugglers were using to get their drugs across various international borders, he learned about the problems they faced trying to prevent the Thai sticks from going mouldy during long journeys; he learned about the mistakes made by some of the smaller, less experienced gangs that had led to them being exposed. He learned the names of all those considered to be the very best in the business. Finally he learned about the farmers in the villages where the crops were grown, their overheads and how much profit they expected to make.

Yet despite his knowledge and eagerness to move on, Daniels seemed destined to be a permanent bit-player in the smuggling world. But then something extraordinary happened: he fell in love with a young Thai woman called Nipaporn and decided to get married. This of itself was nothing unusual – many of the other expats had done the same – but whether through luck or judgement, Daniels had chosen a bride with unique qualities.

Dozens of members of Nipaporn's extended family lived up in the main marijuana growing areas of north-east Thailand and had extensive personal and professional contacts with the farmers. Nipaporn was equally well connected to senior officials in the Vietnamese, Laotian and Thai armies; the very people responsible for controlling the areas where the drugs were grown.

Around the same time, the DEA was starting to crack down hard on cannabis production in Mexico and Latin America, driving up costs and dramatically reducing profits. But the fight against narcotics is often compared to squeezing a big balloon: when you apply pressure to one area, the air simply moves somewhere else. The more the authorities cracked down on other sources of weed, the more incentive there was for the smugglers of the world to look to Thailand instead.

Brian Daniels could not have planned it better. Either by accident or design, he had suddenly found himself in the right place at the right time and with the right contacts to become the most powerful Western figure in the world of South East Asian marijuana.

In the months that followed his marriage, Daniels began to increasingly immerse himself into Thai culture while at the same time withdrawing from the expat scene, earning the respect of his new relatives and a reputation as 'a *farang* that doesn't hang out with other *farangs*'.

Focusing his attention on individual farmers and landowners in the prime growing regions, Daniels was soon at the leading edge of a massive revolution in the way that Thai marijuana was being produced.

Up until then this side of things had been fairly haphazard with individual smugglers making ad hoc arrangements with whoever was willing to deal with them. Harvests were rarely coordinated between villages, the quality of the product varied wildly from one field to another and the techniques used to process and pack the drugs were almost too numerous to be counted.

None of this was too much of a problem when it came to individual smuggling operations getting hold of five or six tons at a time, but Daniels had ambitions far beyond that. He pictured himself at the centre of a massive smuggling ring composed of cells of smugglers, each operating independently from one another. The common factor between them all would be that Daniels would supply the marijuana.

The benefits were clear. Daniels would be able to put out multiple loads each year, often dealing with more than one group at a time. In the event of a shipment being intercepted, the profits from other successful jobs would more than offset the loss. Furthermore, the independent cell structure of The Ring that he envisaged would go a long way to disguising his own involvement.

To add a further layer of protection, Daniels began to ingratiate himself with some of the high-ranking military and law enforcement officials he had begun to associate with as a result of his marriage. In order to successfully move the harvested drugs through the countryside and load them on to boats to take out to the smugglers' mother ships, Daniels would need to bribe dozens of officials. In order to flush those responsible out of the woodwork he quietly began making his intentions known, ensuring those in positions of power that, when the time came, they would be adequately rewarded.

Daniels may not have been the only American active in this field, but he was by far the best connected. Some were cynical about his claims to have friends in high places but most of the teasing ended after a picture of the king of Thailand appeared in the *Bangkok Post*. On the edge of the shot, carrying a walkie talkie, was a high-ranking police officer assigned to protect the Royal Family. Daniels' friends recognised the man instantly – he had been a guest at a dinner party a few days earlier.

One contact proved particularly fruitful. In return for a regular monthly payment, a high-ranking official at the Office of the Narcotics Control Board, the Thai equivalent of the DEA, agreed to provide Daniels with early warning of any investigation focused on his activities.

As Daniels prepared for his first major harvest, the DEA agents in Bangkok and their Thai equivalents were unaware of what was happening right under their noses: that the steady progress they were making in reducing opium cultivation was being offset by a dramatic increase in the marijuana trade.

Not only did Daniels guarantee the farmers a market, he also helped introduce new seed stock, advanced fertilisers and better methods of irrigation. Thanks to Daniels and other American pioneers, the already high potency of Thai marijuana had been increased further still using a process perfected in California. Growers there had discovered that if the male plants were uprooted and destroyed in their infancy, the female plants responded by producing even more THC, the active ingredient in making people high. Within the space of two years, the product known as Thai stick might just as well have had 'Made in America' stamped across every bud.

Daniels also helped to resolve some of the key problems that those early smugglers faced. The biggest of these was the length of the journey across the Pacific. Exposure to the sea air meant that by the time the drugs found their way to America, part of the load would invariably have begun to go mouldy, rendering it impossible to sell. Another difficulty was that the sheer bulk of the product, especially when it was in the form of Thai sticks, severely limited the amount the average pleasure yacht could comfortably fit into its hold.

One of Daniels's subordinates came up with a solution to both problems at once. He adapted a trash compactor to squash the drugs down to a more manageable size, which meant that more marijuana could fit into a much smaller space. He also introduced vacuum packing machines that squeezed out even more air, reducing the space even further and significantly delaying the onset of moulding.

The other issue that needed to be dealt with was that of bribing all the officials and law enforcement officers involved in helping to get the drugs out of the country. Sometimes all the bribes could not be paid in advance but Daniels needed a way to ensure that all those who encountered the drugs would know that they would be entitled to their share. The solution he found was inspired. With the help of friends he designed his own logo: a blue eagle above a line of bold red type that read: PASSED INSPECTION. Word soon spread throughout the smuggling underworld that whenever that sign was seen, officials could rest assured that their payoff was on the way.

During this time Daniels' main competitor was Sunthorn Kraithamjitkul, aka Tony the Thai, the man who worked with Ciro Mancuso, the Coronado Company and dozens of other American smuggling groups, often supplying them with just a few tons of drugs at a time.

But by the early eighties Brian Daniels controlled so much of the Thai marijuana harvest that he was no longer interested in supplying such small loads. He was in a position to dictate to potential buyers what amounts they would take. If anyone was unable or unwilling to deal with the quantities he had, he would simply refuse to deal with them and go to someone else.

It was a system that made perfect sense so far as Daniels was concerned. In purely practical terms, it would cost him roughly the same amount to bribe a customs official to allow one ton of marijuana to pass through his port as it would for five or ten tons. Although there would be more people to pay in terms of truck drivers and guards to bring the stuff through the jungle, the increase was only marginal.

It was simply not financially efficient for Daniels to smuggle small loads the way he had done in the old days. If potential customers couldn't afford to purchase a multi-ton consignment, Daniels was on hand to introduce them to other investors. Together they would form a consortium, sharing the profits but also sharing an element of the risk. It seemed to be a win-win situation all round.

By the time Sunthorn Kraithamjitkul died in a Los Angeles hospital in the spring of 1982, Brian Daniels had already surpassed him and all the other native suppliers in terms of both the quantity and the quality of the marijuana he could provide.

The only cloud on Daniels's horizon related to the way he liked to conduct business. The problem was that the values he held dear put him at a major disadvantage when it came to dealing with the more ruthless and cutthroat smugglers.

As a true hippy, Daniels believed that whenever possible, a sentence should include the word 'man' preferably at the end. He held fast to the principles of karma – the notion that people were generally good to one another – and genuinely hoped that in a situation where there were vast profits to be made, people would simply look after one another without the need for capitalist shackles like contracts and business agreements.

Time and again Daniels would sit in meetings with his fellow

smugglers paying little attention to the fine details of the negotiations and time and time again he would end up being ripped
off or short-changed. The key problem was that Daniels was
such a firm believer in the 'all you need is love' philosophy of
life, that he found it hard to believe that anyone would ever
deliberately take advantage of him.

The best way to avoid such a situation was to have someone
else carry out the negotiations on his behalf. Having once helped
Phil Christensen to smuggle drugs, Daniels was now in a position
to supply them. With 20 tons of premium-quality Thai sticks
ready to go – one of the biggest smuggles ever attempted – Daniels
asked Christensen to help him put together a group of like-minded
investors, financiers, traffickers, offloaders and distributors who
could successfully pull off the operation. It would be the first
cell of The Ring.

It was to be the start of something huge. Ultimately there
would not just be one ring but many, intertwined and linked
through their membership and all supplied by Daniels.

But if that plan was going to succeed, Daniels would need to
ensure the people who smuggled his drugs were able to do so
with the greatest degree of success possible. He was now in a
strong enough position to decide exactly who he wanted to work
with. And he told Christensen that he would only work with the
very best.

9
BAND OF BROTHERS

The first man Phil Christensen turned to with a view to joining the ring was a tall and gangly upper middle-class New Yorker named William LaMorte, who had been involved in the drug trade since 1970.

That very first venture had ended abruptly when LaMorte's boat sank in a storm en route to Jamaica and he and his crew ended up adrift at sea for three weeks before washing ashore in Cuba. But soon afterwards LaMorte had brought his younger brother, Thomas, into the business and gone on to make millions, investing the money in a chain of supermarkets and a luxury multi-million dollar waterfront home in the exclusive Southold community on the north fork of Long Island.

Almost all of his money had come from selling hashish sourced in Lebanon and Morocco but by the beginning of the eighties LaMorte, like so many others, had been drawn to the huge profit potential of Thai product. Having been introduced by Christensen to his friend Bruce Perlowin, the Miami-based smuggler who had visited Bangkok with news of his research findings, LaMorte was soon committed to providing the funding needed to get the drugs processed and loaded on to a mother ship.

With LaMorte's money on board, Christensen knew the next thing that he and Daniels would need was someone to captain the boat that would carry the drugs from Thailand to America. As far as Christensen was concerned, there was only ever one candidate.

Christopher Shaffer was just six years old the day he came home from school to find that a pirate ship had magically appeared in his back garden.

In reality the vessel was just a beaten-up sailboat that his father had brought home to renovate, but in the young boy's mind it was a mighty galleon, captained by the likes of Blackbeard or Henry Morgan, marauding around the seas of the Caribbean and spreading havoc under the banner of the Jolly Roger. It was the start of a love affair with the sea that would come to dominate his life.

Christopher's father had served in the Army Air Corps during the Second World War before moving into the property business in Pittsburgh, Pennsylvania. In 1953 he was offered a job in the army's real estate division on the island of Okinawa and the whole family promptly relocated.

'It was an absolutely idyllic place to be a kid,' Chris recalls. 'I loved it. My dad had a real fascination with boating. We were on the water all the time – sailing, swimming, fishing. I grew up with old boats and rafts and canoes – boating was a passion for me and adventure was a big part of our lives.'

The adventures continued. After a brief return to America, the family moved to France. Christopher's mother, Jeanne, made sure that he and his older siblings, sister Suzanne and brother Bill, saw virtually every European capital, walked through the grounds of every chateau or castle that they came across and toured every museum they found.

Of the two boys it was Chris who enjoyed these excursions the most. Although the brothers were separated by four years they were incredibly close – regularly heading off together on their bicycles in search of excitement. Yet their personalities were poles apart.

'Bill was much more like his father,' recalls Jeanne Shaffer. 'He was very out-going and competitive, a take-charge kind of boy. He took a great deal of pride in his personal accomplishments and recognition was very important to him. He was the youngest Eagle Scout in Europe. He got involved in competitive athletics and was on several all-star teams in baseball and basketball. He always had to be the best at everything he did, win every contest.'

When Christopher was thirteen the family moved again, this time across the English Channel to London. Chris switched schools and over the course of the next five years became increasingly caught up in the cultural and intellectual reforms that were sweeping through the capital at the time.

In 1966 the folk singer Donovan became the first high-profile British star of the counter-culture movement to be busted for possessing pot. Keith Richards and Mick Jagger of the Rolling Stones followed soon after and advocates of the drug realised the time had come to take action.

Following on from a series of smaller protests, more than 3,000 people attended a mass 'smoke-in' at Hyde Park. Later that same month *The Times* carried a pro-legalisation advertisement which declared that: 'the laws against marijuana are immoral in principle and unworkable in practice.' The signatories included such luminaries as David Dimbleby, Bernard Levin and The Beatles.

Christopher was fascinated by the arguments surrounding the pro-legalisation of marijuana and he became an eager participant in the theoretical debates and discussions raging around him, but his own introduction to the practical side of drug-taking was far from conventional.

During the late sixties the eminent Scottish psychiatrist Ronald David Lang began developing a theory that schizophrenia was not truly a disease but merely an alternative way of experiencing the world.

In order to put this to the test, Dr Laing began carrying out experiments using marijuana and LSD. Christopher soon became the youngest of a group of around twenty volunteers who would meet at the Tavistock Institute once or twice a month to drop tabs of acid and smoke joints while Lang and his colleague, Dr David Cooper, monitored them.

Around this time Chris met Tracy Brown, the daughter of an American oil company executive whose family had come London at the same time as the Shaffers. She shared Chris's love of the sea and they were soon utterly inseparable. When Chris returned to the States, Tracy transferred to the same university so they could study and ultimately graduate together. Living with Chris's parents, Tracy soon became one of the family.

The pair then returned to England where they planned to spend a year sailing before returning to their studies. At first Chris waited tables but then the young couple stumbled into the perfect job – delivering yachts. Their very first assignment involved sailing a 40-foot catamaran from the south of France to the south of England on behalf of the owners who had moved.

More deliveries followed and in December 1972 Chris and Tracy found themselves in Rome ready for an eagerly awaited family reunion. Chris's father had been working on a top-secret military project at a nuclear submarine base on the island of Sardinia and it would be the first time in more than a year that the whole Shaffer family would be together in one place.

But instead of their father, the family were approached by a team of officials from the American embassy who told Mrs Shaffer that her husband had apparently eaten some contaminated shellfish, fallen ill with hepatitis and died, all in the space of twenty-four hours. He was just fifty-two years old.

The loss had a devastating effect on the family. Jeanne Shaffer plunged into a cycle of depression and alcoholism from which she would never recover and Bill quit his teaching job and became first a cocaine addict and then ultimately a dealer, primarily as a way of supporting his own habit.

All thoughts of medical school or further study were abandoned and Chris and Tracy moved full time into yacht-delivery work, regularly crossing the Atlantic and travelling around the Caribbean as well as to the Mediterranean and the Far East.

In those early days the vessels they moved were often less than seaworthy. Chris and Tracy would not only have to navigate but they also had to learn how to fix engines and other malfunctioning equipment. They soon became skilled mechanics, great sailors and, in the days before GPS, expert navigators, able to pinpoint locations in the middle of the vast ocean or along a distant coast-line with ease.

Such skills easily lent themselves to the world of trafficking and soon their income from their yacht-delivery business was being boosted by their income from low-level drug smuggling. After a year the couple had enough money to buy a boat of their own, a 105 foot triple-masted schooner called the *Sol*.

Now, instead of smuggling a few pounds of dope here or there, they were in a position to offer their services to gangs looking to shift several hundred pounds of product at a time. With this in mind Chris and Tracy packed up their belongings and headed to Bangkok.

While at Charlie's Superstar, Chris Shaffer became friendly with Phil Christensen who, after learning about the *Sol* and Chris's skill as a sailor, suggested using the yacht to smuggle around a ton of Thai sticks back to the West Coast. Christensen and his partners would pay for the drugs and Shaffer would receive a set fee for transporting them.

Christensen's partners on the deal included two Americans who would be involved at the US end of the operation. They were Dennis Ingham, a cunning, wealthy smuggler whose criminal activities dated back at least to the early seventies and Tommy Smith, a career smuggler who liked to have his fingers in multiple pies. The plan was for Ingham and Smith to meet the *Sol* on the California coast and help with the offload.

It was only when Christensen went to supervise the loading of the drugs on to the *Sol* that he realised that Tracy Brown was not just Chris's girlfriend but also a key member of his crew.

'When I got there Chris was on his boat with his Tracy. I wasn't very happy about having a woman involved because as far as I was concerned, women couldn't be trusted when it came to marijuana smuggling. But Chris said she was an equal partner and that she would be staying. I wasn't happy, but there was nothing I could do about it.'

Ingham also had concerns, not about Tracy but about Chris.

He insisted on having a friend of his named Michael join the crew for the return journey, in order to protect his investment. Chris had no choice but to agree.

When the loading was complete, Chris and Tracy set off across the Pacific, arriving in California around two months later to find a motley band of highly experienced smugglers waiting for them.

Eager to have familiar, friendly faces greeting them, Chris had arranged for his brother Bill – who had been actively selling cocaine in and around Los Angeles – to join the boat as it approached the coastline and assist with the offload as well. His presence was not welcomed.

'Bill was more of a cocaine smuggler than a marijuana smuggler,' Tommy Smith said later. 'I didn't like cocaine people. I liked Chris and his girlfriend. I thought she was a better captain than he was, but Bill I could have done without. I just didn't get along with him.'

Bill became even less popular when he tried to hijack the entire load of drugs with a view to increasing the price he and Chris would be paid for smuggling it in. After the boat docked and several of the crew, including Michael, had got off – but before the drugs had been unloaded – Bill got Chris to sail away and hide while he opened negotiations.

The negotiations were brief to say the least. Michael produced a gun, grabbed Bill by the scruff of the neck and forced the end of the barrel so far down his throat it made him want to gag. 'Just tell us where the fucking boat is,' Michael hissed.

Having failed at their first rip-off, the pair tried again. This time they kept back a portion of the load and handed it over to another group of smugglers, hoping they could collect it later and sell it for their own benefit. However, the ship they chose to trust with holding the drugs was captained by a man who was a good friend of Dennis Ingham. He immediately arranged to give the drugs back and told Ingham what the Shaffers had done.

'It just wasn't the way things worked back then,' Tommy Smith added. 'In the whole of the seventies I never had a problem with anyone except them. All the other smugglers I worked with, they had some honour, but I didn't find any among the Shaffers, not at that time.'

Despite the troubles, the smuggle was ultimately considered to be a big success. Christensen, who had invested $20,000 in the load, received a return of more than $100,000 when the drugs were sold. Chris had more than proved his worth as a captain and Christensen soon made use of his services again on one condition – that Bill kept his distance.

And so it was that in the summer of 1983, with Brian Daniels in the background pulling all the strings, that Phil Christensen got in touch with Chris Shaffer and asked if he would be interested in joining a consortium to smuggle up to 20 tons of top quality Thai marijuana into California. He agreed. But if Shaffer, LaMorte and Christensen were an unlikely band of brothers, the final two investors in Daniels' first major venture were even more unlikely still.

Resplendent in their white turbans, long flowing robes and with ragged beards covering their faces and reaching all the way down to their bellies, the men looked as if they had just emerged from the heart of the Punjab. It was only when they spoke, their American accents ringing through as clear as bells, that their true ethnic origins emerged.

Robert Taylor and Albert Ellis were both members of a curious yoga-loving Sikh group known as the Happy, Healthy, Holy organization or 3HO for short.

The group had been founded in the late sixties by an émigré former tax inspector from India, named Yogi Bhajan, who had arrived in Los Angeles in 1968 and quickly persuaded the flower children that the spiritual salvation they had been seeking through drugs and free love could more easily be found through the practice of Kundalini yoga. Not only that, but the yoga would boost their energy levels, protect them from disease and make them smarter.

Word about the classes that taught you how to get 'high without drugs' spread like wildfire and students flocked to his training camps in droves. By the mid-seventies the Yogi had more than 10,000 followers living in a specially built compound in New Mexico, including the man formerly known as Robert Alvin Taylor. Born in Altoona, Pennsylvania into a family as American as apple pie, he joined 3HO in 1974 and within the space of a few months had become completely unrecognisable. He was even given a new name: Gurujot Singh Khalsa.

Gurujot rose rapidly through the 3HO ranks. It wasn't just that he had instantly managed to grasp the key concepts behind the Yogi's teachings but also that he had managed to uncover the best way to impress his master: with cold hard cash.

With Chris Shaffer, Khalsa, Ellis and LaMorte on board, Daniels could at last see his grand scheme coming together. What he envisaged was a huge umbrella network of smugglers, all more or less working under his control.

As the final preparations were being made, the investors were taken up to remote areas of Thailand to meet the farmers and inspect the drugs they would be buying. After the harvest Shaffer and the others were taken to a warehouse to watch the drugs being packed. First they were vacuum-sealed into clear mylar bags which had been flushed through with pure nitrogen. The mylar was then heat-sealed into large plastic bags lined with aluminium, allowing them to be heat-sealed as well. The idea was that the absence of oxygen within the pack would delay the onset of decay. Two machines were at work and could package a ton of Thai sticks every hour.

It was then time to move the drugs to the coast and load them on to small Thai fishing boats which in turn would carry them out to the mother ship.

In the event, two of the trucks carrying the marijuana down towards the coastal village where they were to be loaded were seized by renegade authorities and only 14 tons were loaded on to the ship. But it was more than enough.

The drugs arrived safely in San Francisco and in the weeks that followed the investors travelled back and forth across the States to collect their money.

Daniels had successfully pulled off his first major importation. Never one to rest on his laurels, he immediately began working on his next load. And this time around he felt secure and confident enough to plunge in and make all the arrangements himself.

10
STUMBLE

The new consignment was to weigh in at just under 13 tons and, to deliver it, Daniels chose a cell led by Dennis Ingham, the same smuggler who had worked alongside Chris Shaffer in the late seventies.

In the years since, Ingham had developed a reputation as a solid and reliable smuggler, despite living a life filled with drug-world stereotypes from fast women and fast boats to shoot-outs and rip-offs. Not only had Ingham come through it all unscathed but he had also managed to father three children by three separate women, all of whom just happened to be sisters.

Ingham worked closely with Harry Kreamer, a San Francisco attorney who managed the finances of the smuggling operation, buying equipment and helping to set up companies to launder money and charter the boats needed to bring the drugs across the Pacific. The final key member of the Ingham ring was Rufus Aylwin, another long-time smuggler with convictions going back to the late sixties, who worked closely with his brother, Robert.

Ingham's most important partner in crime, however, was someone whose existence he preferred to keep quiet. Stephen Swanson was a former DEA agent who had been highly decorated during his career and respected for his many successes against high-ranking drug dealers. It would be years before anyone would realise exactly why he had been so successful. In many cases, rather than simply gathering information, Swanson preferred to sell it to the dealers themselves.

At harvest time Daniels purchased the marijuana for a price between $40 and $100 per pound depending on the rate he had negotiated with the farmer. The load was then transported by lorry down to the coast where a small group of Thai fishing trawlers took it out into the Gulf of Thailand to rendezvous with a freighter called the *Allison*, which would the make the trip across the Pacific.

The drugs were loaded smoothly on board and the *Allison*, captained by Timothy Peterson, set off for the nineteen-day trip to Alaska. During the journey another member of the gang was given the task of keeping an eye out for the coastguard and the DEA, forwarding the information to the ship via a daily satellite telephone call.

As the *Allison* got closer to its destination, Rufus and Robert Aylwin checked into the Captain Cook Hotel in Anchorage, Alaska where they received regular updates from Peterson on the progress of the load. The brothers also began to make preparations for the drugs to be transferred onto a barge which would take them down the coast to Seattle. It was a route the gang had used successfully in the past, taking advantage of the fact that the drug market in Alaska is so small that there are few checks made on arriving cargo.

By transferring the drugs after arrival and making it seem as though the containers had originated in Alaska, they hoped to mislead the local law enforcement officials in Seattle about the nature of the contents.

On the morning of 5 May 1984, the *Allison* arrived and loaded three cargo containers on a barge under the supervision of the Aylwin brothers. In order to further throw the authorities off the scent, Aylwin arranged for the containers carrying the marijuana to be painted white so they would not be recognisable as the ones that had left the *Allison* and would better blend in with others on the barge. Three trucks were hired to drive the containers from Seattle to California where the drugs were to be sold.

It seemed like a textbook operation and Brian Daniels was wondering when to make a call to Bruce Aitken for help with laundering the proceeds of the smuggle when disaster struck.

On 22 May, just as the barge arrived in Seattle, Rufus Aylwin arrived at the dock in order to supervise the offload of the containers and found himself face to face with a DEA special agent who was waiting to board the barge. The agent spotted Aylwin and gave chase but lost him among the maze of containers and machinery that made up the dock area.

Once the barge had docked, the three freshly painted containers were searched and the marijuana worth $125 million was seized. Documents on board the barge pointed to the fact that the containers had originally come via Thailand on the *Allison*, which had docked in Alaska a few days earlier.

Immediate arrangements were made for the *Allison* to be searched and although no more drugs were found, there was plenty of evidence pointing to a highly organised drug conspiracy including dozens of radios and scanners tuned to law enforcement frequencies.

Although the drugs had been seized, all the key members of the Ingham group were still at liberty. They met in California the following week in order to discuss how to proceed. The top priority was to destroy all the records relating to the charter of the boat and communications while the vessel was at sea in order to ensure nothing led back to any of them. As an extra precaution, the gang decided that everyone should obtain false identity papers and go into hiding, at least for a short time.

In the days that followed, Dennis Ingham made a flurry of phone calls to estate agents and other businessmen that he had utilised while arranging the load. He informed them that a shipload of marijuana had been seized and that federal agents might contact them about the ownership of one of the businesses he had created. 'Whatever you do, don't mention my name,' he urged them all.

Daniels was furious and demanded answers but no one knew exactly what had gone wrong. The route had been tried and tested and the smugglers had taken all the usual precautions. What on earth had happened?

Daniels and the rest of the team noticed that, despite the size of the bust, it received barely any media coverage at all – it was hardly even picked up by the local press. Daniels was immediately suspicious. The lack of coverage could be a sign that the bust was the result of an undercover operation, which meant that one of the elements of The Ring had been compromised. If that was the case, it would only be a matter of time before other arrests were made and he himself were indicted.

But just as his panic started to threaten to rage out of control, an explanation for the bust finally emerged. Relying on confidential sources a Seattle newspaper reported that the authorities had been tipped off about the smuggling attempt when a low-ranking member of the crew had unwittingly bragged about the forthcoming operation to a man in a bar. The man, it emerged, was an undercover customs officer.

Although the loss was a financial disaster, The Ring, it seemed, was safe. Daniels and Ingham immediately agreed to set up a second shipment, this time comprising 20 tons of marijuana, in a bid to recoup the losses from the *Allison* and still make a tidy profit.

The problem now was that the seizure of the *Allison* had left the gang without a boat. A new one had to be obtained as quickly as possible. After a brief search, the gang settled on a 150-foot Panamanian tugboat named the *Pacific Star* as the best vessel to use to import the drugs.

Once again Timothy Peterson would be the captain. Ingham assured Daniels that this time around the shipment would be safe.

On 10 November 1983 the *Pacific Star* was loaded from a series of fishing boats and left Bangkok. Almost immediately there were mechanical problems in the South China Sea and it seemed as though the boat would not be able to make the journey. Daniels was forced to travel out to the boat with a series of spare parts in order for repairs to be made.

Throughout December the *Pacific Star* slowly made its way through the Singapore Straits to the Gulf of Thailand where it met with another boat, captained by Daniels, to pick up fresh supplies.

The *Star* then headed towards Mexico. Near Hawaii Peterson managed to make radio contact with the offload vessel and confirm that they were finally on their way.

On 31 December the *Pacific Star* was around 600 miles off the coast of San Diego, waiting to meet up with the offload vessels, when the captain spotted a coastguard cutter, the *Citrus*, on the horizon.

The cutter began racing towards the much slower tugboat and signalled their intention to board. Peterson, doing his best to remain calm, refused and tried to outrun the law enforcement vessel. He began to prepare a coded message to send to Daniels and Ingham to let them know what was going on but, before he had a chance to send it, the coastguard vessel was almost on top of him. A small rubber dinghy had been despatched and the customs officers were carrying out a daring boarding of the vessel despite the *Star* travelling at full speed through the bumpy seas.

The chase had been going on for twelve hours. Peterson knew there was no way to get away and that he was in huge trouble whatever he did. So he made the decision to attempt an all-or-nothing escape bid. If he could get rid of the marijuana as quickly as possible, there was a slim chance he could avoid the most serious of charges.

He ordered the crew to set fire to the ship and then open all the watertight hatches. As the first members of the boarding crew jumped aboard, Peterson turned the now burning *Pacific Star* towards the *Citrus* and set the controls for full power. The coastguard officers could only look on in horror as the burning ship rammed into the *Citrus* at the midpoint.

The impact knocked everyone off their feet and made a horrific noise of metal grinding against metal as further holes were torn in the *Pacific Star*'s hull. The *Citrus*, which had armour plating on its side panels, suffered only slight damage above the waterline and no one was injured. The *Pacific Star*, on the other hand, was unarmoured and began sinking rapidly.

But Peterson had overlooked one factor. The hole in the side of the *Pacific Star* ripped all the way into the cargo hold where the marijuana was being held. As the ship went down, dozens of small packages of marijuana emerged from the hole and began to float to the surface.

Only around 3,000 pounds of the 20 tons the ship had been carrying were seized but it was enough to provide the Coastguard with all the evidence they needed. Peterson and his seven crew members were arrested and charged with drug smuggling.

The Dennis Ingham division of the Brian Daniels Ring were not the only ones experiencing problems getting drugs into America.

In early April 1985 a rusting, 78-foot stern trawler named the *Oregon Beaver* cruised into San Francisco Bay and was soon approached by the coastguard cutter *Point Chico*.

'We asked them on the radio how long they'd been at sea, and if they had any cargo,' says the skipper, Master Petty Officer Gary Keen. 'They came back and said they'd been out for days and had no cargo. But when you're in the fishing business, you don't go out to sea for four days and come back empty. You'd go broke. We could also see that she was lying low in the water, so we knew she was carrying something.

'We gave them the old cliché – told them that we were going to board so we could determine whether the boat was following all applicable safety regulations and federal laws and escorted her to pier 45. Even on the radio, we could pretty much tell that they knew they'd been had.'

In fact the *Point Chico* had been waiting for the *Oregon Beaver* when she headed back into port. Coastguard officers had learned that she had taken on 7,000 gallons of fuel at Bodega Bay and then travelled to San Francisco to take on a further 2,000 gallons. It was around twice as much fuel as a boat of that size would expect to use during a typical fishing trip and immediately alarm bells rang in the minds of the coastguard officers who suspected she was heading out to meet with a mother ship.

Although the officers boarded with the expectation of finding drugs, they were still surprised at what they encountered. 'I looked around,' says Keen, 'and my first thoughts were "Holy Shit, it's everywhere!"'

There was pot in the hold, pot in the engine room, pot in every conceivable space on the boat. With the street value of the drugs estimated at around $3,000 per pound, the haul was estimated at $195 million. It was the biggest haul captured on the West Coast for more than a decade.

The arrested crewmen – all locals – told their captors that they worked twelve hours to take on their cargo and were bound for a small shipyard in San Francisco when they were busted.

Soon into their interrogation, they admitted that the crew had been dining together in a Bodega Bay restaurant when they had been approached by two men who said they wanted to use the vessel for about a week.

When crew-members told the men they made about $1000 per week, the two men pulled rolls of money out of their pockets and paid the six crewmen who were later arrested $1000 in $50 bills.

The seized drugs on the *Oregon Beaver* had been supplied by Brian Daniels and the shipment itself arranged by another division of The Ring, run by William LaMorte along with Gurujot Singh Khalsa. If Daniels had felt the net closing in on him before, he felt it even more keenly now.

Losing the money wasn't the worst part of it. For Brian Daniels the really galling part of having a shipment seized was that it was effectively handing his competitors a free pass.

While his own fledgling organisation was repeatedly stumbling, another business that was being run by Daniels' former smuggling buddy and co-owner of the Superstar, Robert Lietzman, was absolutely thriving.

Recognising the fact that the real market for Thai sticks lay in America rather than Australia, Lietzman and Michael Forwell had switched their efforts there soon after setting up their bar.

The pair formed a company called *Dari Laut* – Malay for 'from the sea' and began air-freighting crates of live tropical fish from Bangkok to San Francisco where they were supposedly destined to fill the aquariums of fancy restaurants. It was a scam of course, but with customs unwilling to carry out too close an inspection for fear of killing off the numerous high-priced species, the drug that Lietzman and Forwell packed inside the crates alongside the fish were never discovered.

When the pair first came up with the idea, Lietzman had wanted to use fake fish but Forwell, knowing the importance of having a totally convincing cover story, insisted on using the real thing and soon became a genuine expert on exotic tropical varieties.

As the money rolled in Forwell bought a house in Singapore while Lietzman invested his money in a huge ranch in New Mexico. Never the kind of men to be tied down, the pair also decided they needed a home with a little more mobility.

Together they purchased a 180-foot barge and each built a luxury three-storey home on its flat surface. It soon became a competition, not just to see whose home was finished first but also which was the more elaborate. Eventually, after spending hundreds of thousands of dollars trying to outdo each other, they agreed to call it a draw. From that moment on they simply bought two of everything – two powerboats, two seaplanes, two satellite receivers – so they could focus on their real business of smuggling drugs and making money.

While they had initially run the Superstar themselves they now found they were spending so much time out of the country that they needed assistance. They soon found the manpower they needed. Twin brothers Sam and Robert Colflesh had been born in Pennsylvania. They had joined the army soon after leaving school and both ended up in the elite special forces squad, the Green Berets. They had served in Vietnam soon after the end of the war and, like so many soliders before them, had fallen in love with the country and the lifestyle. When the opportunity to help run the Superstar came up, it could not have been a better time.

The twins excelled at running the bar but Forwell and Lietzman knew that the skills they had learned in the military could also be put to other use. Both brothers were gifted boat captains and navigators and it was only a matter of time before they were offered the opportunity to get involved in the real business of the Superstar owners.

The first year they sailed a Thai fishing vessel called the *Yellow Bull* to San Francisco and offloaded around half a ton of marijuana. The following year they doubled the amount using a boat called the *Cape Elizabeth*.

In 1982 Forwell and Lietzman bought a 43-foot landing craft called the *Diver Delight*. They engineered a false bottom for the vessel and used it to conceal and ship around a ton of marijuana to the States. For that one trip alone, Samuel Colflesh was paid more than $380,000.

More importations followed but while the business relationship between the two principle owners of the Superstar continued to blossom, their personal relationship began to fall apart. When a dispute over the ownership of the bar erupted, the only thing to do was call in a solicitor. He in turn despatched an experienced investigator to Bangkok in order to delve into the rival claims of the two sides. The investigator was none other than Jack Palladino, the man who had previously worked on behalf of the lawyer for the Coronado Company.

It didn't take Palladino long to realise that his clients were involved in the marijuana trade, but it was none of his concern. He himself was doing nothing illegal and, thanks to the experience he had gained researching into the lives of Louis Villar and the rest of the company, he soon felt right at home.

With Palladino's assistance, it was only a matter of time before the dispute was resolved. Lietzman agreed to hand ownership of the Superstar to Forwell and the Colflesh brothers, and effectively retired from the business, spending an increasing amount of time at his vast estate in New Mexico.

In the meantime the brothers and Forwell continued their smuggling activities, using the *Cape Elizabeth* to bring more drugs directly into San Francisco Bay. By now Samuel Colflesh was so confident about their chances of success that he was investing hundreds of thousands of dollars of his own money into each venture and well on his way to becoming a multi-millionaire.

11
PRIMARY COLOURS

Not only did Brian Daniels have to face his former colleagues out-doing him in the smuggling stakes, but his biggest competitor had seemingly returned to haunt him, literally from beyond the grave.

Although Sunthorn Kraithamjitkul had indeed perished back in 1982, almost immediately a new Thai supplier had risen up out of his ashes and begun using the same name.

Thanong Siripreechapong had the kind of name that proved too tricky for most of the smugglers he was dealing with to remember. It is not clear whether Thanong himself chose 'Tony the Thai' or whether the name was suggested by others. Either way, many of those in the smuggling underworld believed both men to be the same, a detail that would cause problems in years to come.

Thanong exercised ultimate control over many of the fields in the Nakhon Phanom region in the north-east of Thailand, the source of much of the finest marijuana. With seemingly endless contacts at all levels of government and beyond, Tony the Thai was able to produce vast quantities at bargain prices and ease their path from the fields to the docks where they could be loaded on to ships bound for America and Europe.

Thanong's parents ran a small shop selling electrical appliances, glassware and various household accessories. At an early age, along with his twelve brothers and sisters, Thanong was drafted in to help. Using a bicycle he would take some of the shop goods and cycle dozens of miles to offer them for sale in neighbouring districts.

A born entrepreneur, Thanong soon recognised that an even

more lucrative market lay closer to hand. Nakhon Phanom saw some of the most serious fighting between North Vietnamese insurgents and the US Army during the Vietnam War (or American War as the Vietnamese called it). As conditions in Laos, the site of a secret war between the CIA and the Vietcong, became increasingly chaotic, economic opportunities that had not previously existed suddenly emerged.

Goods of all kinds could be bought cheaply there and resold at a substantial profit in Thailand. Televisions, radios, watches and sound equipment were in high demand and Thanong would take them over, bringing other goods that had a higher resale value back in Thailand back with him.

Taking his bicycle across the Mekong river to Laos was a huge risk but soon proved worthwhile. In 1965, at the tender age of thirteen, Thanong was able to replace his bicycle with a motorcycle, an unusual acquisition for anyone in the north-east of Thailand, let alone someone who was only barely a teenager.

The business continued to grow and when Thanong finished school he bought a large truck. Able to travel further and carry more, Thanong found his wealth increasing at a rapid rate. By the end of the war in 1975 many people had become financially successful and Thanong was chief among them. Not only that but he had excellent contacts among the Vietnamese military who now effectively ruled Laos.

As the business grew Thanong could easily have focused on nothing else, but he decided to continue his education, attending teacher training college during the evening and working during the day.

As his status and wealth increased, he found himself courting the daughter of another wealthy businessman and soon made another jump up the social ladder with his advantageous marriage.

The north-east of Thailand has always been one of the poorest regions. It consists mostly of a large barren plateau which is prone to flooding. Every rainy season the lowlands turn into swamps while the uplands are too salty for much vegetation to grow. The region contains more than half of Thailand's paddy land but produces only a little more than a third of the entire rice crop. Its 17 million residents are a mixture of Thai, Lao and Khmer but the culture is predominately Laos-based, leaving locals often subject to discrimination and racism by other Thais.

Even today 90 per cent of the residents live in small villages and the same percentage count farming as their chief economic activity. The average income is half that of the average with 40 per cent of Nakhon Phanom's farmers living below the poverty line.

Much of this disparity came from the fact that Thailand's seat of power was far to the south in Bangkok, but during the eighties this began to change, with the parliament being largely controlled by rural areas at the expense of the urban regions.

Thailand had become an ally of America after the Second World War and had troops in South Vietnam until the early seventies. During this time the country underwent a series of military coups and counter-coups, with martial law being imposed from 1976 under the command of various generals.

In 1973 university students led a civilian revolt against the government and for the next three years democracy reigned. This ended in October 1976 after a huge riot by conservative groups who attacked radical students at the Thammasat University in Bangkok leaving up to forty dead, hundreds injured and thousands under arrest.

The army stepped in and took control until 1979 when democratic elections were held once again.

According to Thanong, his success was all about being in the right place at the right time. 'A good plot of land sometimes fetched as much as 30 million baht after a deposit payment of only 1 million bhat was given. I once bought a plot of land at Nongprue sub-district worth 20 million bhat and, because of my personal credit and soaring price of the land, was able to mortgage it with a bank for as much as 120 million bhat.'

Thanong's increasing wealth was just the kind of situation the government had lived in fear over ever since Thailand became synonymous with the drug trade. Speaking in 1986 the head of the country's Narcotics Control Board, Police General Chavalit Yodamini described the trade in marijuana as 'a threat to Thai society' and called for urgent assistance in tackling it.

'If I make millions from marijuana, I could instigate a lot of trouble,' he explained. 'Money is power, power is money. If we do not get the problem under control, criminal money is going to mix with politics.'

Becoming increasingly prominent in the national community, Thanong took advantage of his status to enter politics. In 1980 he ran for parliament for the first time in the Nakhon Phanom region. He was unsuccessful but the candidacy increased his exposure. Soon there was no one in his home town or in the surrounding areas that had not heard of him.

On his next attempt, he succeeded in being elected to parliament as an MP.

Brian Daniels was only too well aware of the rise of the new Thai Tony, but what really got to him was the news that the Shaffer brothers were to be his first major customers.

Eager to show off his wares, Thai Tony invited the Shaffers to visit Thailand and inspect the marijuana he had available. Wary that they might be walking into some kind of trap, the brothers chose to send one of their team in their place.

By now the Shaffers had surrounded themselves with a team composed of adrenaline junkies. They had also bought a boat capable of transporting large amounts of marijuana across the Pacific and had therefore made themselves ready to join the big boys of smuggling.

In the autumn of 1984 the Shaffer brothers entered negotiations with a man called Byron Evans to buy his ship, the *Six Pac*. Evans was a long-time smuggler and had been using the *Six Pac* to bring hashish from Afghanistan to the West Coast of the States ever since 1980. It had made its last trip in July that same year, successfully landing twenty tons of the product.

The *Six Pac* had many advantages. For one it had already been fitted out with many essentials for drug smuggling. Better still, it came with a crew who were highly experienced in the business. Whereas in the past they had bought ships and then had them adapted and trained their own crew, the *Six Pac* would come as a ready-made package.

A price of $1 million was agreed on the understanding that Evans would refit the ship to bring her completely up to date and would supply a captain familiar with the vessel's operations in order to carry out the Shaffers' next Thai marijuana smuggle.

That captain turned out to be Terry Restall, a former British merchant mariner who had been employed by Evans for several years carrying out both legal and illegal work.

Gutsy and intelligent, Restall wasn't just a fantastic captain, he was also a genius when it came to inventing schemes to ensure that smuggles were always successful. Soon after the boat was sold Restall took it to Malaysia where he picked up three large containers. He had them modified with cement bottoms and then fitted rails to the deck of the *Six Pac*.

The drugs would be stored inside the containers and, in the event that they were compromised and approached by law enforcement or other authorities, the containers could be rolled off the rails and would instantly sink to the bottom of the ocean. So long as no drugs were found on board the ship, it would be impossible for any charges to be brought.

It was Restall that the Shaffers chose to send to see Thai Tony. Meeting in Bangkok, he and Thai Tony then flew to Chang Mai before crossing the border into Laos. There, they were met by a senior army official in full uniform who escorted them to a heavily guarded warehouse where Tony had stashed 200 tons of dope. The message was clear: whatever quantity the Shaffer brothers could comfortably get out of the country, Thai Tony would be able to provide.

Within two months Restall had sailed the *Six Pac* to the Gulf of Thailand and taken on seven tons of marijuana from two

Vietnamese fishing vessels. He brought the drugs back to a rendezvous point 600 miles off the coast of San Diego and transferred them to an American fishing vessel which brought the drugs ashore close to Santa Cruz.

Having successfully brought in a load of marijuana from Thai Tony in early 1985, the brothers were keen to put together another load as soon as possible. But when Christopher travelled to Bangkok in July 1985 he was told that all the available marijuana had already been snapped up by other gangs.

Having given up and returned home, Shaffer was pleasantly surprised when, a few weeks later, he received a call from a contact to say that 10 tons had suddenly become available. The gang that had purchased the drugs had been in the process of smuggling them out of the country when their boat had started to sink. The marijuana that had been recovered by the gang now urgently needed someone else to come in and help with the transportation. The brothers immediately despatched Restall to Santa Barbara to find out more.

The owner of the 10-ton load turned out to be none other than David Ortiz, the early pioneer of Thai marijuana smuggling who had started out having small packages sent to him using military mail from soldiers based in South East Asia. Ortiz and his brothers had since expanded their operations and become investors in far larger loads. Their main role, however, was to act as the offload crew for dozens of smugglers.

As Ortiz spoke with Restall, it soon became obvious to him that he wasn't the main player. Although Restall was reluctant to say exactly who he was working for, Ortiz – eager to move up in the smugglers' league – insisted on being introduced to the boss of the organisation.

In late August David Ortiz met Chris Shaffer. He had heard of him, of course, and only barely managed to control his excitement as the pair reached an agreement in which the Shaffers agreed to provide the long haul transportation for Ortiz's ten tons of pot in exchange for $3 million. Under the terms of the agreement, the Shaffers would also receive a proportion of the drugs and help out with the offload.

Ortiz return to Los Angeles and began contacting members of his crew. He was like an excited schoolboy. 'We're working for the fucking Shaffer brothers,' he said. Almost everyone had heard of them but for those who had not, Ortiz was more than happy to fill in the details.

But the sense of admiration was far from mutual. Chris and Bill dubbed David and his siblings as the 'Beaner' brothers and made no secret of the fact that they neither liked nor respected them. So far as Bill was concerned, David Ortiz could not be trusted and the family was far too exposed. Working with them meant risking the Shaffer organisation too, but because the drugs had originated with them, the Shaffers simply had no choice.

The offload was to take place over two nights. During the first, the portion of the drugs belonging to the Shaffers would be taken ashore at Santa Cruz and the following night the remainder of the marijuana would come ashore at Santa Barbara.

By now the business of offloading had been turned into something of an art form.

The twenty-strong crew met in the auxiliary car park of the Dream Inn in Santa Cruz. Numerous trucks were dotted around nearby, some carrying workers, other carrying the equipment that they would be using.

Just before midnight the signal was received that the small fishing boat that had taken the marijuana from the mother ship had anchored a little way off the shore and the team set off from the staging area to the offload beach.

Half the crew had been provided by David Ortiz, the remainder by the Shaffers. Chris and Bill were there too, personally supervising their employees. David Ortiz was immediately impressed by what he saw. Compared to his own operation, the Shaffers were in a league of their own. As preparations continued he nudged one of his colleagues and nodded towards one of the Shaffer men who was wearing a full wetsuit and clutching a medical bag. 'Look,' said Ortiz. 'They've even got their own fucking paramedic.'

As one member of the crew checked all the vehicles for bugs, another backed up the truck carrying the equipment along the road leading down to the beach until a water pipe across the road meant he could go no further.

The equipment was then carried from the trucks by the crew down to close by the water's edge. It included two 20-foot long Zodiac boats, plenty of rope, camouflage netting, wheelbarrows, air pumps, batteries and two-way radios.

A rope line was attached to the front of the Zodiacs and a second line was attached to the rear. Two members of the crew in wetsuits paddled out to the offload vessel on surfboards towing the front lines attached to the inflatable boats. The front line was than attached to the offload vessel and the lines to the rear ran to the beach.

Crew members on the offload vessel loaded the marijuana and then the Zodiacs were pulled back to the beach using the ropes. The offload crew removed the marijuana and piled it on the beach, covering it with camouflage netting. At this point other members of the crew carried the marijuana up the path and loaded it on to the equipment truck.

Early on a small portion of the marijuana was placed on a separate truck and driven away. The idea was that if the offload was discovered and everyone was arrested, the return from this small cache would provide enough money to pay everyone's legal fees.

In the event such caution proved entirely unnecessary and by 3.30 a.m. the offload was finished and the fishing boat with the remainder of the drugs was heading back out to deeper, safer waters. The Shaffer brothers had pulled it off once again. Even though they despised the Ortiz brothers, they couldn't help but get a thrill from the way David constantly complimented their operation and skills.

Little wonder they were beginning to feel as if they were utterly invincible.

But then came news that shocked everyone at the Superstar and beyond, Brian Daniels in particular. Robert Lietzman was dead, killed in a crash involving his own helicopter. That news had been bad enough but the word being put out by his widow was more disturbing still. She didn't believe his death was an accident. As far as she was concerned, Robert Lietzman had been murdered.

12
FALLEN

Nothing about the crash that killed Robert Lietzman made any sense, and everyone in The Ring knew it.

Of all the marijuana smugglers working in Bangkok at the time, Lietzman had been the one they had all aspired to be. He had worked at the sharp end of the business, made tens of millions of dollars, invested wisely and then retired without ever having felt the long arm of the law.

However, falling out with his one-time partner, Michael Forwell, and leaving first the Superstar and then Thailand altogether had left the forty-seven-year-old Lietzman outside The Ring's circle of trust. At first, none of the remaining members had any reason to believe he would ever betray them, but from the moment his helicopter smashed into the western slope of Carrizo Mountain in New Mexico, everyone that had ever worked with him felt incredibly vulnerable.

Even if his death turned out to be nothing more than an accident, the disposal of Lietzman's assets could still cast an uncomfortable spotlight on the activities of his former colleagues. And if something more sinister had taken place, there was no telling who might be the next target.

For Brian Daniels, having lost his two most recent shipments, the trickle of information being fed back about the crash only added to his growing concern that somehow or other, his fledgling operation had been compromised.

The crash site was just a few miles from the remote O-Bar-O Ranch that Lietzman had bought two years earlier for $10 million in cash. He had spent millions more refurbishing the property, telling friends he wanted 'somewhere remote to go to get away from it all.'

But as the mystery over exactly what had taken place began to deepen, Daniels and others could not help but wonder if the Ranch had been used to plan something far more devious.

Lietzman had last been seen alive on the evening of Sunday 12 May 1985 when he returned a rental car at Albuquerque airport. V.D. Robertson, owner of the nearby airfield where the helicopter was kept, told police that he had seen the aircraft, tail number N8618A, around 5 p.m on Wednesday 15 May but that it was missing when he arrived back at work the following day. Someone – presumably Lietzman – had checked it out early on the Thursday morning, but no one could explain what the ranch owner had been doing during the three days in between.

The wreck was discovered when an Emergency Locator Transmitter signal (ELT), triggered in the event of a crash, was detected at 7 a.m. on the morning of 17 May. But when Lietzman's body was found it was bloated beyond all recognition. Flies and maggots were pouring out of his mouth and nose. A pathologist concluded that Lietzman had been dead at least four days – two days before he had supposedly taken his final flight.

A large pool of Lietzman's blood was found 24 feet from the crash site, yet his actual body was discovered right next to the wreckage, his right leg dangling over the pilot's seat cushion.

A briefcase containing £10,000 in cash and traveller's cheques was found in the remains of the cockpit and Lietzman had thousands more dollars stuffed in his pockets.

The mysteries didn't end there. The fuel tanks of the Enstrom, which had been topped off earlier in the week, were completely empty, even though the flight-time meter showed the engine had only been running for 1.6 hours. Even at full throttle, the Enstrom would have been expected to have at least half a tank left. But there was so little fuel in the aircraft that the crash did not produce any fire – a highly unusual occurrence.

Although the Federal Aviation Administration requires all aircraft to carry ELTs, the cheap systems used on small planes and helicopters are notoriously unreliable. More than 98 per cent of activations are as the result of hard landings rather than crashes, or simple, inadvertent activation of the off switch. In many cases, the devices fail to activate in the event of an actual crash.

The beacons send out an anonymous warble, similar to the sound made by a telephone that has been left off the hook, which can be picked up by passing satellites. To reduce false alarms, each signal that is detected must be confirmed by a second satellite pass. This means it takes between four and seven hours for notice of a crash to be passed on to a search team.

In Lietzman's case this indicated a likely crash time of between 10 p.m. and 2 a.m., but that only added to the mystery further. It would have meant that he had been flying at night, something he was hopelessly under-qualified to do.

Lietzman only ever flew periodically and his student licence had expired more than sixth months earlier. He had owned the helicopter for two years and once had a full-time pilot on his payroll, but had taken the decision to let him go shortly before Christmas. He had last flown the helicopter a month before the crash, when V.D. Robertson watched as he flew up to a low altitude, manoeuvred a short distance and then landed. Lietzman told Robertson he would be back soon and asked for the helicopter to be serviced and fuelled ready for him.

Back at the Superstar, the rumour mill began working at full speed. One theory was that Lietzman had been kidnapped and killed soon after Sunday and his corpse placed near the crash site to make it look as though his death was an accident – that would explain why the advanced state of decomposition his body was found in. Another was that the bloated body was not Lietzman at all and that the cunning ex-smuggler had arranged the whole thing in order to fake his own death.

He certainly had reason to want to disappear. Though Lietzman had always managed to avoid the attention of government officials while actively smuggling, he was finding it increasingly difficult to do so during his retirement.

The Internal Revenue Service had entered the picture. Ever

since the Chicago gangster Al Capone was convicted of tax fraud by a government unable to prove his underworld links, the Internal Revenue Service has been the thorn in the side of every successful criminal.

The vast sums of cash used to purchase the O-Bar-O Ranch soon attracted the attention of IRS investigators who, a year or so before the crash, declared that Lietzman owed at least $6.3 million in back taxes. Even if they couldn't prove the money came from the drug trade, they could still seize the cash, and if Lietzman refused to pay, he could go to jail.

In January 1984, soon after the IRS issued its demand, Lietzman had been arrested trying to enter the States with a fake passport. He was held briefly but released after claiming what is known as a 'greymail' defence. This means he claimed he was effectively working for the CIA in South East Asia and that the fake passport was an essential part of his cover. To take him to trial and probe any deeper could potentially undermine national security. Incredibly, the charges were dismissed.

At the time members of The Ring saw this as nothing more than further proof of Lietzman's ability to talk his way out of trouble. But with hindsight they began to see things differently. Had Lietzman done the unthinkable and somehow struck a deal? Had he been silenced before he had been able to?

'There were people who didn't think he was that terrific. We could well be looking at a murder here,' his wife Carolyn told her local paper the day after his body was found. 'I'm trying not to be conclusive on the circumstances of his death. I am trying to remain objective until I have all the information.'

Friends and relations were not the only ones with suspicions. The FBI, IRS, DEA and even the CIA all sent representatives to New Mexico to dig around and find out more about the circumstances behind the crash.

By the time the National Transportation Safety Board began their own investigation into the incident, the smuggling underworld was buzzing with a number of wild conspiracy theories.

The truth, when it finally emerged, was almost as strange as the fiction.

The key problem turned out to be Lietzman's failure to file a flight plan. If he had done so before he left Albuquerque, a search would have begun as soon as he was thirty minutes overdue. In the event, the fact that there was no easy way to establish exactly when he had left the airfield was the first in a chain of events that would ultimately become responsible for the confusion that surrounded his death.

It also transpired that a key eyewitness had made an unfortunate mistake. V.D. Robertson had been convinced he had seen Lietzman's helicopter in the middle of the week but later realised he had actually confused it with a similar craft.

Tapes from the control tower proved conclusively that Lietzman had actually taken off on 12 May, soon after he had been seen returning his rental car to the airport.

A signal from the helicopter's Emergency Locator Transmitter had first been sent out on Sunday evening and was picked up by Scott Air Force Base in Illinois. However, the signal had been disregarded as Lietzman had not filed a flight plan so there were no reports of any aircraft going missing.

Five or six hours later staff at the base received a second signal. At this time there was still no word about a downed craft so Scott notified airliners to be alert for the signal as they flew around in order to get a more precise fix on its location.

According to NTSB investigators, many such signals exist in the airwaves at any one time. Because there are so many signals bouncing around, no one acts on them until they receive notification by local authorities. However, because this signal was repeated over the course of several days in the same place, Scott Air Force Base eventually contacted local Civil Air Patrol units in the area to carry out a search. An airplane pilot spotted the crash and emergency crews were alerted.

Examination of the wreckage revealed the helicopter's fuel pump had been faulty. Instead of feeding the engine, the pump had been venting the fuel, slowly emptying the tanks as Lietzman flew along. This, combined with a faulty gauge, meant he would have had no idea that anything was wrong until it was too late.

As the Enstrom neared the mountain range, the engine suddenly failed. Lietzman desperately tried to keep the rotors moving as fast as possible to maintain lift, a tricky procedure known as autorotation, but he simply didn't have the experience to pull it off.

As he plummeted towards the ground the tail section hit some trees, knocking the whole vehicle forward into some rocks which shattered the cockpit. The force of the impact and remaining energy from the rotor lifted the helicopter up and made it bounce several times before it finally came to a rest.

At some point in the crash, Lietzman had been thrown from the helicopter and crawled his way back to the cockpit to flip the ELT switch. The Office of the Medical Examiner's report said Lietzman's injuries were consistent which his being able to move after the crash.

His head was uninjured but he had multiple fractures to his arms, legs and ribs, and was bleeding internally from a number of key organs. Having dragged himself back to the cockpit, Lietzman appears to have passed out. He remained alive for another day or two, waiting in vain for rescue, before finally succumbing to his injuries.

The NTSB report found the probable cause of the accident was: inadequate planning and preparation by the pilot, poor decision making by the pilot and a failure to perform refuelling. It also cited over-confidence in the pilot's personal ability.

For Brian Daniels and the others in Bangkok, the official report and investigation into Lietzman's death offered little comfort. It left open the worrying possibility that someone had sabotaged the helicopter, and it was clear that no good could come of so many government agencies probing around, looking for clues about The Ring.

Daniels spent the months after the crash feeling increasingly paranoid. He repeatedly visited the Superstar and hung out with the expat crowd trying to pick up clues about what was happening. He also leaned on his contacts within the Thai police force and Narcotics Control Board to find out if any investigation was underway and whether or not his name had come up.

Having lost his last two shipments and having seen a former smuggling partner die in such mysterious circumstances, Daniels simply didn't feel comfortable putting out any fresh drug loads during the whole of the 85–86 season, allowing his competitors to regain much of the ground they had lost.

For a time Daniels truly believed his days as a marijuana broker might be well and truly over, but after a few tense weeks his contacts reported back that he was in the clear. But just when it seemed that the potential crisis was finally over, a fresh one popped up to take its place.

Timothy Milner, the Briton who had caused such massive scandal in Australia in 1979 after escaping severe punishment for being caught with a load of Thai sticks, had all but retired from the drug business.

In the aftermath of the publicity of his case he had left Bangkok, moved down to the popular holiday island of Phuket and set up home in Chalong Bay, living off his earlier drug earnings and trading on the currency market. Although he was no longer in the capital, Milner maintained his close friendship with both Brian Daniels and the money launderer Bruce Aitken.

During the summer of 1986 Milner started to have concerns that he was being followed. He shared his concerns with his friends but soon decided he was simply being paranoid. The two drug seizures and investigation into Lietzman's crash were weighing heavily on everyone's mind.

But then, on 23 July 1986, Milner was viciously attacked in the street. He had never seen the men who assaulted him before.

Milner went straight to the police and told them he had no idea why anyone would want to harm him.

About three weeks later, on the night of 15 August, Milner got out of his car to remove a log that was blocking the road when he was suddenly set upon by two men. He was kicked and punched, handcuffed, gagged and shoved into the back of his own car, which was then driven off at speed.

At Patong Beach he was given an injection that knocked him out. His next recollection was of waking up in a bedroom on the second floor of a rented house in suburban Bangkok with a massive pain in his side – six of his ribs were broken.

He was told by his captors – two men with strong German accents – that he would be questioned the next day and was given some spiked tea and noodles, which knocked him out again.

The next day he was handcuffed to a chair and questioned about his background, friends and financial status. The men wanted to know most of all if it was true that he had made a fortune from dealing in Thai marijuana. When he refused to answer, he was hit in the face and was kicked and punched in his already broken ribs.

Eventually Milner told his alleged abductors what they wanted to know, and also wrote and signed a telex form to First Financial – Bruce Aitken's company and the place where all his monies were stored – asking for more than $1 million to be transferred to a Hong Kong bank account.

Over the days that followed, Milner was constantly drugged and tortured while his kidnappers waited for the money to arrive. But instead of the money, Milner received a message from First Financial questioning whether the unusual request was genuine.

Milner was then forced to speak to Bruce Aitken personally and urge him to make the transfer as soon as possible. But Aitken remained suspicious. He called Brian Daniels in Bangkok who immediately sensed something was wrong.

He remembered the assault in the street a few weeks earlier and was convinced that Milner had been kidnapped. After deliberating for a few minutes he knew there was only one thing he could do. He called the police.

Detectives quickly traced the call Milner had made to Aitken and located the house where he was being held captive.

The following morning Milner woke up from his drug-induced sleep to hear voices shouting from outside the building. Before he knew what was happening, his abductors took him downstairs and pushed him out into the backyard.

The police were there in force. So were the press. And so was Brian Daniels.

The kidnap and ransom plot had been foiled but Daniels had good reason to feel even more paranoid. The *Bangkok Post* covered the story in depth, making much of the role Daniels and Aitken had played in the dramatic rescue of their friend. The papers also reprinted all the details of Milner's extensive involvement in the Thai marijuana trade.

Milner and Aitken had been there before but for Daniels this level of public recognition was completely new and utterly unwelcome. Although none of the papers went so far as to suggest he had any involvement in drug smuggling himself, even the most slow-witted DEA agent would be able to put two and two together and see the connection.

For the first time in his smuggling career, he was completely exposed.

Unwilling to put out a fresh shipment for fear of coming under law-enforcement scrutiny, Daniels could do nothing but sit back and watch as the Shaffer brothers, in combination with his biggest rival Thai Tony, began to plan their biggest score to date.

13
OPPORTUNITY KNOCKS

Tony Franulovich was born with seawater in his blood.

His father, George, was a master mariner and the youngest ever graduate of the Royal Yugoslav Maritime Academy to be offered his own command. During the Second World War George saw action as a captain in the Yugoslav Navy and faked sympathy for the Nazi cause in order to gather information which he then passed on to the Allies. As the war drew to a close and the Third Reich began to collapse in on itself he fled to Italy, Venezuela and finally America, settling in the picturesque town of Anacortes, fifty miles north of Seattle.

Situated on Fidalgo, the easternmost of the San Juan Islands and once known as The Magic City, Anacortes boasts twelve and a half miles of saltwater shoreline and majestic views said to be almost identical to portions of the Baltic coast. Croatians have flocked to the town ever since the Alaskan Gold Rush and now make up more than a quarter of the population.

With his naval background, George Franulovich naturally gravitated towards the commercial fishing industry that, alongside oil refining and lumber, formed a significant source of employment in the area. He was soon spending his summers sailing up into the treacherous waters of the Bering Sea to hunt for cod, halibut and king crab.

Tony was just eight years old when he went to sea with his father for the first time. The sight of huge waves crashing over the slippery deck, the biting winds, the violent rocking of the boat as it rode the swells, the deafening clatter of the heavy crab pots and the pungent smell of diesel fuel: none of it deterred the young boy in the slightest. From that moment on, the sea dominated his life.

At the age of eighteen, Tony became captain of the family boat, the *St Peter*, and took sole charge of its six-man crew during the annual May to September fishing season. It was not a job for the faint of heart.

On good days the spray coming over the bow of the *St Peter* would freeze in mid air and shatter on the deck like fine china. On bad days the water would freeze only after it hit the rigging, the rails, the deck and the machinery. The weight of the ice unbalanced the boat's centre of gravity leaving it liable to capsize. To prevent this happening the crew members would have to brave the slippery deck and sub-zero temperatures to smash and remove the ice with baseball bats and sledge hammers before shovelling it over the side.

For anyone unfortunate enough to be swept over the side, survival time in the icy waters can be measured in mere minutes. In the winter, a man overboard will die in the time it takes a boat to turn around and fish him out.

In the late seventies the Bering Sea was the site of a modern-day gold rush. Like the wild marijuana grown on the roadsides of Kansas, the cod, pollock, salmon and crab were everywhere – all you had to do was dip a net into the water and it would emerge overflowing with fish.

For those who managed to combine the best of luck with the best of timing, fortunes could be made. In less than three months, an experienced boat captain could earn more than $150,000. During the five-month season a lucky teenager with no previous fishing experience could come away with as much as $50,000.

But the extraordinarily high rewards were counterbalanced by the extraordinarily high risks of working in what is widely acknowledged to be one of the deadliest professions anywhere in the world.

According to the coastguard, the death rate for fishermen is seven times the national average for all workers and twice that for mining, the nation's second most dangerous occupation. Each year around fifty fishermen die in the Bering Sea, the vast majority of them from in and around the Seattle area.

The risks increased as fish and crab stocks in the calmer waters began to dry up, forcing the boats into the more treacherous regions. The seasons, once virtually all-year-round, became shorter and shorter in an attempt to let stocks recover. Then came the introduction of quotas, which operated on a first past the post basis. Under this system, a limit on the quantity of each kind of fish was imposed, but no limit was placed on the number of boats that could attempt to catch them.

It meant that, as soon as the season opened, regardless of the weather, hundreds of boats would head out and crew members would be forced to work frenzied shifts day and night with hardly any sleep. The first boats to find the big schools would load up as much fish as they could possibly carry then race back to port to secure the highest possible prices. The season might have lasted a full three months but eight per cent of the catch was usually landed in the first two weeks.

Seventy mile-an-hour winds and 35-foot waves – conditions that would normally send boats rushing for the shelter of the nearest harbour – were being ignored in pursuit of the best possible catch. To make matters worse boats would head out without even the most basic safety equipment and then use the extra space to land so much fish that they were left dangerously unbalanced.

Where once captains would check the weather forecast and calmly wait out storms from the safety of the nearest harbour, they found themselves compelled to continue fishing even in the midst of high winds and seas. Bravado became everything. If someone else was out there fishing, you had to go too or risk missing out on a share of the quota.

By the mid-eighties, on average, 146 fishing vessels and forty lives were being lost in the waters stretching up from the Pacific North-west each year.

The town of Anacortes is accustomed to the loss of its men and women at sea. An obelisk close to the harbour is inscribed with names of fishermen lost over the last fifty years. The figure, which grows almost every week, is already three times more than the numbers listed on the local memorials to casualties of World War Two, Korea and Vietnam. Similar memorials can be found at towns all the way down the Washington coast.

Drugs and alcohol play a significant part in poor decision making on board ship. Fishermen are famous for their hard-drinking lifestyles, often going on endless benders when they get back to port. Most abstain while out at sea, but some are unable to resist.

Like many fishermen, Tony quickly developed a dependence on alcohol followed by a quest for other ways to reach oblivion. At high school he discovered marijuana and by the time he was nineteen he was using amphetamines on a regular basis. While fishing in Alaska soon afterwards, he became increasingly hooked on cocaine.

He would do his best to sober up and stay clear of drugs during the fishing season, partly because he was responsible for so many lives but also because his supply of drugs dried up once he was on board. However, back on shore he would often spend days or weeks at a time lost in a drunken, drug-fuelled stupor.

By 1986 life was getting tougher. The risk remained high but the introduction of a new quota system meant that while some fishermen got richer, others saw their profits fall sharply. Unforeseen expenses, including urgent engine repairs and the replacement of some dangerously old equipment, had left Tony in a position where each and every trip had to make a substantial profit or risk bringing the whole business crashing down.

Little wonder that when an opportunity came along to earn almost as much money as he did back in the golden days of fishing, but with only a tiny fraction of the risk, Franulovich jumped at it.

It started with a simple act of kindness. A family friend who lived up in Alaska was getting increasingly worried about his daughter, Darla, who was running around with the wrong kind of people and getting into trouble. Her parents were at their wits' end when Tony stepped in and suggested that Darla come to Anacortes and move in with his parents.

Within a few weeks of her arrival Darla had settled down and begun dating a local man, Hank Sheppard. Through Darla, Tony got to know Hank and the pair became friends.

But Hank was the wrong kind of people too. A long-time scam artist and chancer, he had been involved in drugs and petty crime ever since he was a child in his native Newfoundland. Soon after meeting Tony he began talking about marijuana smuggling and in particular the use of fishing boats to offload mother ships.

'I've got connections around the world, guys who are deep into this kind of thing, top people,' Hank explained. 'They're bringing tons of the stuff into the country. Now, if you can get me a few fishing boats to work the offload, then we could get a piece of that action. I'm telling you Tony, if you get involved in this, we could make serious coin. I'm talking millions of dollars, telephone numbers.'

At first the conversations were so few and far between that to Tony the whole thing seemed like some kind of joke, but within a few weeks, when the relationship with Darla had ended and a destitute Hank had moved in with Tony, the talk of working together on a smuggling venture became far more persistent.

'It's all set up already,' Hank explained. 'I just need you to give me the go ahead. My people with the drugs are waiting for the green light and we can all be rich.'

But none of it was true. At the same time that Hank was telling Tony that the marijuana was all lined up and ready to go, he was telling others that he had boat crews ready to do a major offload in Washington. He was playing both ends against the middle in the hope of pulling off a deal.

Hank's main drug contact was Brian O'Dea, a fellow Newfoundlander and the well-to-do son of a prominent brewery owner and politician who, by the start of 1986, had risen to prominence within the Shaffer organisation and become a trusted member of their inner circle. Confident, competent and hugely experienced, he was the kind of man the brothers could trust to take care of whole aspects of a smuggling operation, and he had enough brain power to deal with any problems that might come along.

Years earlier, O'Dea and Hank had launched a legitimate business together, importing hair products from America to Canada. The pair set up a complex, quasi-legal scheme to avoid paying import tax but were accused of defrauding the Canadian government who were already suspicious that, given O'Dea's prior drug convictions, the whole business was simply a cover for smuggling. Hank fled, leaving O'Dea to take the heat alone.

A few years later the pair reunited and did some more deals but once again fell out badly. Their last meeting had not gone well. O'Dea, by then a full-blown coke addict, had woken after an afternoon snooze on the sofa of his country home to find Hank and a hired thug bearing down on him.

Almost five years later Hank called O'Dea again.

'Hey Brian, I know you and me have had our problems in the past but I have an opportunity here and I need your connections. And your connections need me,' he explained. 'I have without doubt the very best offload situation you could ever imagine. If you can get in touch with your guys and get them to come and take a look at it, I just know they're gonna like what they see.'

O'Dea had recently gotten out of rehab and was putting his life on a different track, away from the drug trade. He was working on a new business plan – creating designer jewellery from fossilised dinosaur bone fragments – and believed he could make a success of it. He was also wary of mentioning Hank's deal to the Shaffer brothers because they had invested $250,000 of their own money into the dinosaur-bone scheme and he didn't want to blow it.

But Hank wasn't about to give up and strike out on both ends of his non-existent deal. He increased the pressure on both O'Dea and Tony Franulovich, emphasising the urgency of making a decision and the once-in-a-lifetime nature of the opportunity. He called and called and badgered and made sure it was a constant topic of conversation.

Hank pressed O'Dea as much as he pressed Franulovich and he kept on pressing both men until they finally bowed to his will. Franulovich agreed to meet with his contacts and O'Dea said he would mention the offload site in passing to the Shaffer brothers, though it would ultimately be their decision, not his, as to whether to go ahead.

As it happened the Shaffers were already looking to the state of Washington as the site of their next offload. All of their previous offloads had taken place in California but now the authorities had stepped up the number of patrols and it was getting more difficult. Offloading on beaches left the gang too exposed for too many hours. What they needed was a place where the drugs could be offloaded privately, perhaps masquerading as a fishing catch. Once they had agreed on the location, they knew it would be in their interests to utilise locals to assist them. Hank's timing could not have been more perfect.

In January 1986, within days of O'Dea mentioning the idea, he and the Shaffers and a few other members of the team flew up to Washington and met with Hank at the Crowne Plaza Hotel in Seattle. From there the group went up to Anacortes where Hank introduced them to Tony, who in turned showed them around Lovric's Marina, the proposed offload site.

The brothers saw the potential immediately. A private driveway and large yard area meant trucks could be driven in and loaded up away from prying eyes while the dock itself was secluded enough to ensure that anyone passing by during the offload would simply assume it was business as usual. The only potential onlookers would be other fishermen hanging out at the dockside bars or unloading catches of their own.

O'Dea, wary of his past dealings with Hank, was careful to cover his back. He took the Shaffers to one side and explained that he didn't really know the man they were dealing with that well and that their relationship had not always run smoothly. But Hank had done a superb job of selling himself and an even better job of selling Tony Franulovich as the best man for the operation.

The *St Peter* was the perfect boat and Tony would be the perfect captain. All the Shaffers had to do was provide the mother ship and the drugs, and the rest of the operation would practically run itself.

Tony's boat was well known in the local area and a regular visitor to both its home port and those around the state. No one would look at it twice once it was loaded with drugs and the customs and coastguard officers would be far more likely to smile and wave them by than they would a new ship in town.

It was almost too good to be true and by the time their plane had landed back in California, the Shaffers had agreed to use Anacortes as the offload site for their 1986 importation.

14
THE A TEAM

The importation in Anacortes was not set to take place until May at the earliest – around the time of the next harvest – but there was plenty to keep all those involved in the conspiracy busy in the interim.

Everyone had their role. Chris would be in charge of training the offload crew, Bill would make the arrangements for purchasing the drugs in Thailand and getting them onto the mother ship, O'Dea would be in charge of transporting the drugs once they were inside the United States.

O'Dea started by creating SeaCal Fisheries, an Alaska-based salmon-packing company, to land, vacuum-pack and conceal the marijuana among its boxes of fresh fish. He then leased five trucks and had them painted in the name of Zip Kit, a vending machine refurbishing company run by his business partner on the dinosaur-bone business which had now taken a back seat to drug smuggling.

O'Dea began sending trucks up and down Highway 5 from Los Angeles to Seattle. Every couple of weeks they'd drive up and then they'd drive back, and then they'd drive up and then they'd drive back. 'We had to know the road conditions at all times and the procedures at the inspection stations. We couldn't afford any problems at the stations. Everybody had to know how to keep their log. You can't send a truck up and down the road with nothing in it all the time, or with the same waybill. You need new waybills every time you go. The inspectors read your log, they read your waybill to see what you're carrying.'

And to ensure that every state trooper and weigh-scale operator on US Interstate 5 should believe his company was legitimate, he set up a phantom roofing company to provide his trucks with cargo and waybills. For the next few months, one of his trucks drove up and down the highway with the same load of cedar shingles, just to create cover.

By April Hank was starting to show his true colours. He was still living with Tony Franulovich, but he was also taking increasingly large amounts of coke and bringing prostitutes home. None of it would have been a problem anywhere else but this was a small town and the last thing the gang needed was to have any attention brought upon them at such a delicate time.

After it happened again and again, eventually the decision was made to take Hank out of the picture. O'Dea and a few others went up mob-handed to Seattle and told him to leave for Florida to stay with relatives.

But Hank wasn't about to go anywhere. Paranoid as a result of his drug use, he refused to see that he was jeopardising the operation and instead became convinced that the others were trying to edge him out of the deal; the deal that would not have been put together but for his efforts. O'Dea managed to convince him that his money was safe and the gang wanted nothing more than to ensure the importation went smoothly. Hank reluctantly agreed to leave the area.

The first and most importation decision the Shaffer brothers had to make was to decide who among Tony Franulovich's crew should be invited to take part in the operation. Many of the crew were related to their captain and a few were extremely young, in the late teens or early twenties.

Not only was it important to choose people who were comfortable with breaking the law and could handle the pressure of a multi-million-dollar smuggling operation, the Shaffers also wanted to ensure the people they surrounded themselves with would not crack at the first sign of trouble. The brothers soon reached the conclusion that the best way to ensure only the most trustworthy people were involved was to arrange to evaluate them all.

By the beginning of August the decisions had been made and, as the *St Peter* sat tied up at the dock next to Tony's new boat, the *Kathy B*, each member of the crew that had passed the assessment was approached and told that their presence was required on the other vessel. Once there, they were introduced to Chris Shaffer.

'So here's what's happening. We're planning to import a large shipment of marijuana into the United States in the near future and we'd like you to help,' said Shaffer who went on to negotiate an individual fee for each person.

While Chris worked on picking the perfect crew, Bill set about recruiting others for land-based tasks that would be needed for a successful smuggle. He also set about negotiating with his sources in Thailand in order to buy the drugs.

By now Bill Shaffer knew all about Brian Daniels and in an ideal world he would have wanted to work with him. Compared to the product supplied by Thai Tony, Daniels' was of better quality and produced and packaged to higher standards. Daniels also ran a slicker operation at the Thai and Vietnamese end and his extensive contacts throughout the governments of the key South East Asian countries almost guaranteed a trouble-free loading.

Bill Shaffer had heard other things about Daniels too – that he was a bit of a soft touch; that he wasn't the kind of man to send out the thugs if he didn't get paid. The 'lack of honour' a fellow smuggler had detected among the Shaffer brothers many years earlier had not faded away even in the slightest.

Rather than being paid what they were owed, many of those who had invested money into the two shipments in 1985 had been encouraged to roll their money over into the 1986 shipment with the promise of even greater profits. While on the one hand this seemed to present a genuine opportunity to make huge amounts of cash, the reality was that it gave Chris and Bill the means to put together huge smuggling operations and generate massive profits without ever risking any of their cash.

If they could find the right people to work with – the kind of people who didn't kick up too much of a fuss when money didn't flow their way fast enough – then there seemed to be no reason why they would ever have to pay any of the investors. They could keep stringing them along for years. And if one of their larger shipments was ever seized, the Shaffer brothers would not be left out of pocket.

But while the combination of Daniels' marijuana and the Shaffers' smuggling skills seemed to represent the coming together of the ultimate dream team, Bill knew it was not to be. He had heard that, having lost two shipments and seen several members of The Ring arrested, Brian Daniels had taken a back step from the business for a year and was not putting out any loads for the 1986 season. If Bill wanted marijuana, he would have to go elsewhere. And he if wanted to work with Brian Daniels, he would have to wait until the supplier was once more in the clear.

In the meantime Bill Shaffer learned that Thai Tony had arranged to purchase 75 tons of marijuana from military personnel in Vietnam. After a series of discussions and inspections, Bill agreed to buy 23 tons of the product. Bill then had to look for a ship to transport the drugs.

The *Six Pac* was no longer an option. Earlier that same year the Shaffers experienced a close call of their own. They had made a modest investment in a 5-ton load of Thai marijuana that another group were transporting. The drugs had been seized by US Customs near Hawaii and, worried that vessels from their old operation might now be flagged up to the authorities, the brothers were keen to employ a vessel which had never been used for drug smuggling before.

Bill Shaffer found it in the *Niki Maru*, a 110-foot oil supply ship which they spent hundreds of thousands of dollars converting to make it look like a Japanese fishing boat, and thus more easily go undetected on the journey across the Pacific.

On 22 August 1986 everything was ready to go. The *St Peter* and the *Kathy B* were tied up together and Chris Shaffer went aboard both boats and swept them for bugs. The two crews then got together in order to discuss the offloads.

Crew members were shown how to work the radio equipment and the scrambler that would be in the surveillance plane. Other members of the team made sure the hold of the *Kathy B* was completely dry and measured it carefully to ensure it was large enough to hold 23 tons of dope.

The gang needed a way to communicate with the boats out at sea. In Anacortes they moved a 34-foot motor home into a campground and put a single side band radio in it that was capable of transmitting all over the world. It needed huge amounts of power and a large antenna. The radio was so powerful that anyone touching the antenna risked electrocution, so the gang rigged up a hidden cable and mounted the antenna through the branches of a nearby tree.

But the problem with using high power radio is that the signals can be intercepted from further away.

Concerned that their radio transmission might be intercepted, the Shaffers came up with a novel solution. They bought dozens of copies of the latest edition of the *Webster's* dictionary and gave one out to every member of the gang. The code was simple: look up each word in the dictionary and then quote the page number. The conversations would sound like coordinates but they would make no sense whatsoever and when the actual details of latitude and longitude were mixed in among them, it would be impossible for anyone to work out where the boats actually were.

By July the boats were at sea, fishing for herring and waiting for the mother ship to arrive. The plan was in place. Once the drugs were on board the *Kathy B* the ship would make its way into the fjords of Alaska and hide out while the drugs were taken out of their original packaging and placed in wet-lock boxes – specially constructed fibreboard boxes treated with waterproofing material on the inside and out. One hundred per cent leak-proof, they are normally used to hold fresh fish packed in ice but were ideal for transporting drugs. That way, should anyone stumble into Lorvic's Dock while the offload was taking place, it would look just like any other load of fish that had been boxed at sea.

The final safety precaution before the boats came into shore with the drugs was to ensure there were no law enforcement vessels either looking out for them or simply coming across them on a routine patrol that might demand a spot inspection.

If for some reason news of the operation had leaked out, coastguard cutters and DEA speedboats would be in the area, ready to strike. With a plane scouting out the waters ahead, there would be plenty of time for the *Kathy B* to turn and run or, as an absolute last resort, pitch the drugs into the sea.

The Shaffers didn't know any pilots in the area and in any case were keen to find a local to do the job. They asked Tony Franulovich for suggestions. 'No problem. I know the perfect guy,' he told them.

Like many of the boat captains operating in the Bering Sea, Franulovich rarely relied on luck alone when it came to finding the fish. Specialist spotter pilots criss-crossed the skies in the region, searching out the dark shadows formed by schools of herring or salmon and then radioed the location to the fleets.

With frequent spells of bad weather and a large number of planes circling the same part of the sky, the job is almost as dangerous as being on the sea below. Alaska-based Terry Cratty was widely regarded as being one of the best in the business, had known the Franulovich family for years and had often worked for the *St Peter*.

Tony approached him, explained about the drug importation and offered him $35,000 to spend a couple of days flying his plane ahead of the fishing boats as they made their way back to Anacortes.

Cratty pondered the offer. Although he had tried marijuana as a teenager, it had been years since his last joint and he had never taken any other drugs. Both his parents had been alcoholics and as a result he himself was now teetotal. He had no criminal convictions and had never broken any significant law in his life – but Tony was talking about a lot of money and he was struggling to make ends meet.

He soon managed to justify it in his mind. He would have no direct contact with the drugs and would probably not even see them. While important to the operation, his role was minimal and the drug would be coming in the country whether he flew for them or not. 'OK Tony,' he said softly. 'I'll do it.'

On 24 August the *Niki Maru* rendezvoused with the *Kathy B* in south-east Alaskan waters. Terry Restall, Tony Franulovich, and others helped to transfer the drugs from one boat to the other.

Between 25 and 27 August Terry Cratty flew ahead of the *St Peter* and the *Kathy B* as they travelled down from Alaska to Anacortes with the 23 tons of Thai marijuana. By the time he landed and got to the dock, Tony Franulovich told him the drugs had already been loaded on the trucks and were on their way down to California. It could not have gone more smoothly and had been such a resounding success that they would do it all again as soon as possible.

The boat crew celebrated their success with a couple of ounces of cocaine and a party that lasted right through until the end of the following day.

Back in Thailand, Daniels began to celebrate too but his own party was rudely interrupted.

Just as the Shaffers had landed their load, the US Attorney's office in Seattle made public the results of a secret investigation by a federal grand jury into the seizure of the 12 tons of marijuana carried by the *Allison*.

The indictment named sixteen defendants including Dennis Ingham, Harry Kreamer and Rufus Aylwyn as well as all the other main conspirators Daniels had worked with. But almost miraculously, Daniels' name did not appear on the list.

There had also been the news that Dennis Ingham had been arrested. With the loss of both the *Pacific Star* and the *Allison*,

Ingham was hurting for cash. All his money had been invested in the two unsuccessful loads and what he had left would last him only a few months at the most.

What he had needed most was a scheme to generate enough stake money to buy another big load of marijuana. The two seizures had been a disaster but just one successful smuggle would generate enough cash to make up for both losses.

And just as Ingham started looking around for a possible deal, one fell into his lap. In his desperation and excitement, Ingham forgot the one key rule of the drug business: if someone appears to be too good to be true, he almost certainly is.

In Honolulu Ingham was introduced to a man who offered to sell him 1,000 pounds of Thai marijuana for $1 million. The man explained that he had obtained the drugs in lieu of payment of a debt but that he did not have the contacts to move such a large amount of dope.

At that price Ingham knew he would be able to double his money almost overnight. Initially suspicious, Ingham relaxed when the man explained that he knew he was underselling the drugs but his priority was to get rid of them as quickly as possible rather than maximise his return. The million dollars would cover the debt that was being repaid, and that was all he cared about.

Eager to proceed, Ingham, who was using the name 'Fred' throughout, showed up in downtown Los Angeles the following evening with $400,000 to put down as a deposit on the dope. The rest of the money would be paid once he had sold the drugs on.

The moment he handed over the money, Ingham was surrounded by a dozen heavily armed federal agents and was placed under arrest. His contact then revealed himself to be an undercover DEA agent.

Ingham believed it was simply his greed and lack of caution that had led to his downfall and that his arrest was little more than a continuation of the bad luck he had suffered from ever since the seizure of the *Allison* little more than a year earlier.

But although the capture of the *Allison* had been made to look like a random seizure and stories were leaked to the press about a member of the crew having unwittingly spoken to a customs officer, the truth was somewhat different. The authorities had actually been acting on a tip off from an informant based in Thailand who had fallen out with one of the key organisers of the load – Dennis Ingham.

In a bizarre twist of fate, the informant was keen to see Ingham put away for as long as possible but was a good friend of Brian Daniels and did not want to see anything bad happen to him. Although he gave investigators all the information they needed to intercept the *Allison* and later the *Pacific Star*, he said nothing about Daniels.

The DEA had their suspicions. Brian Daniels had been cropping up on their radar ever since the late seventies, partly as a result of intelligence gathered from the Australian authorities in the Cessna-Milner case and partly as a result of small seizures made in the US. But Ingham was also a big fish and one who had eluded capture for some time. In total the Dennis Ingham organisation was believed to have smuggled up to 124 tons of marijuana worth around $250 million in the space of just five years.

As Ingham made his way to jail, Brian Daniels was planning his next smuggling venture and had little notion of just how close the authorities had come to catching up with him.

Ingham would post bail of $275,000 and not return to court, preferring instead to drop out of sight. But although he was still free and able to actively participate in future smuggling activity, Daniels believed that, like Milner, he was now too exposed, at least for a few months.

The only thing left to do was to carry on. Once the Shaffer brothers paid him what they owed for the load they had just landed, he would begin talking to them about the next.

Once the money from the load landed by the *Kathy B* started to come in, it quite literally arrived by the ton.

A simple rule of thumb in the world of drug dealing says that for every pound or kilo of marijuana that you sell, you receive back twice the weight in cash. (For cocaine the ratio is six to one.) Having successfully brought in the drugs, the Shaffer brothers now had some 46 tons of paper money coming their way from all over the country.

Although most of the drugs they brought in were sold wholesale to trusted dealers up and down the West Coast, they also supplied wholesalers as far away as New York. That meant arranging for trucks filled with dope to criss-cross the country and, more importantly, for someone to pick up the cash that resulted from East Coast sales.

The Shaffers' main contact in the Big Apple was a man who worked hard to keep his true identity under wraps and was known only as 'Sonny'.

In his fifties, stocky, with a mop of wild grey hair and a thick Amish-style beard, Sonny's reputation was such that the brothers were happy to let him take their marijuana on tick and pay only after he had sold it on.

A few weeks after each new delivery, he would send a message asking the Shaffers to send one of their couriers to New York to collect what was due. The man would be instructed to check into a suite at the Plaza Hotel on Central Park West and then to call a pager, the number of which would change with every trip. An hour of so after the call was made, Sonny would show up outside the door of the courier's hotel room, drop off a couple of hefty suitcases, then make a quick exit.

Between them the two suitcases would contain anything up to $3 million. Similar meetings would take place on a monthly basis for as long as it took for all the drugs to be sold on. At the end of four months, Sonny had paid the Shaffers more than $18 million.

Sonny rarely hung around long enough to get involved in anything more than the most rudimentary small talk, but one evening after dropping off the cases he mentioned in passing that he had not eaten since the early morning and invited the courier to join him for dinner.

Over the course of the meal, Sonny slowly began to open up. It was clear that the drug trade had been good to him and that he had tens of millions of dollars at his disposal, but Sonny confessed there was one dream that no amount of money was able to buy.

'I got no real complaints about my life,' he confessed. 'Except one. I wish I'd tried a little harder to pursue my dream.'

'What dream is that?'

'I always wanted to be an actor, you know, make it in the movies, that kind of thing. I kept trying all through my twenties but you know how it is, a one in a million chance that anyone ever makes it. Tell you what though, I got my first real break coming up. My new girlfriend works for an ad agency and she's gonna get me a part in a commercial. It's only television but hey, it's good enough for me.'

By the time the meal had finished, Sonny was back to his usual reticent self and vanished into the night with little more than a cursory goodbye. Perhaps, somewhere deep down, he already felt that he had said too much and that one day, the seemingly innocent dinner conversation would come back to haunt him.

Dealing with such enormous quantities of cash, the vast majority of it in used small-denomination bills, is an art in itself. Hollywood films that show dealers with slim briefcases full of neatly packed stacks of crisp notes are somewhat wide of the mark. Used bills take up significantly more space than those straight out of the bank and can be almost impossible to stack straight. Duffel bags, suitcases and cardboard boxes are a far better bet.

The Shaffers had spent years refining every aspect of their operation and the money laundering and cash management side of the enterprise was no exception.

Common sense dictated that this money and that generated from West Coast sales should be dealt with at a location as far removed from the stash house as possible. Bill recruited a couple of old friends to help him out by renting a large house in the fashionable Brentwood district of Los Angeles as a place to count money, and another in the Hollywood Hills for storage.

Not everybody could be trusted to know the truth about where the money came from but the brothers' work in the marine salvage and treasure-diving industry turned out to be the ideal cover story.

In 1986 the *Sol* was the site of filming for a segment on the leading US documentary news programme, *20/20*. The segment was titled 'Slave Ships of the Sulu Sea' and was eventually nominated for an Emmy. Chris helped track down the wreck of the *Griffin*, a cargo ship of the English East India Company, which sank in 1761. He would ultimately invest more than $5 million of his own money into the *Griffin* project alone.

Everyone knew about the wreck of the *Griffin* and about the huge amounts of valuable porcelain Bill and Chris had salvaged. This proved to be serendipitous in more ways than one as it provided an explanation of the cash that they had come by. The cover story for those outside the inner circle of trust was that the money had been generated through sales of the porcelain and needed to be counted and collated before being banked.

Counting and storing the money was only part of the problem. Tough new laws on disclosure meant it was impossible to simply go out and spend it the way you could in the old days. Instead it had to be 'laundered' into the banking system using a variety of methods that would ultimately disguise its illegal origins.

One of the simplest methods of achieving this was to take the money to one of the many countries with no such restrictions and, ideally, a long-standing tradition of banking secrecy.

By 20 October 1986 more than $20 million had gone through the counting house and was being stored in the Hollywood Hills. Bill and his friend Leslie Berkowitz packed the money into cardboard cartons stamped 'Computer Equipment', loaded them into a motor home and drove the lot to a private airfield at Salt Lake City in Utah.

There a twin-engined, twelve-seater Gulfstream II jet, which had been had been leased from Louisiana Pacific at a cost of $116,000, was waiting on the tarmac.

Detail was everything. Berkowitz had printed a series of business cards, complete with official titles for each of the plane's passengers, and Shaffer had purchased a set of matching lapel pins to serve as makeshift company logos. To all intents and purposes, the party looked like a serious business trip for a group of dynamic business executives.

It was just the image that Shaffer wanted the group to portray and he had chosen carefully among his friends, selecting only those able to pull off such an act. In return for their services, each participant received $10,000 with the exception of Berkowitz who paid himself $200,000 as the de facto company accountant.

The pilot looked on as forty A4-size boxes were loaded into the plane's cargo hold. Berkowitz smiled and explained that the boxes contained computer equipment that he and his colleagues planned to use to establish a European branch of their company, Bi-Continental Computers.

The pilot nodded politely then made his way to the plane's cockpit, scribbling 'computer related equipment' on his copy of the manifest to be handed to Swiss customs officials on landing.

The flight was smooth and the mood cheerful, assisted by the copious amounts of champagne and upmarket nibbles on offer to the passengers. The following morning the plane touched down in Zurich and in a few minutes the passengers and their cargo were unloaded.

The pilot handed his manifest to the official who had come to meet them. The man walked a quick circle around the cart that the boxes had been piled onto and then opened one at random. Instead of computer equipment, he found stacks of $20 and $50 bills.

'What the hell's going on,' he demanded. 'Why have you made a false declaration?' The pilot's mouth fell open. He was just as shocked and surprised as he customs officer and had no answer. Both men turned to the passengers. Berkowitz had no choice but to admit that he and the others had lied and that every single one of the forty boxes contained hundreds of thousands of dollars.

The customs official shook his head with frustration. 'Look, there's no problem bringing cash into Switzerland. Bring as much as you like. We do, however, have a problem with computer equipment. So next time, just declare the cash, don't try to fake it. OK?'

The three couples nodded sheepishly. The official then stood to one side and gestured for the travellers and their booty to continue on their way. 'Then all that remains for me to say,' he said, 'is welcome to Switzerland.'

As news of the success of the laundering operation spread throughout the members of the gang, Hank Sheppard – who had been down in Florida cooling his heels – had turned up at Tony Franulovich's house in Anacortes looking to get paid.

'The way I see it, I've got at least a million dollars coming,' said Hank as he stepped through the door. 'And that's just the first instalment.'

He was right, of course, but there were two problems. The first was that much of the money was still tied up in Europe and it would take some time before it could be laundered and safely filtered back to the States. The second was that, even if there had been cash around, no one in the gang was keen to hand anything over to Hank during such a delicate part of the operation.

The last thing they wanted was for him to draw too much attention to them at a time when the final negotiations over prices and quantities were still being hammered out. In his most reassuring tone of voice, Tony explained that the money was indeed on its way and that Hank had absolutely nothing to worry about. In fact, the enterprise had been so successful that the Shaffers were already starting to plan for the next year. Hank reluctantly accepted this explanation and he returned to Florida. However, he wasn't to be mollified for long.

It took just two weeks for Hank's patience to run out and for him to return to Anacortes in anticipation of his big pay day. This time around, for the sake of a quiet life, the group had agreed to let Hank have a modest amount of cash, enough to get him off their backs, but not enough to let him get into too much trouble.

Tony carefully, diplomatically explained the situation then invited Hank into his kitchen where he nodded towards a large black bag sitting on the table.

'How much?' asked Hank.

'Fifty.'

'Fifty grand!' Hank let the words hang in the air for a few moments. When he spoke again the anger in his voice was as clear as a bell. 'You guys are screwing with me.'

Tony shook his head. 'That's not what's happening here Hank, it's not like that...'

But Hank was already heading out of the door.

He got into his car and sped south along the I-5 for 80 miles or so until he reached downtown Seattle. He parked on Roy Street and walked around the block to 2nd Avenue and into the divisional office for the Washington State branch of the Drug Enforcement Administration, demanding to be seen immediately.

Ten minutes later Hank found himself in an interview room sitting opposite Special Agent Gary Annunziata.

'Six weeks ago, a bunch of guys brought in 23 tons of Thai dope into a private dock in Anacortes,' Hank explained. 'I know because I set the whole thing up, but the bastards didn't pay me what they said they would. They've already started planning the next load and when it comes in, I think you and your buddies should be waiting for them.'

PART THREE

PART THREE

15
SPY GAME

In April 1987, CBS News despatched a camera team to Geneva to cover the Sotheby's sale of jewellery from the collection of the Duchess of Windsor, the woman for whom King Edward VIII had abdicated his throne.

In the run-up to the start of the auction, the crew moved through the conspicuously affluent crowd milling about the venue – a marquee overlooking Lake Geneva – carrying out ad hoc interviews. Their cameras soon settled on the figure of a tall, immaculately groomed, fair-haired man in an expensive suit and Italian leather shoes. He held a glass of champagne in one hand and on his other arm was a stunningly beautiful woman.

'And what is your name, sir' asked the eager young reporter.

Caught off guard, a slightly startled expression filled the face of Bill Shaffer for a moment or two as he struggled to compose himself. 'Bill Ryan,' he replied at last.

'And are you planning on buying something here today Mr Ryan?'

Shaffer smiled then looked into the camera, his eyes flashing with mischief.

'Well, there are times when you just have to go for it.'

As a matter of fact, the Shaffer brothers *were* going for it full throttle, and with some considerable style.

Life could not have been much better for Chris and Bill. The 1986 importation alone had earned them more than $20 million. Bill chose to spend his share of this fortune on traditional pursuits: beautiful women, fast cars and incredible homes. Together the brothers bought art, jewellery and high-performance sports cars that they began racing around Europe, once even entering the

187

Paris–Dakar rally together. They bought houses in California, England and elsewhere in Europe. They covered the walls of their many homes with paintings by the likes of Picasso and Warhol and had items in their wardrobes handmade by the finest tailors around.

But Chris opted to use at least some of his money to indulge his true passion – documentary film making. Whereas most film-makers struggle to make ends meet, Chris was able to get involved in projects that interested him, even if there was no promise of a pay cheque at the end of them.

Chris would use a combination of his nautical, diving and photography skills to assist those who needed to film in remote parts of the world or access difficult and dangerous spots within the oceans.

One of his first films was about Japanese vessels sunk during the Second World War. Soon afterwards he worked with the BBC on a film about sea snakes in the South China Sea, part of David Attenborough's 'Life on Earth' series.

In 1986 Chris made a documentary called *The Muro-Ami Dilemma* about young boys who were being exploited for fishing on the coral reefs of the Philippines. The film received a prize at the Cannes film festival.

Chris and Bill Shaffer had only one dark cloud on their horizon. Although the 1986 importation had been a huge success, the marijuana that had been supplied by Tony the Thai had been of rather poor quality. The pair soon learned that the reason so much marijuana had been stored in the warehouse that Tony had escorted Terry Restall to was because this was where marijuana purchased by other gangs and seized on its way down to be shipped out of the country was brought.

Tony the Thai may have had virtually unlimited access to this marijuana, but because much of it had been seized many months before, it had started to go mouldy long before its journey across the ocean. It had led to a massive argument when Tony the Thai had travelled to San Francisco to collect the $4 million that he believed he was owed.

Bill Shaffer flat out refused to pay anything more than $1 million. Tony could do nothing except swear that he would never, ever work with the Shaffers again.

The brothers were keen to begin planning a new shipment as quickly as possible for the summer of 1987 but were in desperate need of a new supplier. Wary of repeating the same mistakes all over again, they knew they needed someone who could not only provide bulk quantities of the product but also supply it direct from the growers and processors to ensure its freshness.

It was at this time that fate intervened, arranging a series of introductions that, when combined, provided the Shaffers with everything they needed and far, far more besides.

Michael Carter and Gary Waldon were known throughout the marijuana underworld as two of the best offloaders in the business. Former fishermen who had turned to drug smuggling during lean periods, the pair had coordinated and successfully landed drugs for pretty much every major smuggler operating out of South East Asia since the late seventies.

The pair had helped the Shaffers with their first 1985 offload and a few weeks later at the same location, had offloaded drugs for another group that had been supplied by none other than Brian Daniels. This part of The Ring was run by a man named David Boese, an international playboy character and one of Daniels' few close, non-Thai personal friends.

Hearing of the Shaffers' dilemma and keen to see them fixed up with a new supplier so that they themselves would get the offload contract, Carter and Waldon introduced the Shaffers to David Boese, who in turn introduced the brothers to Brian Daniels.

In the history of the global trade in Thai marijuana, there are certain moments that, with the benefit of hindsight, stand out as having been key to the creation, expansion and continuation of the market. Ciro Mancuso being arrested in Kansas is one; Louis Villar being approached by two of his former students and being asked to travel to Mexico is another, as is the chance encounter between the fugitive Robert Lietzman and the carefree traveller Michael Forwell.

But that first meeting between the Shaffer brothers and Brian Daniels eclipsed them all. The Ring had reached its ultimate configuration. The biggest and the best marijuana broker in all of South East Asia had at last teamed up with the cleverest and most sophisticated smugglers around. It was a match made in heaven.

The deal was struck immediately and the confidence each party had in the other was obvious. At 42 tons, the shipment would be the largest single amount of marijuana that Daniels had ever put on the water. It was special for other reasons too. Normally Daniels demanded partial payment up front on the understanding that he would receive the remainder when the drugs were success-fully landed and sold. But such was his confidence in the Shaffers that Daniels decide to invest in the shipment himself. The Shaffers would foot the bill all the logistics and transportation needed to move and offload the drugs, but would pay nothing for the marijuana.

Instead, the brothers would keep half the marijuana for them-selves once it arrived in California. The remainder belonged to Daniels and would be sold and distributed by workers employed by David Boese. The offloaders, Carter and Waldon, were impressed with the pairing they had brought together too, so much so that Michael Carter decided to invest $1 million of his own money into the deal.

Another reason for the widespread confidence was the presence of Boese's right hand man, a long-time smuggler by the name of Robert Kimball. He had been involved in the marijuana trade since the early seventies and was a firm friend of Daniels. He had been off the smuggling scene after being caught in Thailand and sentenced to forty-five years. After just five he had been issued with a pardon by the King and, on his release, had contacted Boese and Daniels with a view to getting right back to work.

It was a true coming together of a dream team and all the

pieces were falling into place. This really was the big one. If they could pull it off, everyone would make big money. Daniels anticipated personal profits of around $30 million from this one deal. The Shaffers estimated they would come away with some $35 million. It was going to be a very, very good year.

With a supplier finally in place, detailed planning for the latest shipment began in earnest.

The success of the previous venture showed that, despite his numerous shortcomings, Hank Sheppard had been dead right about the suitability of Anacortes as an offload site and, with no indication that the DEA or any other law enforcement agency were on to them, the Shaffers saw no reason not to use the site and Tony Franulovich's fleet once again.

Brian O'Dea once again became a regular fixture around the Anacortes area as he and Franulovich prepared the boats they planned to use to transfer the drugs from the mother ship.

In March 1987 in Hong Kong the brothers met with leading representatives of their group to discuss progress. Chris announced that, under the terms of the deal they had with Daniels, they needed to pay around $4 million to initiate the movement of the marijuana through Thailand. The brothers would be investing much of this themselves but called on other senior members of the team to also make a contribution and thus have a vested interest in the success of the mission.

The planning continued to go smoothly but as the months went by O'Dea and the rest of the gang were getting increasingly paranoid and edgy.

By the end of the summer, several members of the gang began to get the first fleeting suspicions that they were being watched. There was nothing concrete: a sense of déjà vu about a van parked at the end of the street for days on end; clicks, buzzes and echoes while talking on the phone; strangers at distant tables in bars and restaurants holding their stares just a little too long.

Although Hank had been acting slightly strangely ever since

the start of the year, he was not the most obvious suspect. In April 1987 a mid-ranking member of the gang had sold a large quantity of last year's marijuana to one of his near neighbours in Hawaii. The neighbour had subsequently been arrested and ever since the Shaffers had become increasingly concerned that the police investigation into the source of the drugs might end up exposing the whole operation.

There was also Tony Franulovich. During several of the planning meetings he had clearly been under the influence of cocaine and had began making a nuisance of himself.

Michael Carter was brought in to keep an eye both on Franulovich and on the boats in Seattle, and make sure they were not being watched.

The Shaffers also took other security measures, issuing every member of the team in Seattle with radio scanners pre-programmed with the frequencies of all the federal law enforcement agencies. Should an agent watching one of the group radio details of their movements back to their base station, the scanners would light up, lock on to the message and allow the gang members to overhear what was being said.

It was while Carter was fulfilling his new role as security chief that Hank turned up again to see Tony Franulovich.

The conversation between the three men started out casually enough. Carter let it slip that the organisation was having trouble with the boats on the other side and that this was causing a delay with the launch of the mother ship. Carter also said this was particularly annoying for him as he had personally invested a million dollars in the load. But as the questions continued Carter became increasingly uncomfortable.

He took Hank to one side. 'I don't think you should be coming around here no more and talking about our business. I'm telling you now, I don't want to see you here again and I don't want to hear that you've been speaking to Tony or anyone else.'

Carter's suspicions were right on the money. After their initial meeting in November, DEA Special Agent Gary Annunziata had designated Hank CI#1 – Confidential Informant 1 – wired him for sound and sent him back into the organisation. Since the start of the New Year Annunziata had been compiling a series of detailed intelligence reports about the planning of the load.

On 8 January 1987 CI#1, working in an undercover capacity, met with Tony Franulovich. The meeting was videotaped. At the meeting Franulovich discusses that the 1986 load had come in August 1986 and that Chris Shaffer and Bill Shaffer were personally present at the offload. In the video tape Franulovich further indicated that the same organisation had begun planning a 1987 marijuana importation which was expected to arrive in July or August 1987.

On 17 February 1987 CI#1 met with Tony Franulovich. After approximately five minutes of conversation Franulovich told CI#1 that he had just purchased a fishing vessel in Seward, Alaska, which he planned to utilise as the primary offload vessel for the 1987 marijuana importation. Franulovich subsequently identified it as the F/V Stormbird.

On May 19 1987 I observed Brian O'Dea at a location in Anacortes where Tony Franulovich was constructing a new warehouse. Brian O'Dea was identified by CI#1 as the individual who had introduced Franulovich to the Shaffer organisation and who had coordinated many of the offload activities of the 1986 importation. Later on the same day I observed a 1978 GMC Jimmy at Franlovich's Anacortes residence. Washington state records indicate in March 1987 this vehicle was registered to David Romei. I have obtained copies of driver's licences issued to David Romei and Gary Waldon and determined from the photographs that David Romei and Gary Waldon are the same person.

CI#1 learned that the *Kathy B* would not be large enough; that $200,000 had been despatched to Seattle to pay for refitting the new boat; that a mysterious new source in Thailand would be supplying the drugs.

Slowly but surely, Annunziata and his team began to identify all the individuals and vessels involved. They were placed on extensive surveillance by a team of experienced male and female agents.

They identified the hired cars they were using, found the applications for passports in false names, tracked down the mail boxes they used to send mail and uncovered the list of code names they used while staying in hotels.

The net was closing in. But suspicions within the gang were still bubbling over and, increasingly, the finger began to point at the man who was indeed feeding information back to the authorities.

In early September 1987 Hank was called to a meeting at the Four Seasons hotel in Seattle. O'Dea's suspicions had finally got the better of him and he and Michael Carter asked Hank directly if he was cooperating with the authorities.

'Jesus Hank,' said O'Dea. 'This is getting to be like an overhead, having to keep travelling here and there to talk to you.'

Hank was determined to front out the situation. 'Never mind spending money on travelling, Brian. How about paying me my share of this operation.'

'You'll get your share. Why wouldn't you? If you didn't, next thing we know you might be knocking on the DEA doors and we'd have people parked outside our houses, you know, studying the racing forms and peeking at us from under their fucking fedoras.'

'What the hell are you trying to say? I'd rat you out?'

'We're worried Hank, that's all. More worried than you need to be.'

'That's bullshit. That's total bullshit. You think I'd do something like that? You're crazy. All I want is my money.'

Carter finally joined in the conversation. 'Yeah, but if it was you buddy, you know what would happen, don't you?'

Hank's denials continued and eventually the tension eased and the meeting was over.

Annunziata had caught it all on tape and now had more than

enough evidence to charge all those concerned with conspiracy. But for the eager agent, having had what promised to be one of the bigger cases of his career land right into his lap, that was not enough. Without the drugs themselves, a good lawyer would be able to have most of the charges against them thrown out.

Annunziata knew that to make the case stick, he had to catch them all red-handed. Otherwise he might just as well not catch them at all.

16
INSIDE MAN

Brian Daniels had arranged for the Shaffer mother ship, the *Manuia*, to rendezvous with two Vietnamese fishing vessels a couple of hundred miles off the coast of Vietnam, to transfer the 42 tons of marijuana.

But a few days before the transfer was due to take place, word reached the Shaffers that the marijuana was stuck in Da Nang harbour, had been impounded by the army, and would not be released until they paid $1 million ransom. The generals, suddenly aware of just how much money was being made from the trade, had decided to up their own stake.

Paying ransom on drug deals in that part of the world carries something of a health warning. It is not unknown for those responsible to collect the money, kill the buyers and dangle the exact same marijuana as a lure for the next victims. The Shaffers knew the risks they were running, and Bill and Chris had no intention of being anywhere nearby when the money was handed over.

That job went to Restall and a few other junior members of the gang. The Shaffers gave them a duffel bag containing $1 million and they sailed with it on the *Manuia* out of Malaysia. A couple of nights later, in total darkness in the middle of the South China Sea, they paid the ransom to a high-ranking Vietnamese army officer in full uniform.

Watched by machine-gun toting soldiers, the officer pretended to count the money. Restall held his breath, not knowing what the men with the machine guns would do next. The officer barked an order. Much to Restall's relief, the soldiers began loading the dope on to his boat.

The following day, with the danger now over, Chris and Bill went to visit the mother ship and inspected the marijuana to make sure it was exactly what they had ordered. It was, and the shipment was finally on its way. The ultimate configuration of The Ring was about to make its first score.

Three weeks later the *Stormbird* met the *Manuia* off the coast of Alaska. A conveyer belt was placed between the two boats and around 2,200 boxes containing 40 pounds of marijuana each were transferred. Hank – or CI#1 as he was known to the DEA – ensured a steady stream of reports made their way back to the authorities. Now at last the importation onto US soil was imminent and Annunziata and his men were poised to strike.

In late September 1987 Tony Franulovich and his first mate on the *St Peter* flew from Alaska to Seattle where they were picked up by Brian O'Dea in his brown Chevrolet Suburban SUV.

The boat crews were busy repacking the marijuana into wetlock boxes and O'Dea was keen to go over the final details of the offload to ensure all went smoothly. From Sea-Tac airport he joined the I-5 freeway heading north towards Anacortes where he planned to do a step-by-step dress rehearsal.

As they got close to their destination, O'Dea's scanner crackled into life, picking up a burst of nearby radio traffic: 'Uh, yeah, a brown Suburban. We're right behind it. We should be pulling up into Anacortes in about twenty minutes.'

The three men froze. O'Dea glanced at his rear view mirror and saw a large jeep with tinted windows and several antenna following a little way behind. It was the DEA.

'Oh no. Oh shit,' said Franulovich.

They had no idea if other members of the gang had been arrested or if the boat crews had been intercepted. They were completely in the dark. For two hours they drove in silence.

'What are we doing to do Brian?' said Tony at last.

'Shit. I don't know what the fuck we're doing to do. We're going to drive.'

'Where are we going?'

'How the fuck do I know?'

'You OK Brian?' Tony asked.

'I'm fucking freaked.'

There was no sense in heading to Anacortes, but where to go instead? O'Dea left the highway at the next exit and headed east, inland, away from the sea. Convinced they would be pulled over at any moment, the trio drove in silence for the next few hours, covering more than 200 miles of back roads and dirt tracks until it was clear they were no longer being followed.

O'Dea pulled up at a phone box and called the safe house. He soon learned that he was not alone – other members of the gang had also reported being followed and so had two other groups. It was now clear that their earlier suspicions had been entirely correct. Furthermore, there could be only one reason for the sudden increase in the level of surveillance – the DEA clearly knew the drugs had been transferred from the mother ship and that the importation was imminent. They were hoping to catch them red-handed.

The safe house reported back that all those who had been followed had managed to lose their pursuers and were scattered far and wide across the state of Washington – no one had risked going home. A plan had been drawn up for an emergency meeting at a motor home in Bellingham, up near the Canadian border, the following day.

There could be no doubt about it – the DEA were onto them. But just how much did they really know about the forthcoming operation and when did they plan to strike?

To get the answers, the Shaffers turned to Stephen Swanson, the former DEA agent who had previously assisted the Dennis Ingham branch of the organisation by providing them with inside information about the investigation into their activities.

William Shaffer flew to Los Angeles and personally delivered $120,000 to Swanson's office, a down payment for the investigation he would undertake on the organisation's behalf. In the meantime, the operation was placed on hold. The 42 tons of marijuana would remain on the *Stormbird*, which in turn would remain in hiding somewhere in the Alaskan fjords.

Within the space of a few days Swanson had delivered his report and fingered Hank Sheppard as the man who had turned informant. The bad news was thatthe DEA knew about the *Stormbird* and, with the help of the navy and the coastguard, was regularly sending out air and sea patrols to look for it. They also knew that the mother ship, the *Manuia*, had delivered the marijuana and was already headed back to South East Asia. They were simply waiting for the fishing boats to come into port and then they would strike.

There was good news too. The DEA knew nothing about the fake trucking company which O'Dea had set up to transport the drugs down to California. Wary of their previous dealings, O'Dea had never mentioned anything about this to Hank meaning that, in turn, Hank was unable to pass details on to the authorities. Most importantly, the DEA had no idea its operation had been compromised.

Exact details of the day-to-day surveillance operation were not available but they had to assume that their every move was being monitored and that their phones were being tapped. They wouldn't be able to catch a cold without the DEA knowing about it. The sensible thing to do would have been to dump the drugs overboard and bring the two boats in clean, putting the loss down to bad luck.

But Chris and Bill didn't feel like being sensible. The odds were stacked against them and they would be taking on the combined resources of two powerful government agencies along with one arm of the military. Despite that, they had some things in their favour and were aware of the limitations of the information held by those working against them. It might just be possible to pull it off anyway. As was the case with the Duchess of Windsor's jewels, sometimes you just have to go for it.

The other ace in the hand for the Shaffers was that the DEA had no idea that Hank had been identified as the source of the leak. The brothers knew that whatever they told him, he would faithfully report back to the authorities. With a little careful handling, it would be easy to make sure the authorities were looking in the wrong direction when the drugs came in.

Although everyone in the organisation was furious with Hank, it made sense to use the fact that he had become an informant to their advantage, rather than try to seek revenge right away. It meant there was a chance that he would ultimately get away with his betrayal – but bringing in the load was a far bigger priority.

The next day Bill Shaffer gathered the crews of the *Stormbird* and the *St Peter* together and announced that they had discovered they were under surveillance by the DEA and that anybody who wanted out was free to leave there and then. 'I got to tell you now that it looks bad, looks bad for all of us,' he explained. 'And even though we're at a critical phase of the operation I want you to know that you can walk away from it and that no one is going to think any the less of you for doing so.' However, Shaffer explained that he and his brother had come up with a plan to defeat the authorities and bring the drugs in right under their noses.

The confidence the brothers displayed was infectious; everyone on board the two boats decided to remain with the operation.

Bill Shaffer turned to his brother. It was time to put the first part of his plan into action. 'The *Stormbird*'s been burned, it's no good to us. Our priority right now,' he explained, 'is to get ourselves a new boat.'

17
THE TRAP

Throughout the sleepy farming community of Fir Island in northern Washington State, Jeff Koetje was known as the kind of guy that people liked to look up to: a local farm boy made good.

Koetje had tried his hand at a number of odd jobs – milking cows, picking berries, farm labouring and mechanics – before turning to the fishing trade. Within the space of a few years Koetje had married his high school sweetheart, bought his first home and, in partnership with two friends, bought a pair of larger boats, the *Prelude* and the *Blue Fin*, to fish for tuna, salmon and herring.

Late in September 1987 an old school friend who happened to be working for the Shaffers approached Koetje and asked to lease the *Blue Fin* for a few days. At first it seemed as though everything would be on the level but then the friend carefully explained that there would be no written agreement for fear of leaving a paper trail. They would, he said, be using the boat to bring in several tons of marijuana. At that point, Koetje began to feel extremely uncomfortable.

Never wanting to let anyone down, Koetje had developed a strategy for avoiding this kind of situation. All his life, whenever he felt he was being pressured, instead of saying no he would simply make up a series of excuses. This time the strategy failed him.

'I'm not sure it's a good idea,' Koetje mumbled. 'The *Blue Fin*, she's got all kinds of mechanical problems. She might not even make it out of the dock.'

'Don't worry about that,' replied the friend. 'I've got a guy who can fix anything.'

Koetje stared at the floor and said nothing.

'Look, are you gonna let us have the boat or what?'

Koetje didn't like the 'or what?' He hesitated once more, desperately trying to think of another, better excuse. The old school friend finally lost his patience. He leaned forward so his face was directly in front of Koetje, close enough to feel his breath.

'You listen and you listen good. We need a boat and yours is the only one in this area that's right. I don't think you know who you are dealing with. The people I work for are accustomed to getting their own way; they don't take any shit. They've been bringing pot into this country for years; we're talking tons and tons and tons. Nothing stands in their way, not even the DEA. Shit, they've got those guys paid off anyway.'

The following day the Shaffers themselves arrived in Koetje's office to press home the point. By now he was convinced that they were a pair of ruthless international drug dealers, the kind of men who would not hesitate to kill to get what they wanted.

'They seemed so powerful,' he said later. 'I genuinely feared they might hurt my family.'

He already knew too much about their plans and there was no way they were going to walk away and leave them alone. He knew there was only one way out: if he agreed to lease the boat he would become part of the conspiracy with as much to lose as they had. Only then might they leave him alone. Koetje handed over the keys.

Fir Island residents rarely lock their doors and windows. Crime is so infrequent and the community so strong that it is simply unnecessary. After meeting the Shaffers, Koetje began locking the doors and double-checking them obsessively. The following day he bought a handgun and took his wife out behind the house to teach her how to shoot.

From that night on Koetje slept with the gun under his pillow.

*   *   *

The day after securing the new boat, Bill Shaffer flew up to Alaska by private plane. He returned to Seattle airport a few days later, all too well aware that he was under surveillance.

Feeling cocky and confident about the new plan, he couldn't resist teasing his pursuers. He looked around and soon identified one of the agents keeping an eye on him and walked straight towards the man.

'I just wanted to say, good luck to your team.' And with that Shaffer turned and left the airport.

The *Blue Fin* left its dock at Bellingham on 10 September 1987 and travelled north to Alaska where it met up with the *Stormbird*. The two boats tied together and the crew transferred the drugs from the *Stormbird* to the *Blue Fin*.

As with the year before, spotter pilot Terry Cratty was brought in to fly ahead of the *Blue Fin* as it made its way to port. Cratty, still uncomfortable with his role in the 1986 operation, had hesitated but finally agreed after learning that, because the load was significantly larger, he would be paid considerably more.

Once news of the DEA operation emerged, Cratty tried to pull out completely but Franulovich and others in the gang began pressuring him to fulfil his obligation, pressure that culminated in a series of lightly veiled threats, until Cratty finally agreed to do what had been asked of him.

With the usual air escort in place, the fully loaded *Blue Fin* then made its way back to the public dock at Bellingham. Unlike Anacortes, this was the least perfect offload site imaginable, the last place anyone in their right mind would choose to bring in a consignment of drugs. For one thing it was far too exposed: a small coffee shop overlooked the main loading area and dozens of bystanders could see everything that was going on. It was so wrong that it simply had to be right. The Shaffers had decided that, under the circumstances, the best place to hide was in plain sight.

Throughout the journey Terry Cratty was not the only aircraft in the sky. DEA and Royal Canadian Mounted Police airplanes roared overhead, looking out for the *Kathy B* and the *Stormbird*, which were expected to attempt to make their run at any time. Brian O'Dea stood on the dock, convinced they were all about to be arrested at any moment. Many of those on the *Blue Fin* felt the same way. As they got closer to the dock, several members of the crew began waving nervously at O'Dea from the deck of the ship. But absolutely nothing happened.

As the *Blue Fin* tied off, the first of the five trucks backed up. Each had four pallets of cedar shingles as a cover which first had to be removed using forklift trucks. Once they were clear, the wet-lock boxes were piled up in the back. Though all the boxes were identical, a few of the boxes actually contained fish and ice so the offloaders made a show of dropping one, spilling a couple of large salmon on the ground. To those looking on, it all looked totally innocent.

As the trucks were filled up, the pallets of cedar were hauled back into place and the trucks headed off towards California, each one being followed at a discreet distance by a 'safety car' which would report back in the event of the load running into problems. The whole operation had taken less than six hours.

Two days later, back at Anacortes, Special Agent Annunziata and his team were anticipating a glorious end to the operation that had begun almost a year earlier when Hank Sheppard had come to the DEA office.

It was to be a spectacular raid – one of the biggest to take place in the Pacific North-west for many years. The prize would be marijuana with a street value of more than $100 million dollars and the resulting case would see millions of dollars of assets forfeited and dozens jailed. The anticipation was so great you could feel it in the air. Helicopters, airplanes, coastguard and navy cutters and DEA zodiac boats were all poised to strike the moment that Annunziata gave the word.

That word was finally given just after 4 p.m. on a breezy Tuesday afternoon in September when the *Stormbird* and the *St*

Peter crossed the Canada-US border in the Inside Passage and found themselves illuminated under a flood of spotlights from all directions.

The two boats cut their engines and drifted to a halt as the mass of law enforcement vehicles around and above them began to close in. There would be no escape, no opportunity to destroy evidence, no chance to avoid paying the consequences for attempting such an audacious smuggle.

Annunziata was one of the first to board. He tried hard not to be too eager, too smug about what he expected to find. Although difficult to conceal at first, it rapidly became easier as his search became increasingly fruitless. He found the holds packed with freshly caught fish and the crew calmly drinking coffee, but no drugs, not so much as a single joint.

Annunziata was speechless. He moved about the *Stormbird* once more, frantically searching every nook and cranny, checking for hidden compartments or signs of recent welding work. There was nothing and after several hours of work with absolutely nothing to show for it, he had to accept the drugs were simply not there.

What on earth had gone wrong? He had been working the case for almost a year, compiled dozens of reports, spent hundreds of hours cramped up in his car on stake-outs, pleaded with his bosses to be able to allocate more time and resources to the investigation because they were virtually 100 per cent certain to get a good result. But he had come away empty-handed. Against all the odds, the smugglers had pulled off the impossible.

The depth of Annunziata's despair was easily matched by the heights of the joy felt by the Shaffers and their team. A few hours after the crew of the *Stormbird* had returned to port, they were handed bundles of airline tickets along with wads of spending money. The following day everyone who had been involved in the operations flew down to Mexico for a party to end all parties.

The ultimate configuration of The Ring – Brian Daniels and

the Shaffer brothers – had lived up to all expectations. They were truly unstoppable; invincible. And so far as Daniels in particular was concerned, the only way to go was up.

18
CASH CRISIS

Everyone involved in the smuggle had come away with their pockets bulging. The payments made the previous year had been large enough but this time around they made it seem as though everyone involved had won the lottery. Terry Cratty, for example, had been paid $35,000 for his flying services in 1986, this time around that went up to $170,000.

When the Shaffers' money-laundering system swung back into action the brothers found they had flown more than $35 million to Switzerland in the space of a few weeks. And that represented profits from the sales of only half the marijuana they had smuggled in; the other half of the cargo belonging to Daniels himself. This portion of the load would be sold and distributed by a newly established division of The Ring set up by Bruce Aitken.

After years of laundering millions of dollars on behalf of all the top Thai marijuana smugglers, Bruce Aitken had decided to quit while he was still at the top and announced his plans to retire from the business. As soon as he made his intentions known his old friend and California attorney Edward Seltzer was given the opportunity to take over the business.

With $50 million soon heading his way from the sale of the Daniels's marijuana, Seltzer threw himself into his new role as an international money launderer and immediately began seeking contacts with whom he would be able to do business. In October 1987 he called William Henry Harris, a British citizen living in Los Angeles, to enquire whether he knew anyone who could help move large amounts of currency.

At the time Harris was a member of a charitable organisation called the Knights of Malta and had just received a call from another member, Joseph Stedino, offering him the chance to get involved in a legitimate business opportunity.

During the conversation Harris sensed that Stedino was the kind of man he could trust, the kind of guy who had connections, the kind of guy who had served a little time in the past; all of which was true. Harris called Stedino back and went straight to his main question without hesitation: do you have any contacts who could launder between fifty and one hundred million dollars in US currency?

Harris's instincts were right on the money. Stedino may have liked to dabble in charity work but, above all, he was a businessman. 'Sure, I can deal with all of that,' he told Harris, explaining that he had a friend who owned a casino in Reno, Nevada who would happily launder the money in return for a 3 per cent slice of the total.

Harris replied that he had already agreed with the people behind the venture that in total 10 per cent of the sum would be available as commission and that the casino worker and their own personal share – including money due to Seltzer – would be divided up among that.

When Seltzer heard the news he was initially pleased but then he began to get extremely nervous. As the reality of what he was planning began to dawn on him, Seltzer became increasingly concerned about the project. He had agreed to launder $50 million in cash. Not only that, he would be doing it through a contact and a casino boss he had never met. Harris assured him that everything would be fine, and that Stedino seemed like a good guy. There was nothing to worry about.

On 22 October 1987 Harris and Seltzer flew to Reno from LA. They were met by Stedino who introduced them to his casino contact, Daniel Camillo. The group made their way to a room in a nearby hotel and as soon as the door was closed, Seltzer began searching the suite, looking for recording devices. He pulled the curtains closed, looked behind pictures on the walls, inside cabinets, checked the underside of drawers and then turned up the TV to almost full volume.

'I don't mind telling you I'm a bit uncomfortable with this whole thing,' he told Camillo. 'I mean, say you got a bunch of guns hidden away here or something. I don't know you at all. You could be trying anything.'

'We're cool,' said Camillo. 'You can relax.'

Eventually Seltzer calmed down and told everyone in the room that there was $30 million immediately available for laundering with another $20 million to follow in a week or so. Within an hour Camillo had agreed to accept the cash, hiding it among the cashflow of his casino and then using his business accounts to wire it to Europe and Hong Kong.

At around 5 p.m. on 4 November 1987, Harris and Seltzer arrived in Reno and met with David Boese and Robert Kimball who transferred numerous suitcases and duffel-bags to their vehicle. Each of the bags was stuffed with cash and the whole lot weighed close to a ton. The men all smiled at one another as they loaded the vehicle. This was really going to happen. Thanks to the commission they had been promised, each of them would be a millionaire in the space of a few days.

The money was taken to room 352 of the Airport Plaza Hotel in Reno where Camillo and Stedino were waiting. Once the four men were safely inside and the doors secured, the money was taken out of the bag and they began to count. And count, and count.

Only Seltzer had the vaguest idea exactly what line of business the money they were counting had been derived from but it wasn't long before others in the group began to speculate.

STEDINO: You know what I'm worried about doing this. I'm worried about residue and getting a contact high. Can I sniff it, any of these bulls and get high? I think there's still some c-o-k-e on them.

SELTZER: No, no, no. It's not that kind of money. It's not. It's a different kind of money.

STEDINO: Huh?

SELTZER: It's hashish.

CAMILLO: This much from hashish? How much does that stuff sell for?

SELTZER: Well. . . this may be some chicken shit cocaine money, I don't know these guys. I mean I was introduced through someone else and that, see that's why I was real jumpy, remember the first time you met me how jumpy I was. . .

CAMILLO: Yeah. Why are they paying us to take it out when they had to bring it in?

SELTZER: They didn't bring it in here. This has got to be domestic. So, maybe, maybe, Joey's right. Maybe this is blow money. I met one guy and he's not a blow guy. I know what they look like. He's a hash guy. It's a whole different trip, but you don't have the violence with it. You know, it's nothing like that.

CAMILLO: And these are twenties, we're not dealing in straight hundreds. These are twenties.

SELTZER: Cocaine dealers, they're all hundreds. This looks like marijuana money.

Three, four and five hours passed and still the counting continued. By now the room had descended into a state of sheer chaos. There were bags and boxes and piles of money everywhere – on the floor, on the tables, on the bed, on every item of furniture. Some of it was wrapped and tagged, some of it was not. After a while, no one was sure exactly what had been counted and what hadn't.

Each man tried to count their own piles of money and each man did it out loud. They then introduced a new system: each person would count a different type of bill – twenties, fifties, hundreds and so on, but that just made things even more confusing. Eventually they realised they had no option but to stop and start over again.

The count reached $6.6 million but then Camillo found some

notes on the floor that appeared to have been missed. Then Seltzer picked up what appeared to be $320,000 in twenty dollar bills that had got mixed in with a bunch of fifties. Another bag full of cash seemed to have been kicked under the bed and none of them was sure what was going on.

'We have $6.6 million packed away,' announced Stedino confidently.

'That's not right,' said Seltzer.

'How do you know?' came the reply.

Harris jumped into the conversation: 'He doesn't know.'

Suddenly Camillo groaned: 'Shit, I just dropped my money on the floor.'

The group recalculated from the bundles of cash that they knew had definitely been counted. It brought them up $70,000 short. They decided to double check the figures and this time came up $108,000 short. Then they found a few loose bills and realised the true figure is actually $106,000 short.

Finally, at close to 1 a.m., after more than eight solid hours of counting, they determined they had a total of $7,618,570 in US currency, just over $105,000 short of what they were supposed to have.

With everyone eager to take a well-deserved break, Camillo began to take drinks orders. Seltzer had a regular Coke, Harris a Diet. Stedino was happy to stick with coffee, but before Camillo was halfway to the door it burst open.

Twenty men, some in sharp suits, others in tactical body armour, rushed in, guns drawn. 'FBI,' said one, 'Everybody's under arrest.'

At the same time other agents swooped on nearby hotels to arrest Robert Kimball, and David Boese – who had a further $2.4 million in cash on him. The youngest division of The Ring had turned out to be the most notorious for all the wrong reasons – they had provided the agents who arrested them with the largest cash seizure in US history.

* * *

The first Brian Daniels knew of the seizure of the money was an urgent message from a man who had risen to become one of the top distributors of his marijuana in the US.

Thomas Sherrett had joined The Ring in the mid-eighties and had quickly proved himself to be among the most talented and sophisticated smugglers around. Unlike the Shaffer brothers, Dennis Ingham or even Robert Lietzman, Sherrett had mastered the art of keeping a low profile to such a degree that no law enforcement agency had ever even heard of him.

Based in Oregon, he had perfected his cover by living in a modest home and working part-time for his local refugee centre, earning around $900 per month. Outwardly at least he presented few clues to the fact that he earned several million dollars each year from the marijuana trade.

The pair's most recent collaboration had taken place just a few weeks earlier when Sherrett had successfully offloaded 12 tons of marijuana, with the assistance of none other than the Ortiz brothers, a short time after the Shaffers had brought in their 42-ton load. Another reason for his trip had been to arrange to hand over to Daniels some of the first monies from the sale of the drugs, but now Sherrett was not so sure it was safe.

'Man you've got a fucking problem,' Sherrett told Daniels urgently. 'They've got your address. They're going to fuck your arse.'

Daniels listened carefully to the first accounts of what had happened and then began to make a series of urgent phone calls to everyone he could get hold of. The news that filtered its way back to him was anything but good.

Within a few days the newspapers were reporting that Dan Camillo, the casino executive, had actually been an FBI agent. That meant that one of the men who had been involved in making the introduction had to be a mole. Sherrett was right: Daniels had a problem.

From what he could ascertain, at least $3 million had been due to be wired to his personal bank accounts in the next few days. That was now lost. That still left more than $25 million, but with so many members of The Ring in custody it was touch and go as to whether he would ever be able to get hold of it.

Some of the older, more experienced smugglers who had been taken into custody would have been smart enough to ensure any cash they had access to was safe from raids on their homes and businesses, but Daniels was concerned that some of the newer recruits might not have the backbone to withstand the pressure of a police interrogation.

His instincts turned out to be right on the money. In his very first interview with the FBI, William Henry Harris had cracked like a dried twig and given up everything that he had known right away.

'Well, Seltzer, the lawyer guy, he knows this guy by the name of Aitken in Hong Kong,' Harris told the Feds. 'He used to launder money but he doesn't do it any more because he's got a bunch of problems in the Far East. He's retired. You know, I think this Aitken guy, he must be the Kingpin.'

Ever since the Cessna-Milner scandal and subsequent kidnap, Daniels' name had always been associated with that of Aitken, and the fact that his friend's name was now tied to the money that had been seized in Reno was a massive cause for concern.

But a far bigger problem was the lack of cashflow that the seizure was set to create. Like many major smugglers, Daniels liked to invest the profits from each operation into the next. It was a system that worked well and generated a phenomenal turnover just so long as the shipments kept getting through. Each seizure – be it of drugs or money – was little short of a financial catastrophe which threatened to bring the whole ring crashing down around his ears.

Daniels got back in touch with Sherrett. 'Listen Tom, right now I got this problem. I need some cash. So send me a gift box, OK?'

Sherrett promised to comply but only a day later he landed in Hong Kong, his sense of panic and paranoia stronger than ever.

He called Aitken and told him that it was simply too hot and that he wouldn't be able to pay any money to anyone at that time.

Sherrett told Aitken that although the 12 tons of marijuana he had received the previous month had been successfully landed, he was having trouble selling the drugs on. One issue was that the local market had been flooded by the earlier load that had been brought in by the Shaffers. Another was that the seals on the packets of drugs had been faulty and some had begun to go mouldy, dramatically reducing the amount of cash they could be sold for.

'I walk into a market that my friend Bri has just dumped 40 tons in with different groups: the Shaffers, Kimball, the offload group and Boese. They had no coordinated programme, they're each out there saying 'OK, we'll coordinate the price' and then they're just fucking each other every time they got the chance. Because everybody wants the money that people have saved. Now I jump into the market, nobody has money saved and everybody's got the same problem that I do.'

So far as Daniels was concerned, Sherrett was simply making pathetic excuses. Like far too many of those with whom he worked in The Ring, Sherrett had realised that Daniels was a soft touch, not the kind of guy to make a fuss if money he was owed didn't come his way when it was due.

Sherret was a firm believer in shipping small quantities of marijuana – 12 tons at the very most but preferably between five and ten tons at a time. He had spent months trying to convince Daniels to drop the size of his shipments but Daniels had refused because financially, it simply wasn't worth his while to get involved in smaller deals. Now so far as Daniels was concerned Sherrett was trying to punish him for having brought in 42 tons in one sitting.

His claims about not being able to sell the marijuana because the market was flooded just didn't ring true. In Daniels' mind there were only two issues at play. First, Sherrett had lost his nerve as a result of the Reno seizure. Second, he was trying to drive up the price by holding back on his marijuana stock and selling it at a later date.

Daniels could do nothing but sit back and wait for Sherrett to send through what he owed, while at the same time seeing if there was another way to get hold of the money that David Boese and Robert Kimball and the others had made from selling their portion of the drugs.

Of the two men, Kimball was the better bet. Daniels had known him longer and their friendship was solid. Even though he was in jail and looking at being there for many, many years to come, Kimball would believe in fair play. If he had any of Daniels' money stashed away, he would more than willingly hand it over.

But just as Daniels was dealing with this one set of bad news, a knock-on effect of the same seizure soon provided another.

At the time that the money was seized the Shaffer brothers were in Zurich with their own share of the money from the 42-ton load. Having provided the transportation, they did not owe any of their profits to Daniels and, using their traditional laundering system, had managed to safely deposit all of their cash into their usual bank accounts and shell companies.

But over cocktails at Zurich's Central Hotel the fallout of the seizure was discussed. Up until that point the brothers were feeling so pleased with themselves for having defeated the DEA that they were considering bringing in another shipment the following year.

The seizure of the money brought it home to them that the success of their last mission had been as much down to luck as their skills as smugglers. Someone within The Ring, someone far too close to their end of the operation, was leaking information to the authorities and, for all they knew, the FBI might have them all under surveillance.

It seemed as if it was only a matter of time before the authorities caught up with them. It was a depressing thought and a dark cloud descended over the room until someone pointed out that they still had millions of dollars to spend and no real reason to save the cash for the future.

The days of the Shaffer brothers may have been numbered, but each and every one of those days would be lived to the full.

Not so for Daniels. The ultimate configuration of The Ring, that had brought Daniels his greatest success and smuggled in the largest ever single load of marijuana he had put onto the water, was no more. And now he needed to find a way to recoup his losses.

19
SMOOTH OPERATOR

If Brian Daniels was suffering from a lack of cash, Michael Forwell, the sole surviving owner of the Superstar and former partner of Robert Lietzman, had the opposite problem.

He and the Colflesh brothers had continued their smuggling activities after taking over the bar from Lietzman and had seen their earnings increase every year since.

One night in New York Forwell was flicking through a boating magazine when he saw an advertisement for the *Delfino II*, a 130-foot motor yacht costing $1 million dollars. He picked up the phone, dialled the number of the owners and said: 'I just bought your boat.'

Berthing her on the seafront at Miami, Forwell had the en-suite bathroom kitted out in marble and glazed tiles imported from Italy. The fittings were finished in 24-carat gold. Four million dollars-worth of additions later, the *Delfino* could stay self-sufficient at sea for up to six months. She had jet skis, sports boats, fishing and scuba gear, a landing pad and her own five-passenger helicopter.

By now Forwell was making so much money from smuggling that he no longer had any respect for it. One time he suspected members of the crew of the *Delfino* were pilfering supplies. He lined up his crew on the deck and held out his hand with a bundle of $5,000. He then told those in front of him that money meant nothing compared to the loyalty he expected from then. And with that, he tossed the money into the sea. When it was time to make money rather than spend it or throw it away, Forwell sold the *Delfino* for $3.5 million and bought the *Encounter Bay*.

The *Bay* was a legacy of the recession in the oil business that struck around the mid-eighties. With dozens of rigs out in the middle of the ocean that needed to be supplied and serviced on a regular basis, oil companies commissioned and built dozens of ships specifically for that purpose.

The vessels were incredibly powerful, had a large carrying capacity to enable them to transport supplies and could travel in any weather. The ships were not particularly fast but they were incredibly sturdy.

When the recession struck, the price of such vessels fell dramatically. The high cost of storage and maintenance meant it made more economic sense for the oil companies to sell the ships off cheaply at a huge loss than to keep them on, waiting for the recession to lift. Ships that had originally cost several million dollars to build were suddenly coming on to the market for a few hundred thousand dollars at a time.

Such vessels soon became the marijuana smugglers' vessel of choice. They could haul tons at a time in all kinds of conditions. They could travel via the polar routes to avoid coastguard patrols and, if things got bad, they could happily sit around in the middle of the ocean for weeks at a time waiting for the situation to improve. For anyone in the smuggling business, it would have been impossible to design a ship more suited to the task at hand[1]

Once the *Encounter Bay* had been taken to Singapore and fitted out for its new role as a drug carrier, Forwell and Sam Colflesh took it on a journey to the Gulf of Thailand where they met with Sam's brother Robert who was in a smaller boat loaded with hundreds of pounds of marijuana.

Earlier, Forwell had bought two 40-foot racing powerboats, the *Kimono* and the *Mariposa*. Capable of around 90 mph, Forwell had come up with a novel way of getting the drugs from the *Encounter Bay* and into America. The cigarette boats would be loaded on to the back of the freighter, stocked up with marijuana and then launched off, like planes leaving an aircraft carrier.

---

[1]Not everyone involved in the marijuana smuggling business was quite so enamoured of the vessels however. When Thomas Sherrett was offered one he told the seller: 'How am I gonna take chicks on an oil rig supply boat and get laid? It's not going to work. I'd look like an idiot. But if I buy a yacht . . . I'm in business.'

On that first trip the two boats were put into the water at a point 150 miles off San Francisco Bay. Forwell drove one and Sam the other right into the bay. The journey from ship to shore took eight hours and the two men, along with their precious cargo, passed under the Golden Gate Bridge at 60 mph in broad daylight. Forwell was so excited about the venture that he even hired a helicopter to film his arrival.

Although it seemed like pure bravado, nothing was left to chance. Forwell backed up everything with meticulous organisation and planning. At any sign of police activity, teams of lookouts on the coast would send messages to the cigarette boats to put into beaches rather than the bay. There, Forwell and Colflesh would have stripped off their racing suits to reveal the business suits – complete with smart shirts and ties – they were wearing underneath.

The escape and evasion plan would call for the drugs to be abandoned and for the whole team to escape on motorbikes making them almost impossible for law enforcement vehicles to follow.

But nothing ever went wrong and for two years, Forwell used the *Encounter Bay* and the two speedboats to ship increasingly large amounts of marijuana into San Francisco without the authorities being any the wiser.

Once time, rather than piloting the boat himself, Forwell travelled to San Francisco direct in order to coordinate the offload and arrange for the sale and marketing of the marijuana. Disguising his British accent, Forwell entered the States using a false American passport in the name Rodney Wayne Boggs.

Whenever he flew anywhere he would buy his first-class tickets at least six months in advance but then switch them at the last minute to another airline which had a reciprocal agreement. This meant that keeping track of him was next to impossible.

Forwell's organisation came up with an equally novel way of dealing with the problem of getting the money they made out of the country. Forwell established an American company called Fast Lane Express. Every year it entered a car for the Macau Grand Prix. It looked like a Formula One car but inside there was only a go-kart engine – barely enough to make it move at all. All of the unused space was stuffed with dollar bills. The car was air-freighted to Hong Kong where customs, not wishing to interfere with preparations for the big race, would wave it through.

The day before the race was due to start, the Fast Lane Express car would report engine trouble and have to withdraw from the competition. The money would then be removed.

More cash left the States in Louis Vuitton cabin trunks bound for Hong Kong's best hotels where they awaited Forwell's arrival. He also had handmade suits designed with special pockets that could carry large sums of cash. Even the pedestal of the captain's seat on the *Encounter Bay* was specially designed with a space where up to $750,000 could be stashed.

In 1987 Forwell decided on a different tactic, switching from the West to the East Coast. The *Encounter Bay*, captained by Sam Colflesh, was again sent to the Gulf of Thailand to receive marijuana. The drugs were then packed into cans, which in turn were concealed in large, British-made spools of steel towing cable which were placed on the deck of the *Encounter Bay*. The boat then sailed to Colombo, Sri Lanka, where it was met by Forwell. He arranged to have the spools sent first to Rotterdam then to London, from where they were sent to New York.

On arrival, the spools appeared to have been sent directly from Europe and were marked 'Maritime supplies in transit'. Customs waved them through without a second glance. The final part of the journey involved sending the spools back to California where the drugs were finally removed.

But this time around the drugs sold poorly. As had been the case with Thomas Sherrett, the marijuana had arrived shortly after the Shaffer brothers successfully unloaded their 42 tons in Washington. The market was flooded and the previously high price had fallen to an all-time low. It was nothing more than a case of bad timing but for a gang that had seen so much success – financial and logistical – it was hugely disappointing. There simply had to be a better way of doing business.

20
ALL YOU NEED IS LOVE

If Brian Daniels was going to continue in the marijuana business, he needed to bring in some new blood, a team with the right level of skill and competence to enable them to successfully smuggle multi-ton loads of drugs into the United States. Most importantly, it should be a team that had yet to make an appearance on any law enforcement radar screen.

The Shaffer brothers had proved themselves to be a cut above the rest but had now all but retired from the business. Thomas Sherrett was a cunning and successful smuggler but he was already messing Daniels around when it came to paying him what he was owed.

But Daniels knew at least one place he could go where he would be sure of finding the kind of people he was looking for. It was time to revisit an old haunt.

In December 1987 Robert Colflesh was working in the back office of the Superstar when one of his staff knocked on the door and informed him that someone was looking for him.

The man waiting in the bar was tall, stocky and balding. He introduced himself as Brian and explained that he was an old friend of Robert Lietzman and had worked with him in Australia during the seventies.

'Tell me about how he died,' said Brian. 'Do you think it was an accident, or something else?'

Although they had never met, Robert Colflesh quickly realised the man he was talking to was none other than Brian Daniels. It was to be another one of those moments that, with the benefit of hindsight, turn out to be key in the history of Thai marijuana smuggling.

It had been many years since Daniels had been a regular at the Superstar. During the years between, he had spent an increasing amount of time with his Thai friends and had become increasingly influenced by their culture. One key element was that spending too much time with *farangs* was seen as leading to a loss of 'face' or social standing. For Daniels to maintain his position of influence within the Thai community he had to all but cut off his ties to the other expats.

That had worked well enough for a while but now, with an urgent need to find new recruits to The Ring, Daniels had no choice but to expand his circle of contacts.

He began to meet with Robert Colflesh on a regular basis, and it didn't take long for the conversation to turn to drug smuggling. Daniels began regaling the bar owner with stories of his adventures with Lietzman on their journeys to Australia. Colflesh soon understood that it was Brian Daniels himself who had been responsible for providing the 42-ton load that had been landed by the Shaffer brothers and flooded the American market.

As the pair grew more comfortable in each other's company, Daniels began to share some of the secrets of his organisation. He told Colflesh that he had a source that gave him law enforcement information. The source came from the Office of the Narcotics Control Board in Bangkok. Daniels claimed he could receive information about telephone taps and surveillance operations on targets, as well as people who were likely to be arrested. Daniels emphasised that he paid his source on a regular basis, regardless of whether the man provided any information or not.

Daniels also explained that he had a secret code that he used with people within The Ring so that they could be sure that any communication received through a third party or other source was genuinely coming from him.

A couple of weeks after he and Daniels had first met, Robert Colflesh arranged to meet up with Michael Forwell and his twin brother, Samuel. He put a proposal to them. 'I think we should abandon our plans to do our own importation in 1988. Instead, we should get together with this Daniels guy and offer to transport whatever load he wants to move with the *Encounter Bay*. We'll collect a flat fee for the transportation and that way we'll be protected from any variation in the market price in the States on the off chance that some other group bring a load in at the same time.'

Forwell was intrigued. 'How big a load are we talking about?'

'Big. Maybe sixty tons.'

Forwell did a quick calculation in his head. For that amount of drugs the profit on the transportation would amount to $25 million. And because they were not buying any of the actual marijuana, Forwell's team would hardly have to put any money up front.

Forwell and the Colflesh brothers knew the good luck they had enjoyed up until now could not possibly last. All around them, the other gangs that frequented the Superstar were falling like flies. They had lost count of the number of people now serving sentences or awaiting trial.

Everyone in the smuggling business worked on the basis of using the profits from one job to fund the next. That worked well just so long as the jobs continued to be successful. Even a single seizure could spell absolute disaster and end up costing tens of million of dollars.

The opportunity to make $25 million with only a minimal investment of their own funds was almost too good to be true. Forwell told Robert Colflesh to tell Brian Daniels that he was interested and that they would meet to discuss the details in the very near future.

With the Colflesh brothers and Forwell expressing an interest in working with him, Daniels felt a renewed confidence in the business. He took Robert to one side with an additional proposal for him: would he and his brother – making full use of the fact that both had served in the military – be willing to travel to the States to collect the money that Thomas Sherrett owed Daniels? With around $10 million outstanding and a hefty commission available for whoever collected it, it would be more than worthwhile.

Daniels needed help because Sherrett was becoming increasingly aggressive in his negotiations, and also increasingly paranoid. Once a mild-mannered hippy type like Daniels himself, Sherrett had found himself on the leading edge of a sea change taking place in the marijuana business. Word of the huge sums of money to be made had reached out beyond those who had traditionally become involved in smuggling. With profits on a par with heroin and Thai marijuana worth more than gold, organised crime proper was getting involved.

In New York, junior members of the Mafia were now controlling the docks and warehouses where the drugs were being stored before being distributed. The violence that had been seen in Mexico during the mid-seventies was now creeping into some of the Thai trade as well. If Daniels was going to have any chance of getting his money and staying in business, he needed to surround himself with tough guys. The two former Green Berets and Vietnam veterans seemed just the ticket.

The Colflesh brothers agreed to meet Sherrett in person to help them to assess what kind of person he was before deciding whether to take on the task. The men got together in the bar of the Shangri-La hotel and Daniels soon lost his temper as Sherrett made excuse after excuse about why the money was not available and moaned about the problems he was having selling the last load of drugs Daniels had provided.

The key issue was the Ortiz brothers, who had been involved in the offload and had a share of the drugs. They had 'stolen' some of Sherrett's marijuana, not only reducing the amount he had left to sell but also leaving him with a high proportion of mouldy marijuana.

'When the landing craft came into the shore, the Ortiz brothers sent out another boat to meet it,' Sherrett explained. 'They told me it was carrying fuel and food but they were lying and they put some of the drugs on it. I know that because the captain on the mother ship had a clicker and was counting the packages as they went on to the landing craft. There was no way he could have been wrong.

'But the Ortiz brothers, David and the others, they just said "fuck you". These guys are old in the business. They've done a lot of offloads for people. They did three loads for the Shaffers. Everyone in the business had heard of them. But every single guy on their crew was doing as much coke as possible the whole time. I mean everybody was just jamming his face. There were even a couple of pistols floating around. Not a stable group of people to work with.

'When it was over, David Ortiz didn't want to give me my stuff until he and his crew had looked through everything and picked out what they wanted, you know, all the good stuff. Finally I went down with some guys that I had with me. We took some Uzis [sub machine guns]. I said I don't give a shit what you say. They had seven guys there. I had two guys with me. I don't give a fuck what you say, I'm taking mine now. I said I had 58 per cent of this thing, you had 20 per cent. The guy with 20 per cent doesn't tell the guy with 58 per cent when he gets to take his.'

Because the Ortiz brothers had taken all the best quality drugs, they had led to Sherrett being short in terms of what he owed Daniels. He explained that in reality, money should be coming from the Ortiz brothers but that they were unlikely to hand over any cash.

'We'll never get the money back from them. They won't pay because they will never admit they did it. We are going to square it up the other way,' Sherrett explained. 'We are going to hospitalise them.'

All the talk of guns and violence did little to inspire the Colflesh brothers to think it would be a good idea to attempt to intimidate Sherrett into handing over the money he owed to Daniels, and the pair soon left Sherrett and Daniels to talk alone.

It was then that Daniels decided to tell Sherrett that he hoped to put together a huge load for 1988 with the Colflesh boys and Michael Forwell.

'How big is huge?' asked Sherrett.

'Sixty, maybe seventy tons.'

'What, on one boat?'

'That's the idea.'

'You're crazy Brian.'

Sherrett was furious. He pointed out the problems that Daniels had created the year before when he flooded the market with just 42 tons. To put sixty or seventy out there at one time would just make things a thousand times worse. It could take months for the market to recover. Daniels would be shooting himself in the foot.

But Daniels didn't see it like that at all. From where he sat, far away from the streets of California, the market seemed more than big enough to handle any amount of drugs. All that really concerned him was putting together a single shipment that was large enough to cover all the losses that he had made up until that point and that made use of a team that were almost guaranteed to pull it off without a hitch.

'What did you think of Sam and Bob?' Daniels asked Sherrett.

'The Superstar boys?'

'Yeah.'

'To be honest, not a lot. Not impressed. They're too young and they don't have enough experience.'

'Really? I was hoping you might want to buy into the load.'

'I've got a better idea. Instead of getting the Superstar boys to do the offload, let me do it. You know my people, that way it's all secure.'

But Daniels was wary. Sherrett buying into the load would be one thing – it would mean he would have to pay Daniels what he owed him and then some on top. But to give Sherrett the offload would mean he would also be entitled to take a proportion of the 70 tons. With Daniels's luck, that would be rolled into the existing debt and he'd never get his money. In the meantime, Sherrett would have several tons of marijuana to sell and make millions of dollars. Millions more dollars that Daniels would never see.

'Look man,' Daniels said slowly. 'We need to clear the balance first before we can even consider any kind of "new business". You know what I'm saying.'

In many ways Sherrett was right, and he had always proved reliable in the past. So far as anyone knew, his name was not even known to any law enforcement agency. The same could not be said of Forwell and the Colflesh brothers. Although they had never come close to being caught, the death of Robert Lietzman had cast a fresh spotlight on activities at the Superstar and everyone associated with it. It might only be a matter of time before they too were exposed.

But despite the risks, Daniels preferred to work with people who hadn't yet screwed him over. He told Sherrett that he would only continue working with him once he handed over the money he owed. As for transporting his next multi-ton load, no deal.

A few days later Sherrett went out drinking in Bangkok with mutual friends of his and Daniels, and could not resist the temptation to vent his spleen about the Daniels situation.

Daniels had cast himself in the role of corporate titan but his empire had become so vast and so far-flung that he regularly lost contact with the rank and file members of the organisation. He was unable to keep tabs on what people were doing with his products or his money. And in a world where most deals are done on a handshake and a word, Daniels simply didn't know who to trust and was getting screwed left, right and centre, usually by the people with the strongest personalities.

'Right now there are two groups of people,' Sherrett explained to his friends. 'There's one group that are afraid to get near Brian because there's heat on him. There's another group that think he's the goose that laid the golden egg – like Sam and Bob

Colflesh. He's not a very strong personality in negotiations. I know they see that. Because they're just real pushy sons of bitches.

'Don't tell this to Brian because he is quite conscious of any criticism, he hates it. He won't ever engage in any self-analysis at all. But I've sat in rooms and watched these very sharp guys from back east that dotted every "i" and crossed every "t" when it was pertaining to their part of the contract. And then I saw this ageing hippy across the table saying "aw, come on man, I know you are going to take care of me" not caring at all about any of the fine print on the contract. And I have found you got to fucking write things on paper and say what if this happens, then what? And you almost got to make them sign in blood. Or record their voice because they will always deny they said that. It's always a power grab for the money once it gets here.

'He wants me to work with the Colflesh brothers but I said no. They are pricks and to tell you the truth I won't work with them. I don't care, honest to God, I won't work this year if I have to work with them. I'll go work with the Pakistanis and do a bunch of Black. Because I'm not going to work with people that are going to be pushy and that I don't enjoy being with. I told him [Brian] I said look, I've come over here to work the books out with you, to find out how much I'm sending you back. You don't give me five minutes to talk about it. You want me to go meet this guy and all that but I don't want to work with them. I will play along. I'll pretend that I'm interested, but I'm not interested Brian. Not in the slightest. They are assholes. They are real pushy mother fuckers.'

The notion of a shipment of over 60 tons was also sticking in Sherrett's throat.

'What is he focusing on? How much weight he puts out or how much money he gets back? Who gives a fuck how much you put out there if 95 per cent of the money is still owed to you?'

In Sherrett's eyes Daniels was becoming increasingly desperate to find new people to add to The Ring but, as had been the case with the money seizure in Reno, each new addition to the group merely added another layer of weakness.

'He's been in Thailand too long. He's getting this face syndrome. He's had it ever since I've known him, but it has grown. I've known him five years, something like that, and I've watched him work every year. When I met him he was portrayed to me as a *farang* that doesn't hang out with *farangs*, that has a lot of Thai friends, that he's very careful, puts out a few loads a year, makes good money and just keeps to himself.

'That's what he could be, but he's not that. He's a *farang* that hangs out at the airport to see if any new *farangs* are coming in so he can say "hey, do you want to work with me?" I mean, he comes up with four or five guys every year that are new.

'Then he has trouble saying no, that's what the problem is. He is not very good at saying no at all. As tough as he can be, he is a sweetheart of a guy. When someone beats him out of money he doesn't send the Thais to shoot them or break their knees, and he talks like "gosh, darn it". You know, that type of thing. But you can't do that. He has a list a mile long of people that owe him millions and millions.'

Less than a month after Brian Daniels had walked into the Superstar and met Robert Colflesh for the first time, he sat down with both Colflesh brothers and Michael Forwell to discuss a joint importation.

The negotiations moved quickly and easily, led by Forwell and Bob Colflesh. Not only would Forwell's people not have to put up any cash to set up the deal or cover the cost of the marijuana but they would receive 20 per cent of the proceeds of the sale in return for providing the transportation.

The majority of the work would be done by Daniels. He would arrange to purchase the marijuana from the growers in Laos (much of the area's production had shifted across the border to Laos following a crackdown on marijuana cultivation by Thai authorities). He would then arrange for the drugs to be processed and packed, packaged and stored and then transported from Laos across Vietnam to a loading point in the South China Sea near Da Nang, Vietnam.

Daniels would even arrange for smaller ships to come out and take the marijuana out to sea to be loaded on to the *Encounter Bay*.

It was a dream of a deal and Forwell could immediately see that, in the very worst case scenario, his organisation stood to make at least $25 million.

He smiled and reached out his hand. The single biggest importation of Thai marijuana into the United States was about to get underway.

21
MADE MEN

Brian Daniels began the New Year with a resolution so life-changing that he immediately wished he'd made it years earlier: no more Mr Nice Guy.

'The way I see it,' he told Phil Christensen, as the two of them sat down to late morning coffee in a small café bar on the outskirts of Bangkok, 'is that everyone sees me as a soft touch, the guy they can fuck in the ass again and again and never hear a single complaint. That's gonna change. That's ancient history. I'm through with that shit.'

Christensen drained the last of his coffee and leaned back in his chair. 'So what are you going to do?'

'Isn't it obvious,' Daniels replied curtly. 'I'm gonna get my fucking money.'

Daniels had heard of two money collectors, linked to the American Mafia, who had made an appearance in the Bangkok area working for some of the other smugglers. They came highly recommended and were just what he needed: ruthless types who never took no for an answer and pursued their quarry with all the determination of a pit bull terrier. They were the kind of men that wouldn't be intimated by the likes of Sherrett and his cronies. 'These guys are the real thing,' he told Christensen. 'If there's money out there, they will track it down and they won't come back without it.'

A few weeks later on 15 February 1988, Daniels was introduced to Bill Bartelucci and Jim Robinson and was instantly impressed by them. Having worked as money collectors for mafia gangs in New York, they looked as tough and as uncompromising as their reputations suggested they were. They were just the kind of people he needed to have on his side.

During the meeting Daniels gave the pair a copy of the Reno criminal indictment issued after the seizure of the $7 million in the fake casino sting. It named Robert Kimball, Daniels himself and all of those who had been involved in counting the cash. Daniels told them that although $3 million of the money that had been seized by the FBI belonged to him, up to $19 million more was still out there somewhere. It hadn't been seized so Kimball, even though he was now in prison, should know how to get his hands on it.

In order to get hold of Kimball, Daniels suggested the two men make the approach via his attorney, Jack Hill, or through Hill's investigator, none other than Jack Palladino. By speaking to them, they would be able to arrange to visit Kimball in jail and track down the cash.

On 20 February Robert Kimball, incarcerated at the Nevada State Prison, was told he had visitors waiting for him. He was not expecting anyone and when he made his way to the visiting room he found himself sitting opposite two men he had never seen before.

'Who the hell are you?' asked Kimball.

'I'm Bill and this is Jim,' said one of the men. 'Brian Daniels sent us. He's after his money. We're here to collect.'

'How the hell did you get in here?'

Bartelucci snorted with laughter. 'We told them we were your cousins. We arranged it all through Jack Hill, it's all legit.'

'Well he never told me about it.'

'Really? Must have slipped his mind or something,' said Robinson. 'He assured us he was going to mention it to you. I mean, we wanted you to be ready for us, not just turn up out of the blue.'

Kimball relaxed a little more when the pair showed him a card from Daniels that contained some of the words from the secret code Daniels had devised for members of The Ring. Now Kimball knew the men were genuine.

Kimball admitted owing the money and said, despite his own predicament, he took the debt seriously and would make the payment. He would have to make a few calls and asked the two men to leave a telephone number so he could contact them in a few days' time.

But Kimball never called them.

Instead, Daniels got a call from Jack Hill who then flew to Bangkok to visit him. Hill was furious that the two men had contacted Kimball and the story of how they had got into the jail had made no sense. As far as Hill was concerned, the men were almost certainly undercover federal agents and Daniels should have nothing more to do with them.

It was this comment that made Daniels and his two Mafia men laugh out loud when he saw them next. It was just the kind of reaction that he had hoped to provoke; in fact, it had worked out even better than expected. Kimball was angry but now he knew that Daniels was determined to get his hands on his money and would stop at nothing. As for Hill suggesting that the men were agents, that was a last-ditch desperate attempt to allow Kimball to get out of paying the money that he owed.

Daniels told the men: 'The only reason he [Jack Hill] came to see me at all was because you guys saw Kimball. If you hadn't gone to see Kimball, they would have sat back on their ass for another six months.'

Undaunted, the two Mafia men started pursuing friends and family members of Kimball, and others connected to the cash, to see if they could track it down.

But Daniels also had another job he wanted the men to do – to collect money from Thomas Sherrett over in Portland, Oregon.

Sherrett lived in a relatively modest house and worked in a local refugee centre where he was regarded as an excellent employee. Yet when the Mafia men came he had no trouble locating the millions of dollars he had made from his last smuggling venture to hand over.

As Sherrett relaxed, he began to talk openly of his feelings about the way Daniels was running his operation and questioned the suppliers' loyalty to Robert Kimball.

'Brian doesn't think things through,' said Sherrett. 'I told him, I said don't be so goddamn enthusiastic to work with this guy. In the long run it will result in his demise unless he takes some steps. But I know he feels like he is going to lose face with the Thais.'

When the Mafia men told him they were also pursuing Kimball for some of the money that Daniels was owed from the 42-ton load brought in by the Shaffer brothers, he was highly sceptical about how much success they were likely to have.

'They don't want to give it up. They have no intention of giving it up. What he has told people is: "Doesn't the son of a bitch [Daniels] understand he isn't going to get paid, period." They don't have to pay him. These people are looking at it like they have no relationship with him. They never met him, why should they pay him? Why would anybody pay him?

'The trouble with Brian, he obviously has a fascination with working with a lot of people. But it has become awkward on this end. He's removed himself so far from this end that he doesn't remember what it's like to have to get out and market things.'

As the conversation began to run dry, Sherrett helped to carry ten cardboard boxes stuffed with $20 bills to Bartelucci's car. Each box contained $600,000 in $10 and $20 bills that he and his girlfriend had counted and double-checked by hand, even passing each note under a black light to ensure none of them were counterfeit.

'When you guys see Daniels, you tell him to be careful. There's a lot of heat on him right now,' Sherrett told the Mafia men. 'I've given him a false British passport and I wish he'd use it. I don't want to see him get pinched. I've got one myself, under the name Sullivan. If you guys need someone, I can get them to you, two grand apiece.'

*   *   *

With the money from Sherrett collected, Bartelucci and Robinson redoubled their efforts to extract cash from Robert Kimball.

They returned to see Daniels in Bangkok and brought with them the first $1 million of Sherrett's money that they had managed to launder. Daniels told them that in their absence, he had received a letter from Kimball which he had destroyed after reading.

The letter said that despite his arrest the money was still around, but that Kimball was very wary of discussing the situation with any new people. He was convinced that several undercover agents were working throughout Bangkok and that the private investigator Jack Palladino was planning to carry out an investigation.

Palladino took a dramatic approach. He flew into Bangkok and started hanging out in the Superstar and a few other bars known to attract drug dealers. Eager to make himself as visible as possible, he handed out flyers blatantly stating that he was seeking information about government informants working with marijuana smugglers.

A firm believer in fair play, Palladino was convinced that some of those involved in the marijuana trade were working both sides of the street, informing on competitors and dealing dope while government agents looked the other way. 'I wanted everybody to come out of the woodwork,' he says. 'I wanted to make a lot of noise.'

He made so much noise in Bangkok that he soon attracted the attention of Bartellucci and Robinson who were desperate to talk to him in order to see if he could help track down the money that Kimball owed Daniels. The men eventually got through but Palladino refused to talk to them: 'I can't help you. I think you guys should go out and look for other things to do,' he told them.

Soon afterwards Palladino delivered his report to Daniels, Sherrett and other members of The Ring. It listed the names of seven men who he believed to be acting as informants. One was a good friend of Thomas Sherrett, another was someone Daniels had confided in many times, the third was a local journalist.

The revelations were startling, but not altogether unexpected. Some of those named had long been suspected of collaborating with the authorities and had been pushed to the outside of The Ring some months earlier.

With the names in circulation, Daniels attempted to limit information about his forthcoming importations in an effort to shield the remaining divisions of The Ring from harm.

Soon after the list of alleged informants was passed out, Bartelucci and Robinson headed back to Reno in a further effort to get Kimball to agree to meet with them. After weeks of encouragement Daniels had finally written a letter to Kimball in prison and faxed it over to his Mafia men.

It urged Kimball to trust the pair and hand over the money that he owed, adding that he should not follow the advice of his lawyers. 'Don't listen to all their shit,' wrote Daniels. 'All lawyers are jerks.'

Daniels faxed the letter to the Mafia men and they immediately sent it to Kimball in prison along with a note for him to call them. Again, Kimball ignored the request.

But the move did provoke one response. Once again Jack Hill arranged to meet with Daniels and told him that Kimball had been very upset to receive the letter and had no intention of dealing with the Mafia men as he simply did not trust them.

Daniels was now between a rock and a hard place. He was in no position to cut Bartelucci and Robinson out of the Kimball payment. The Mafia men had managed to collect more than $6 million from Tom Sherrett and although they had filtered some of it back to him, they were still holding on to most of it. They would be taking a percentage of the total amount as their fee but they were also expecting a percentage of whatever they collected from Kimball. If Daniels switched and started using someone else, he might piss them off so much that they would not give him any more of the Sherrett money.

The solution that finally came to him was simple and, he

hoped, would be acceptable to all. He would get a message through to Kimball that he should arrange to get the remaining money put in a storage locker and then pass the key on to Daniels. That way, the Mafia men would still be involved in the actual collection and transportation of the money to Thailand and therefore entitled to their cut, but Kimball would not have to deal with them directly. It would be a win-win situation all round and, as far as he was concerned, that was as much as he could hope for.

He sent off the message and sat back to await the arrival of the key.

22
OVER THE WALL

Too many things were happening at once, all of them bad.

In March came the news that Gurujot Singh Khalsa – the senior member of the cult-like Sikh yoga organisation 3HO and someone who had invested heavily in some of Daniels early shipments – had been arrested.

This was a huge concern. Khalsa had been negotiating to buy a new load of marijuana all through 1987. He had spent several days in Bangkok and Daniels had sent his representatives out to New Mexico, where Khalsa's team was based, to conduct further talks. If Khalsa talked he would not only be able to give the authorities a blow by blow account of everything Daniels had been involved in for the past few years but he would also be able to expose other parts of The Ring.

As if that wasn't bad enough. To begin with, Dennis Ingham, the leader of another division of The Ring and the man with whom Daniels had been planning a major importation in early spring 1988, had been arrested. Ingham had been a fugitive from justice since skipping bail two years earlier but had been tracked down by Federal Marshals and locked up.

Normally the loss of a single individual would not be a complete disaster but in the case of Dennis Ingham it was just that. His capture made all those who were planning to invest in the deal extremely nervous. They believed that, without Ingham's experience on the ground to co-ordinate the smuggling activities, there was little chance the venture would be a success, especially at a time when informants and undercover agents seemed to be everywhere.

Daniels, who was supplying the marijuana, desperately needed the smuggle to go ahead but as the days went by so the level of doubt in the investors' minds only increased. The gang tried to put someone else forward to co-ordinate the smuggling but the investors made it clear that if they could not work with Ingham, they would not work with the gang at all.

Daniels also had other reasons to be worried. Dennis Ingham wasn't directly involved in the *Encounter Bay* shipment but he certainly knew about it. Although he was considered wholly trustworthy, the longer he stayed behind bars the greater the chance that some snippet of information might somehow slip out. For the first time, Daniels began to have serious doubts about whether his biggest ever importation was really such a good idea after all.

The remaining members of Ingham's group were also in a crisis. They had already invested hundreds of thousands of dollars of their own money in the shipment and none of them were willing to simply write this off.

There was only one thing for it: they were going to have to bust Dennis Ingham out of jail.

Ingham could not have got himself incarcerated at a better prison if he had tried his best.

Although by no means easy, Terminal Island had a reputation as a prison that, with a little ingenuity, it would be possible to escape from. During the early eighties between twenty-five and thirty inmates had escaped each year until armed guards were posted, 50-foot guard towers erected and other security measures added.

But even these had failed to make the prison escape-proof. Just a month or so before Ingham had been taken there two inmates were caught while trying to sneak out inside a stack of wooden pallets. A couple of weeks later two more did get out, climbing up a fence and jumping into a lake which borders one side of the prison. One was caught soon after, the other was found half a mile away, cowering in the cold while nursing a broken ankle suffered in the jump.

Another inmate had made it all the way to the gate wearing a wig, moustache, civilian clothes, and posing as a lawyer. He was stopped by a guard who recognised him as a convicted drug trafficker awaiting sentencing.

Every since Johnny Cash played at Folsom Prison, every up- and-coming band has known that a prison gig is a sure fire way to garner street credibility. For the most part such gigs pay a pittance or often nothing at all but the opportunity for publicity is worth far more than money.

So when a small rock and roll band from San Francisco received a phone call out of the blue asking if they would like to play a show at the Terminal Island Federal Correction Centre for $1,000, they jumped at the chance.

The only problem was that the band did not have enough equipment for a gig of that size and asked what arrangements the prison was making for them. 'Don't worry about that,' the caller explained. 'All the equipment you need will be provided. It's all part of a new public service initiative to keep the prisoners entertained.'

With no need to hire a PA or other equipment, it almost seemed too good to be true. They were about to play their biggest ever gig and have their biggest ever pay day all rolled into one.

The band assumed the call had come direct from the prison and thought little more of it. In fact the call had come from a member of the Dennis Ingham organisation. His next call was to the prison itself.

'Hi, I represent a great up-and-coming rock band and the guys would love to play a gig at the prison as a way of upping their credibility and spreading a little word of mouth. Now you and I both know how good these kind of shows are for morale. And not only will the band play for free but they will also provide all their own equipment . . .'

Dozens of bands had performed at Terminal Island over the preceding years for similar reasons and the jail, eager for anything that would help to entertain the inmates, eagerly agreed.

On the day of the show, soon after the band arrived, a truck carrying all their equipment arrived at the gate. A team of roadies put out mike stands, effects boards, amplifiers and a set of giant concert speakers, each one more than six feet high with a sound cone the size of a small car.

The speakers had been custom built a few days earlier at a cost of $10,000. Each of the four speakers was capable of delivering and ear-splitting 5,000 watts of high fidelity sound.

The concert was a huge success, a mix of well-known covers to warm things up and then a few foot-stomping original tunes. A good time was had by all.

The band packed up their instruments and left, followed closely by the roadies and all their equipment. It wasn't until the 4 p.m. head count, two hours after the concert had finished, that the prison authorities realised that Dennis Ingham and two other inmates had vanished.

'We don't know exactly how they got out. We're checking all possibilities. We're mystified; it's one for the books,' said Sam Cicchino, a US Marshal.

'We've done a thorough search of the institute and the surrounding grounds and we can't find them,' Jim Zangs, assistant to the warden, added.

Two of the three had been in custody awaiting federal trials on narcotics cases, Zangs said. The third man had served four years of a fifteen-year prison sentence for importing heroin.

'We really don't know how they got together,' Zangs said, adding that the three men lived in different housing units within the 1,200-inmate facility, which is surrounded by two fences. As of Thursday afternoon, prison officials had not come up with any evidence to show how the men escaped, Zangs said. 'There is all kinds of truck traffic coming in and out of here. They may have gotten out that way,' he speculated.

Over the hours that followed the story was slowly pieced together. After the concert Ingham and two other men had sneaked back into the auditorium and hidden inside the giant, specially-made speakers.

Incredibly, the two men who said they were roadies with the band had been allowed to enter the prison, pick up the equipment and leave without anyone keeping a record of their names or taking down the licence plate of the truck they were driving.

The band, who had been promised $1,000 for their performance, never received any money despite being told the cheque was in the post. Instead they found themselves being questioned by federal law enforcement officials for potentially aiding and abetting the escape of a group of prisoners.

The next few hours were tense. It was the third escape from the prison that year and in both the other cases, the fugitives had been captured almost immediately. In any fugitive situation the first few hours are key because that is when the trail will be clearest and any scent will be strongest.

By the second day the hunt was no less intense but the enthusiasm had begun to die down. By the third day the Marshals were all too well aware that, though their track record for catching those on the run was good, Dennis Ingham seemed to have evaded their dragnet.

Back in Bangkok the news that Ingham had survived the first few crucial hours of the manhunt and was back at work with the rest of his gang was greeted with elation by Daniels and other members of The Ring.

Not only was Ingham's importation back on but, more importantly, Daniels, along with Michael Forwell and the Colflesh brothers, could now press ahead with their plans for the *Encounter Bay*.

23
THE MOTHER LOAD

Like the Shaffer brothers before them, Forwell's team had earmarked the north-west coast as the best location for the *Encounter Bay* offload. And like the Shaffer brothers, and somewhat in awe of their success in bringing in a load under the noses of the DEA, Forwell's team decided to employ the talents of members of the local fishing fleet.

Just like Tony Franulovich the man they chose to head up the offload, Larry Brant, had seawater in his blood.

As a boy he had sailed with his father and then worked as crew on his uncle's salmon trawler in order to earn enough cash to see him through college. After graduation he had returned to the sea and, after a few lucky seasons, had built up his business to the point that he now owned a fleet of six boats, all based in Blaine Harbor, just a stone's throw from the border with Canada.

But his initial success at sea had soon deserted him. The six ships in his fleet cost a fortune to crew and maintain and with quotas being reduced every years, his business was only barely able to break even. Like dozens of other fishermen in the area, the lure of easy money from the drug business was simply impossible to resist.

After an initial approach was made in Washington and Brant expressed interest, he and his crew chief, Helmut Witt, were asked to fly out to Hong Kong to meet the rest of the team.

The Colflesh brothers and Forwell needed to know they could trust Brant to perform under pressure. His was perhaps the most key role of all. Getting the drugs all the way across the Pacific was one thing but it would all be for nothing if they could not get them inside the US itself. The entire multi-million-dollar operation was going to rest on Brant's personal ability to evade the coastguard and customs services.

The meeting took place on a 50-foot yacht that met the men at the harbour before taking them out to sea. Inside the main cabin, sitting casually on the comfortable sofas with long drinks in their hands, were Michael Forwell and the Colflesh brothers.

With no chance of their conversation being overheard, everyone felt free to talk openly.

Robert Colflesh began talking to Witt about the use of encrypted codes and communications at sea – something all of the boats in Brant's fleet would have to master if the operation was to be a success.

Brant had brought along pictures of his fleet and Colflesh studied them carefully, trying to calculate exactly how much marijuana they would be able to hold.

'So you'll do the offload?'

'Sure,' said Brant.

Michael Forwell had said little during the meeting. If anything he had seemed a little bored by the proceedings. It was his money at stake, but Sam Colflesh had taken control of all the organisational aspects of the operation and there had been little for him to do. Whether or not to hire Brant to do the offload was his decision. But Forwell did have one question.

'On your previous jobs, have you ever been intercepted by the coastguard?'

'Never.'

'What about Canadian customs?'

'No. We have our own private dock. It's never been a problem.'

Colflesh was looking at the pictures once more. The largest of Brant's fleet was a mere 58 feet. The *Encounter Bay* was 187 feet and weighed a massive 800 tonnes. Most of the time, offloading involved the two boats tying up together side by side while nets and cranes were used to swing the marijuana from one boat to another. But the *Encounter Bay* was so large there was a real danger that, if the seas got rough, some of the smaller boats could be crushed.

No sooner had he pondered the question than Colfesh had the answer. 'We'll tether you off the back on a line. My crew will load the product on to rafts and swing them alongside you. If we do that, it will slow us down a little, but we should still be able to get the offload done in two days.'

Brant knew the gang were planning a big load but up until that point he had no idea exactly how large it was going to be. His eyes widened. Two days! The load must be huge. 'How much dope are we talking about?' he asked.

Colflesh didn't even blink. 'Somewhere between forty and sixty tons. Maybe more.'

Brant wanted to know something about the people he was working with. With that amount of dope around, he was taking a risk and wanted to make sure their expertise was at least equal to his own.

Samuel Colflesh explained that he had been in the marijuana smuggling business for fifteen years, had made a trip once per year and had never been caught. He said the largest marijuana load he had ever shipped was 10 to 20 tons.

Colflesh then went on to describe his vessel to the agents: a large twin-engine ship, with a range of 30,000 miles, equipped with satellite equipment – known as SATCOM – that could be used to deliver messages. He also said he could provide hand-held VHF radios set to specific frequencies not normally used for communications.

Sam said it would take twenty-one days to cross the Pacific Ocean to the agreed offloading site. The cargo would be transferred under cover of night. Brant assured the group that he knew of no coastguard patrols in the area.

By the end of the meeting both sides were satisfied. Colflesh knew that Brant was the kind of man who loved the fishing life but hated the financial uncertainty of his work. Brant knew he was dealing with a highly professional team who would stop at nothing to make sure the drugs got through.

Michael and the others stayed in the cabin when the ship got back to the dock at the end of the meeting. 'We're too well known around here,' said Forwell. 'We'd rather not be seen.'

The five met again the following day and Colflesh told Brant he would provide him with a complete communications package that he would need for the operation. This would detail all the code words, radio frequencies and so on that would be used by the mother ship as it approached the rendezvous point.

They also agreed that Brant would meet with either Forwell or another member of the gang in Seattle or San Francisco to pick up the specialist radio equipment that would be needed to contact the mother ship.

So that Brant could get a better idea of the size of the *Encounter Bay*, they made their way to the harbour, where Colflesh pointed out a 150ft oil service vessel anchored up that he said was a pretty good match for their mother ship.

The next meeting took place on 5 May 1988 in room 34 of the Peninsula Hotel in Kowloon, Hong Kong. This time Brian Daniels was there too, and informed the small gathering that the drugs were already on there way down from the Golden Triangle, travelling in Vietnamese army trucks, and would soon be in Da Nang ready for loading.

The final plans were being drawn up. At the Kowloon meeting Daniels used a calculator to determine that the fishing vessels could carry about 67 tons of marijuana from the mother ship to shore.

Colflesh gave everyone codenames – part of his scheme for confusing anyone listening in on the radio. 'From now on you will be known as Gedo, I am Haig, Michael is The Fox.'

Brant had one final question. 'How will I know that the ship is on its way?'

'I'll send you a fax,' replied Colflesh. 'Do you have a machine?'

'I've got a private fax machine in my office at the dock. No one else has access to it. If you send the message there, I'll get it right away and we can head out.'

It took four days to prepare the *Encounter Bay* for her latest and greatest journey across the Pacific. Of those days, some seventeen hours had been spent purely loading the marijuana.

There were 8,250 bales in all, each wrapped in blue waterproof bags, which were heat-sealed and secured with metal grommets. Each bag carried a stamp of a blue eagle over a line of red type which read: 'PASSED INSPECTION'.

Inside each bag there was a layer of polythene covered with tape to ensure there were not leaks. Underneath was a cardboard box containing eight one-kilo packs of prime-grade Thai grass, vacuum packaged using the special machines that Daniels had imported from Switzerland.

With its well-drilled crew looking smart in their military-style uniforms, Sam Colflesh waved goodbye to the coast of Thailand and powered up the boat on a heading of due west.

The journey was uneventful and on 22 June 1988, with the *Encounter Bay* some 800 miles from the US coast, Colflesh contacted his brother by satellite telephone to tell him to proceed to the next stage of the operation, and then sent off a fax to the number Larry Brant had given him.

Brant had heard nothing for almost two months and was beginning to wonder if the smugglers had found another group of offloaders to work with. Every day he checked his fax machine and every day he came away disappointed. When the fax finally arrived, he could barely contain his excitement.

Across the world, the dozens of people connected to the *Encounter Bay* shipment were eagerly awaiting news of her arrival.

All the bases had been covered; every element of the trip, the offload and the distribution had been worked out in advance right down to the smallest detail. Every possible precaution had been taken and a dozen contingency plans were in place. The buyers were waiting and the gang knew the drugs on the boat would be converted to hard cash within hours of arriving on dry land. Rich as they all were, they were soon set to become considerably richer. All they had to do was sit back and wait.

24
CHECK MATE

Not everything that Larry Brant had told Michael Forwell and the Colflesh brothers had been a lie.

He had indeed sailed with his father as a boy and worked as a hired hand on his uncle's salmon trawler to put himself through college. Truth be told, he had omitted just one small detail: at college he had studied police science and criminology and then gone on to become an agent of the Drug Enforcement Administration.

The fax number he had given them was connected to a machine located on the second floor of the agency's Seattle office.

Brant specialised in undercover, sea-borne smuggling operations, often working more than one investigation at the same time. A month or two before his first trip to Hong Kong to meet the Colflesh brothers, Brant had sailed a freighter, supposedly loaded to the gunwales with Thai sticks, to Vancouver Island. When the offloaders came out to collect their drugs, they were immediately arrested.

This time Brant himself had been cast in the role of offloader, but instead of going out to meet the *Encounter Bay*, he would be sending the coastguard. But first he had to find out exactly where the offload was going to take place.

The message on the fax machine was from Haig saying that The Fox was on his way and would meet him at the Red Lion Hotel close to Sea-Tac Airport within a couple of hours. Brant jumped into his car and raced down the freeway. He didn't want to blow the deal by being late.

After the initial meeting in Hong Kong Brant had scanned intelligence reports for clues to the men's identity and finally got lucky when he dug up a 1986 report from Canadian Customs, who had questioned Samuel Colflesh and another man after the pair had delivered the *Encounter Bay* to Vancouver for a refit. With no evidence of any wrongdoing, the pair had been allowed to go on their way, but not before their photographs were taken and their passport details noted.

At last Brant had a full name: Michael Cleave Forwell. From there he soon learned that Forwell had been rumoured to be a big marijuana mover for many years but had never been caught. The meeting at the Red Lion was therefore crucial. Up until then, there was insufficient evidence to tie Forwell to the venture. He could easily claim to have been nothing more than an innocent bystander and a half-decent defence lawyer would get any charges thrown out in a heartbeat.

But when Brant arrived at the Red Lion, it was not Forwell but Robert Colflesh who greeted him. Brant had to fight to hide his disappointment as Colflesh handed over a VHF radio and a fifteen-page operation manual containing maps, radio codes and navigational information.

Colflesh explained that, on the day of the offload, the *Encounter Bay* would be at one of six potential meeting points, each around 600 miles due west of the Seattle coast. 'When the ship gets to within 100 miles of one of the points, they will radio with the exact offload point,' he explained.

As Brant returned to the office he felt nothing but relief. Although he was no closer to Forwell, he at last knew that the drugs were on their way and that he would soon be told exactly where the ship was going to be.

The following morning Brant gave a briefing to officers from the Thirteenth District Pacific North-West Region Coastguard, warning it would be best to send 'the biggest boat they had' to carry out the intercept.

It was wise advice. The *Encounter Bay* was big and heavy. Once Colflesh saw that it was the coastguard rather than a fleet of fishing boats coming to greet him, he might try to run but he might just as well attempt to ram whoever was chasing him.

With its reinforced ice-breaker hull, the *Encounter Bay* was more than capable of causing serious damage to a much larger vessel, even a heavily armoured coastguard cutter.

The *Encounter Bay* was less than twelve hours from the rendezvous point when Samuel Colflesh heard a high-pitched whining noise from the sky above. He looked up and saw a large white plane with four large black propellers spinning in front of its wing-mounted engines. A bright orange stripe was painted slanting forward at the front part of the fuselage. There was no mistaking what he was looking at: a Hercules C130 long-range surveillance aircraft.

For a short time there was hope that the plane might be on routine patrol, or that it might be targeting some other vessel, but as soon as it turned and began to circle the *Encounter Bay*, Colflesh knew he was in big trouble. He had been heading for the Strait of Juan de Fuca, which separates British Columbia and the north-eastern corner of the state of Washington, but no longer. From the bridge he called for full power from the engine room, flipped around so he was heading back east and pulled back on the twin throttles, sending the boat surging forward through the waves.

Half an hour later he spotted a vast ship appear on the horizon. This was the *Boutwell*, a 3,250-tonne coastguard cutter, one of twelve used to patrol the ocean between Alaska and Central America. At 378 feet she was almost twice the size of the *Encounter Bay*. She was also heavily armed with two .50 calibre laser-guided machine guns plus a 76 mm cannon and was capable of 27 knots – compared to the *Encounter Bay*'s 16. There would be no escape.

Within an hour, the *Boutwell* was looming large, less than 1,000 yards from her target. Her captain, Cecil Allison, picked up the radio and called for the *Encounter Bay* to stop. There was no reply.

Allowing for the possibility that her radio was not working,

Allison tried to make contact using flags, lights and bull horns, as well as firing blank charges through the ship's guns, all to no avail.

Video footage shot from the deck of the *Boutwell* shows the *Encounter Bay* heaving up and down, white and grey foam crashing over her bow as, in her desperation to get away, she travels at speeds far too high for such choppy seas.

Twenty minutes later Allison grabbed the radio again. He informed the *Encounter Bay* that he would be firing a series of warning shots across her bow and urged her to stop immediately. Again there was no reply.

Within minutes, a series of sharp cracks could be heard on the video and a line of neat water-spouts appeared in the path of the *Encounter Bay* as the bullets hit the water.

Two further volleys failed to illicit a response so Captain Allison issued a warning that he would disable the boat by firing into its engine, and warned any personnel in that part of the vessel to get out immediately. At last, Sam Colflesh answered the radio call.

'We are a Panamanian vessel in international waters,' he said, his voice clearly cracking under the strain. 'You have no authority.' The *Encounter Bay* was not flying a flag but the word 'Panama' could just be read in partially obscured letters across the back of the ship. A check of the records confirmed that the boat's owner was listed as Countess Shipping Corporation of Panama.

Captain Allison now found himself caught between a rock and a hard place. Maritime law states that to board a ship in international waters, permission must be received from the government whose flag the ship is flying. Each vessel essentially represents the sovereign territory of whichever nation's flag it flies under. For the coastguard or anybody else to board a vessel without obtaining permission from the relevant country would be little short of an act of war. Any evidence gathered during such an operation would not be admissible in court.

Under normal circumstances, it is a relatively simple matter for the captain of the coastguard cutter to obtain permission.

Across the world various legal and political systems are in place to allow such permission to be obtained in a matter of minutes. But at the time that *Encounter Bay* was being chased across the Pacific, circumstances were anything but normal.

Five months earlier the head of Panama's secret police, General Manuel Noriega, had been indicted in Florida on charges of drug trafficking and money laundering. When President Eric Delvalle attempted to fire Noriega as a result, the general and former CIA operative forced the National Assembly to replace Delvalle instead, and appointed himself the country's ruler.

At the end of the bloodless coup Delvalle was placed under house arrest, but fled into hiding soon afterwards. He was attempting to establish a government in exile – one which America had chosen to recognise over that of Noriega's regime – but at that precise moment no one knew exactly where he was.

But there was no time to waste. Moments earlier the crew of the *Boutwell* had seen a puff of white smoke come out of *Encounter Bay*'s exhaust stack. 'It wasn't from the engine; it was too dark for that,' Allison said later. 'We realised they were burning all the records and paperwork. We had to move fast.'

Exactly what happened next has never been fully established. One version of events, which many of those involved in the investigation insist is true, has half a dozen secret service agents bursting through the door of a Panamanian restaurant in Washington DC and ushering the bemused owner out of the door with the words: 'Your presence is urgently required at the White House.'

Within half an hour the man had been sworn in as acting president of Panama and, seconds after that, he carried out his first official duty – signing the order to allow the *Boutwell* to fire on the *Encounter Bay*. Another version of the story has a deal being struck with Noriega himself. In any event, at 4.35 p.m., the *Boutwell* received a teletype message announcing that permission had been granted to fire at the ship itself.

In the meantime, the bridge of the *Encounter Bay* had been a flurry of activity as Colflesh, as well as controlling the ship at full speed, had been frantically trying to make contact with Michael Forwell via satellite phone, finally tracking him down to his home in Singapore.

'The coastguard are on to us, they're right on top of us,' he told him. 'I need permission to abort.'

'Abort? Are you crazy? I can't authorise that.'

'Then get hold of someone who can,' demanded Colflesh. 'We don't have a choice.'

'Look, just calm down Sam. I'm sure it's not that bad.'

'Not that bad? They're shooting at us. They're shooting the life out of us.'

'Don't be silly, they wouldn't do that.'

Colflesh yanked back the side window of the bridge and thrust the receiver outside, just in time to catch the sound of a volley of shots hitting the side of the boat.

Colflesh pulled the phone back in. 'Now do you believe me Michael?' But The Fox had already hung up and started planning his escape.

Seconds later, the video operator on the *Boutwell* zoomed in to capture the sight and sounds of more than fifty armour-piercing rounds smashing through the side of the boat, then pulled back to show the *Encounter Bay* moving slower and slower until it finally grinds to a halt.

The bullets had bounced around the inside, slicing through cables and cracking hydraulic pipes, causing them to leak. Colflesh pushed forward on the throttle but it was no good, he could hear the ship's engines dying and they would soon stop turning altogether. There was not even enough power to try to turn around and ram the *Boutwell*, for all the good it would have done them. He had no choice but to surrender. To risk another volley would be to risk the whole ship going down, something that had happened a number of times in the past but something the coastguard were keen to play down.

In those few moments of silence, Colflesh saw all his hopes and dreams flash before his eyes: the millions of dollars he had hoped to earn for the trip, the life of luxury he was planning to lead, the sense of pride and accomplishment that comes from completing a complex task to the best of your ability. It had all fallen apart in the worst possible way.

Back on the *Boutwell*, the video technician caught the moment that Samuel Colflesh's weary voice came over the radio for the last time. 'We acknowledge your contact with our vessel,' he said. 'We're going to go down and have a look at the damage and we will come back to you shortly to make arrangements for you to board.'

The most audacious and ambitious smuggling attempt The Ring had ever made was over. And now the days of The Ring itself were numbered.

PART FOUR

25
WITHOUT A PADDLE

Zurich, Switzerland, July 1988

'We got a problem, we got a big fucking problem.'

A frantic Robert Colflesh was on the phone to Brian Daniels telling him about the capture of the *Encounter Bay* just minutes before the first coastguard officers boarded the vessel.

'Sam said they were firing at the ship, they had told them to get out of the engine room because they were going to shoot,' Robert continued. 'He said they were right on top of them. That was the last I heard. I think we're fucked, totally fucked.'

As Robert Colflesh spoke, Brian Daniels could hear the sound of his own blood rushing in his ears and felt weak enough to pass out. Not only was it the worst possible news but, along with the severe financial difficulties he was experiencing as a result of the cash seizure in Reno, it had come at the worst possible time.

The year had started out so positively, but now it had all gone horribly wrong. The biggest and most ambitious smuggling venture that anyone in Thailand had ever put together had ended in disaster. Daniels' first collaboration with a team of operators who, in more than fifteen years of multi-ton smuggling, had never once been caught or even come close to being compromised, had somehow gone completely pear-shaped.

Daniels didn't need a calculator or even a pen and paper to work out exactly what the loss meant to him personally. The numbers flew around his head like a swarm of angry bees. He had been due to receive $1 million per ton for the marijuana. When that was added to his other expenses, Daniels was out to the tune of more than $100 million. Almost immediately his bad leg started to bother him more than it had done for many months – the stress of the situation was really starting to get to him.

Daniels needed information and needed it fast, but the fifteen-hour time difference between Bangkok and Seattle, along with the fact that the *Encounter Bay* was still hundreds of miles off the US coastline, meant it was virtually impossible to find out much about what had really happened.

Michael Forwell was not answering any of his phones and the Hong Kong office of the front company that had been used to purchase and maintain the *Encounter Bay* had been cleared out almost as soon as Forwell had received his phone call from Samuel Colflesh. There was absolutely nothing Brian Daniels could do apart from sit back and wait.

Constantly playing on his mind was the arrest of Gurujot Singh Khalsa back in March of that same year. Everything had gone quiet since then and none of his contacts knew if Khalsa had struck some kind of deal with the US Attorney or was agreeing to cooperate with the authorities and help them to target Daniels.

Since that first deal brokered by Phil Christensen, Daniels had been personally involved in negotiations with Khalsa over several other loads of marijuana, though William LaMorte, the other partner from his first big adventure, had moved out of the business. In theory neither Khalsa nor LaMorte knew any of the specifics about the *Encounter Bay* shipment but with so many people involved in the deal, there was no way to guarantee that some information had not leaked out.

There was no concern that the crew of the *Encounter Bay* might give him up. Samuel Colflesh had already been taken care of. Weeks earlier Michael Forwell had set aside $50,000 for each senior member of the crew as a fund to pay their legal fees in the event of an arrest. The majority of the rest of the crew were from Indonesia, spoke little English and knew nothing about those behind the smuggling venture.

Likewise there was no concern about the fact that Dennis Ingham had been captured again just a few days before the drugs had been seized. He had been found hiding in a house along with the two men he had escaped from jail with. Ever since he had been busted out Daniels had been careful to avoid divulging any specific details of his mammoth operation. His arrest was clearly a coincidence, nothing more.

In the hours that followed the call from Robert Colflesh small pieces of news began to filter back, but it wasn't until the end of the following day that Brian Daniels received his first piece of solid information in the form of a faxed copy of an article from the *Seattle Times* dated 2 July 1988.

MARIJUANA SHIP SEIZED UNDER FIRE

A ship containing more than 50 tons of marijuana was seized yesterday under fire a few hundred miles off the Washington coast, according to the coastguard.

No one was injured in the seizure, although the coastguard fired into the engine-room area to stop the ship, authorities said. The street value of the marijuana, stowed in four containers, was estimated by the coastguard at $220 million.

A coastguard aircraft saw the 180-foot *Encounter Bay*, an offshore-oil-rig supply vessel, as it was heading toward the mid-Washington coast Thursday morning, said the coast-guard spokesman.

That type of ship is rare in North-west waters, so the pilot alerted the coastguard cutter *Boutwell* to investigate. As the *Boutwell* closed within 500 yards of the *Encounter Bay*, the coastguard requested permission to board, but the ship operator did not respond or slow the ship.

After receiving no response following several contact attempts, the coastguard asked the US State Department to obtain permission to board and enforce US law on a foreign ship.

The report offered one small comfort. Unfortunate as the seizure was, The Ring appeared to be safe, at least for the time being. The bust had been down to nothing more than dumb luck on the part of the authorities.

This notion that the seizure was the result of nothing more than a chance discovery seemed to be confirmed a few days later when the *Boutwell*, with the *Encounter Bay* in tow, finally arrived at the Pier 36 headquarters of the coastguard in Seattle's port to the cheers of banner-waving relatives of the crew and others who crowded the dock. Eager to make the most of their time in the spotlight, Captain Cecil Allison's shipmates had attached a makeshift flag to their prize, which showed a marijuana leaf with a diagonal red line through it.

At a dockside news conference soon after landing, Captain Allison was asked about the circumstances leading up to the record-breaking bust. 'Did you have any intelligence information about this ship?'

'No,' Allison responded.

'None at all?' the reporter asked again.

'No,' Allison said.

The comments calmed Daniels and the other members of The Ring. Tom Sherrett, already paranoid as hell after the Reno cash seizure, believed the lucky streak he had been enjoying until that point in time seemed set to continue. He once again thanked the stars that his personal dislike of Sam and Robert Colflesh had led to him turning down Daniels's offer to buy into the *Encounter Bay* load.

Just to be on the safe side, Daniels contacted his latest mole – an official at the US Embassy in Bangkok – in an attempt to find out if there was any investigation aimed at him. A few hours later the source had come back with the good news: there were no telephone intercepts in place or on order for any of Daniels' phones. Furthermore, there was no current information linking his name to the seizure of the *Encounter Bay*.

It was an important revelation, not just for his personal peace of mind but also professionally. Although the marijuana contained within the *Encounter Bay* had been a huge, record-breaking shipment, it was far from the only smuggle Daniels had been working on at the time.

Soon after the *Encounter Bay* had been loaded, Daniels had begun working with another division of The Ring, using a boat called the *Lloyd B. Gore*, on a plan to bring in 20 tons of marijuana.

The team involved were new to The Ring but extremely experienced and Daniels had high hopes that, despite so many loads being seized that year, this one would make it through. Tom Sherrett felt the same way and this time around had agreed to invest in the deal. With the *Encounter Bay* gone and no sign of his missing $30 million, Daniels really needed this shipment to be a success. He personally owned 5 tons of the load and was in line to receive at least $10 million from the deal.

For the first time, Daniels demonstrated an element of caution in his dealings. With all the debate flying around Bangkok about possible informants and collaborators, Daniels made sure this new division of The Ring had been kept totally isolated from all the others. He had been especially careful not to discuss the details of the *Lloyd B. Gore* operation with anyone. It was enough to allow him to relax just a little; even if The Ring had somehow been compromised, this latest shipment should still be safe.

There was further light at the end of the tunnel too. The Mafia men had begun trickle-feeding the $7 million they had collected from Thomas Sherrett back to Daniels. It was, Daniels believed, as good as money in the bank.

Daniels may have been down but he was far from out. Once his outstanding bills had been paid, he would be in good shape and able to proceed with his plans for 1989, which would see even greater quantities of marijuana being sent to America. He eagerly told friends he planned to ship out at least 100 tons.

In the interim the priority was to get treatment for his leg. The best doctors and clinics were in Switzerland, a place where he had received treatment before. There was also a chance to kill two birds with one stone – Tom Sherrett was in Zurich and it would give Daniels a chance to pick up some of the remaining cash he was owed.

On 4 July 1988, Independence Day, Daniels bought himself a ticket to Zurich leaving Bangkok on the 7th and booked into a clinic for a week-long course of treatment for his leg. At the end of it, Daniels planned to travel to either the States or Canada in order to meet with some of those who owned him money, in a personal bid to convince them to pay up.

But later that same afternoon, just when everything seemed to be calming down, Daniels got an urgent message to call his secretary. When he got through to her she explained that she had just received a telephone call from an unknown male in the States who had warned Daniels not to speak to anyone in America, especially in the Miami area, because there was a massive leak in The Ring.

That warning followed a call a few days earlier from his former money launderer, Bruce Aitken, who said that someone in The Ring had 'rolled over' and provided the DEA with information about people that Daniels had worked with in the recent past.

Two days later, Daniels' secretary received another call, this time from a woman, who again warned Daniels to be careful because he had a leak in his organisation. When the secretary pointed out to the woman that if she wanted to be truly helpful it would be nice if she provided further details, the caller promised that she would, but only in return for a payment of $25,000.

The woman had promised to call back but he had not heard from her by the time he was due to leave for Zurich. Suspecting it might simply be some kind of scam, Daniels put the call to the back of his mind as he set off to deal with his increasingly troublesome leg.

Soon after arriving in Switzerland, it became clear that the leg was the least of his worries. With Samuel Colflesh and the remainder of the crew of the *Encounter Bay* making their first appearance in court, the story surrounding the circumstances of the seizure had changed in the most alarming way possible.

COASTGUARD OFFICER TELLS
NEW STORY OF SHIP SEIZURE

The coastguard was looking for a specific ship when it stopped and boarded a vessel that was carrying 72 tons of marijuana off the Washington coast on June 30, a coastguard officer acknowledged in federal court in Seattle today.

The information contradicted earlier coastguard descriptions of the seizure of the ship. Capt. Cecil Allison, the *Boutwell*'s commander, said last week the coastguard had no intelligence information about the *Encounter Bay*. But under questioning today by the attorney for the skipper of the *Encounter Bay*, Lt. Thomas Rogers, the *Boutwell*'s weapons officer said the coastguard knew the name of the ship it was looking for and had a general description of the vessel. 'We were on a routine patrol,' Rogers said. 'But we also had a specific target . . . We had the name and possible description.'

Daniels was back at square one. Had The Ring been penetrated or, as was the case with the *Oregon Beaver* four years earlier, had some loud-mouthed member of the crew simply been overheard bragging about the shipment in a bar? There was simply no way of knowing.

Up until that point Daniels had been planning to travel from Switzerland to the US using the false British passport provided to him by Tom Sherrett (who had conveniently left Zurich just before Daniels had arrived). Once there he planned to meet with his Mafia men and get them to assist him in collecting what he was owed. Now, with fresh uncertainty hanging over the *Encounter Bay* seizure, there was no way Daniels would risk the trip to the States. He would not even travel to Canada. Instead he called his Mafia men and told them to come to Zurich to discuss how best to proceed.

Bill Bartelucci and Jim Robinson arrived in Zurich on 19 July and Daniels was pleased to have someone with whom he could talk about his problems.

'I'll tell you what I did wrong,' he told the men. 'I used the Colflesh brothers to handle the transportation. Sherrett was right all along. They were too young and too inexperienced. Did you hear what Sam did with the crew of the *Encounter Bay*? He had them all wearing fucking uniforms! Had them doing drill and parade during the journey. It was way too military.

'All that planning, and then when it started to go wrong they didn't follow their own plan. They were too flashy and with all that electronic equipment on board, they must have been lit up like a Christmas tree.'

Daniels told the men that, contrary to the initial reports, he had now received solid information that the *Encounter Bay* had been the target of a DEA investigation and that at least three separate customs cutters had been out looking for it on the day.

'I'll tell you what guys,' Daniels groaned. 'I don't know anyone who has managed to get any dope into the country so far this year. I'm changing tactics. I'm never going to do one big load like that again. And another thing, I'm never going to use just one ship to make the whole journey. In the future I'm going to use at least two and maybe three. Switch the load a few times before you head to the rendezvous point. That way no one knows what they're supposed to be looking out for.'

His plan was to travel back to Bangkok at the end of the month and then make his way to Hong Kong to meet with one of Robert Kimball's people, to find out the reason for the delay in the delivery of the money. If the cash could only be delivered in the States, Daniels wanted it to be sent to members of his family and would then get his Mafia men to go and collect it from them.

Meanwhile, the *Lloyd B. Gore* and its 20 tons of marijuana were now on their way to the West Coast of America. One way or another, Daniels was due a big pay day in the very near future.

And then disaster struck once again.

On 20 July 1988 William LaMorte was arrested at his expensive home in Greenwich, Connecticut; the home he had moved to two years earlier after leaving eastern Long Island in a bid to put his drug dealing days behind him.

Agents seized financial records, including an IBM computer and twenty-eight disks containing detailed business information. Also seized were boat records, travel receipts, a small amount of heroin and a video cassette marked 'Southold Friends Say Farewell To The LaMortes' – a heartfelt community tribute to LaMorte and his family made by Long Island residents utterly unaware of the true nature of his business and sorry to see him leave.

To his many friends, he was a generous man whose business skills were to be admired, a man who had scored early and big as an investor and the owner of five supermarkets, including one in Cutchogue.

Always ready to help out a new friend or a good cause, he opened his house for a fund-raising party for a Suffolk County police officer from Mattituck wounded in the line of duty and included a spectacular firework display arranged by the leading company of the time.

'Maybe now things add up,' one former Long Island friend, who declined to be identified, told the local paper. 'He was always going somewhere, but he never said where. And two years ago, he just up and left suddenly. You think of drug dealers as real tough people. The astonishing part was that he was so nice, so laid back.'

A detailed, fifty-eight-page affidavit described LaMorte as both an investor in smuggling operations and a distributor, whose drug operations went back as far as 1971. In just a single operation, according to the affidavit, LaMorte's 'organisation could expect gross profits from the sale of the marijuana to be near $50 million.' Prosecutors said LaMorte was 'a major player in an international ring.'

If the arrest of LaMorte sent shockwaves throughout the marijuana underworld, the harshness of his treatment only intensified them. Arraigned in US District Court in Brooklyn, LaMorte was finally released only after agreeing to post an astonishing $20 million bail bond, secured by several of his homes and those owned by members of his immediate family. Before LaMorte left the courtroom, US Magistrate A. Simon Chrein warned him that the government would seize all the property if he fled.

For Daniels there was now no denying that he was in big trouble. In the months that had passed since the Shaffer brothers successfully landed the 42-ton load right under the noses of the DEA, it had been one disaster after another.

Kimball had been arrested, millions of dollars had been seized and virtually every shipment coming out of Thailand had been intercepted. Sam Colflesh was behind bars along with the likes Dennis Ingham, and now William LaMorte.

The net was closing in fast and Daniels wasn't the only one at risk. The Shaffer brothers were somewhere in Europe, living the good life, but for how much longer? Tom Sherrett, who still owed Daniels money, had seemingly vanished off the face of the earth, as had Michael Forwell, the main man behind the *Encounter Bay* scheme.

It took no time at all for a plan of action to form in Daniels' mind. He arranged to take a return flight to Bangkok on 25 July at 7.35 p.m. At around 10 a.m. that morning he walked into the lobby of the Hotel Edan Au Lac for one last meeting with his Mafia men before heading back.

With the arrest of William LaMorte, his world looked bleaker than ever. As he moved through the hotel his mind drifted back through the events of the past six months. What on earth was going to go wrong next?

At that moment a dozen officers from the Zurich State Police appeared around Daniels and told him he was under arrest.

Bemusement and surprise turned to shock and horror when his two Mafia men appeared in the background. Daniels wanted to usher them away – how on earth would he get his money if they got themselves arrested too? – but he need not have worried.

Jim Robinson pulled out a wallet and flipped it open. Inside was a badge and card identifying him as Special Agent James Harper of the Drug Enforcement Administration.

In that instant, Brian Daniels suddenly recalled every single thing he had ever told the two men he thought had been Mafia money collectors. He thought about the cash they had collected on his behalf, the conversations they had had with Tom Sherrett and his other contacts. He thought about the details of past, present and future shipments that he had shared with them.

Kimball, Hill and the others had been right all along but he had been too blind and too stubborn to see it. And now he was going to pay the ultimate price. Daniels knew only too well that, even if the prosecutors back in America uncovered just a fraction of what he had been up to during his time in Bangkok, he was going to spend the rest of his life in prison.

26
TARGET MAN

The name Brian Daniels first appeared on Drug Enforcement Administration intelligence files as a 'person of interest' in 1977, just one year after he had arrived in Bangkok and a few months after he participated in a scheme to smuggle marijuana into America concealed in helicopter engines.

Since that time his name had cropped up in numerous reports on a regular basis but there had not been sufficient information to enable the authorities to launch a proper investigation. It was only a lack of resources and the decision to focus on the problem of heroin in South East Asia that meant that Daniels and many others who based themselves in Bangkok were able to operate with virtual impunity.

Ultimately Daniels had simply been a victim of time. After years of playing catch-up, the government finally got the experience, the knowledge and the skill to trap him.

The seeds of his destruction were first sewn in October 1982 when President Ronald Regan vowed to 'end the drug menace and cripple organised crime' with a $200 million programme that would blanket the United States with federal narcotics task forces.

The President announced plans to form a dozen Organised Crime Drug Enforcement Task Forces (OCDEFs) which would aim to infiltrate the drug mobs and concentrate on long-range investigations, aimed at breaking up networks, rather than street pushers. A grand alliance of United States attorneys, the Drug Enforcement Administration, the Internal Revenue Service, the federal marshals, the coastguard, and other agencies, were to be modelled after a pilot task force formed to combat drug trade in south Florida.

Initially they were targeted mainly at the cocaine trade and established in cities with the biggest coke problems, but as the years went by and the vast profits being made from the Thai marijuana trade became apparent, other cities got in on the act.

Their first big break had come in 1984, the year that Daniels had worked alongside Dennis Ingham to place a 12-ton load on a boat called the *Allison*. The drugs had made it to Alaska but were seized a few days later as they were being barged down to Seattle.

Daniels had always believed the story quoted in the press at the time – that a loose-tongued member of the ship's crew had been overheard by a customs officer bragging about the forthcoming importation. The truth would turn out to be somewhat more alarming.

Around the time the *Allison* shipment was first being prepared, Dennis Ingham had a major falling out with another Bangkok-based marijuana smuggler over a personal matter. For Ingham, at least, the dispute was quickly forgotten but his adversary swore to get his revenge. As the *Allison* was being loaded the man with whom Ingham had fallen out decided his best tactic was to go to the authorities and let them know exactly what Ingham was up to. But while the man hated Ingham with a vengeance, he had a huge soft spot for another man intimately involved in the smuggling venture – Brian Daniels.

After entering into discussions with Seattle-based DEA officers, the man agreed to assist the authorities on one condition and one condition alone – in the inevitable round up and indicting of individuals linked to the *Allison* load that would follow the seizure, Daniels' name could not be included.

At first the DEA and the local branch of the US Attorney's office objected but the man was steadfast. Without him there could be no case and the only way he would agree to help was if his friend did not suffer as a result. The deal was done, the *Allison* load was seized and Brian Daniels was left to ponder his extraordinary good luck in having escaped indictment.

The prosecutor assigned to the original Ingham case was Peter Mueller, based in the Seattle office of the US Attorney. 'I remember looking at the paperwork, coming across the name of Brian Daniels and saying hey, why the hell aren't we going after this guy? When they told me the reason I was furious. I said that made no sense and tried to kick up a real fuss, but there was no way around it. That was the deal that had been made and we had to stick to it.

'As far as I was aware, he was the single biggest broker of South East Asian marijuana around. He put the distributors together with the growers and was responsible for packaging large shipments. He had done more of that in the last seven or eight years than anybody else but we were letting him go.'

Mueller knew the only way he would be ever able to prosecute Daniels would be to start a brand new case against him and gather the evidence independently of the man who had assisted them in building the case against Ingham.

After years of frustration, that had finally happened during the early part of 1988 when undercover DEA agents had managed to infiltrate The Ring on two fronts. The first had involved Larry Brant posing as a fisherman willing to help offload the marijuana that would be travelling on the *Encounter Bay*; the second had involved two other DEA men posing as Mafia money collectors trying to help Daniels get hold of his cash.

The second part of the scheme had been particularly satisfying for Mueller. Many large-scale operations aimed at drug kingpins like Daniels fall apart because the law enforcement agencies are simply not able to risk investing millions of dollars in a plan that ultimately might actually work. In this case, however, all the money that was spent on putting the *Encounter Bay* shipment together had come from Daniels himself and it had not cost the government a single penny.

But the capture of Daniels was just the beginning. As the head of The Ring, he was the absolute priority and dozens of other cases and investigations linked to the *Encounter Bay* had been essentially put on hold until it had been confirmed that Daniels was in custody. The news of arrest was like the sound of a starting pistol to law enforcement agencies across America and beyond.

In Oregon, DEA agents burst into the home of Thomas Sherrett. Investigators had dearly wanted to arrest him far earlier but to have done so would have tipped their hand to Daniels too early.

The house was deserted, of course, but in his haste to get away, Sherrett had left valuable clues behind. Agents seized a variety of items as evidence, including about $277,000 in cash, two safes, a money-counting machine, two 1-pound bricks of marijuana, and drug sales records. Among the mass of paperwork recovered were receipts relating to the repair of a former World War II minesweeper called the *Lloyd B. Gore.*

Up until that point Mueller and his colleagues had gotten an inkling that Daniels was planning a new shipment a few weeks after the *Encounter Bay* – he had told the men he believed were his Mafia money collectors that he had another job lined up for them – but they did not know what the vessel transporting the drugs was called.

Mueller soon learned that the *Gore* had come ashore at Steveston, a fishing community south of Vancouver, on 27 July. Acting on his behalf, officers from the Royal Canadian Mounted Police soon tracked the 22 tons of marijuana it had been carrying to a remote beach on the south end of Moresby Island in the Queen Charlotte Islands. The RCMP officers camped on the island and kept the large plastic-wrapped bundles, hidden in brush above the high tideline, under surveillance as the smugglers waited to move them. As soon as the smugglers moved in, they were all arrested.

On 29 July Robert Colflesh was arrested by Thai police officials as he arrived at his office at the Superstar in Bangkok. Thai officers also raided a house that had once belonged to Michael Forwell but this too had long been deserted.

That same day Mueller finally issued the indictment which had been burning a hole in his pocket ever since he had worked on the investigation into Dennis Ingham four years earlier.

It named Daniels, Michael Forwell, both Colflesh brothers, all seventeen junior members of the crew of the *Encounter Bay* and two other minor characters linked to the conspiracy. The ten counts included possession with intent to distribute the 72 tons of marijuana found aboard the *Encounter Bay*, conspiracy to import marijuana, aiding and abetting the importation of marijuana, and using a telephone to facilitate a drug conspiracy.

Daniels' name also cropped up elsewhere. A fresh indictment in Reno linked him and the money launderer Bruce Aitken to the seizure of the $7 million dollars in the phoney casino sting. New indictments issued out of San Diego named him as the supplier of the marijuana that had been seized from the *Pacific Star* in 1985.

A few days later an affidavit filed by the Internal Revenue Service in Portland, Oregon, detailed how Thomas Sherrett had passed to undercover federal agents more than $7 million in cash that he owed to Brian Daniels for a 15 ton shipment of marijuana delivered in 1987.

For Daniels, languishing in a Swiss prison, it was time to start fighting back. Mueller had hoped to have him returned to the United States in a matter of weeks, but the world's biggest marijuana broker made it clear that he would not come quietly.

Daniels hired one of Switzerland's top lawyers and extradition experts to fight his case and made it clear that he would attempt to hold out for as long as possible.

In the meantime, Mueller set about dealing with those already in the States. By the end of October the entire crew of the *Encounter Bay* along with Robert Colflesh had been dealt with in the court of US District Judge John Coughenour – the man assigned to handle all the Thai marijuana cases coming out of Seattle.

Samuel and Robert Colflesh pleaded guilty and were each sentenced to ten years as part of an agreement in which they would have to testify against Brian Daniels when he was eventually brought to trial. The remainder of the crew received sentences ranging from six months to a few years depending on the level of their involvement.

It was not until February 1989 that Brian Daniels himself was finally returned to the States and made his own appearance before Judge Coughenour. Initially choosing to go to trial, Daniels changed his mind a month before the proceedings were due to start. Under a carefully negotiated plea agreement, charges in Seattle, San Diego and Reno were packaged into a single plea agreement filed in Seattle while others were dropped.

Daniels ultimately pleaded guilty to smuggling nearly 200 tons of marijuana into the US in a four-year period. He was sentenced to twenty-five years in prison and fined $6.25 million.

And now that the prosecutors finally had the head of The Ring under their belt, it was time to go after the rest.

It was during the DEA investigation of Brian Daniels that Gary Annunziata finally learned why he had failed to find any drugs aboard the *Stormbird*, the ship his informant had told him the Shaffer brothers were using to bring in their 42-ton load of marijuana.

Up until then, Annunziata had assumed that the gang had somehow gotten wind of the DEA operation and abandoned the project or simply jettisoned the drugs at sea. He had not even wanted to consider the truth – that the gang had simply outsmarted the authorities and brought the drugs in anyway.

To make matters worse, the snippets of information that filtered back to him about what the Shaffers had been up to since the importation only added to his sense that justice had simply not been done.

Both brothers had developed a fascination with racing cars,

and used their wealth to purchase state-of-the-art models and buy their way into major events like the Monte Carlo rally.

Together the brothers bought an ocean-going yacht for $1.2 million. They called it the *Henry Morgan* after the infamous pirate, and Bill even arranged for a low-ranking member of their now disbanded smuggling team to go to Europe and work as his personal assistant on a salary of $60,000 per year plus expenses including 'reasonable food, transportation and lodging', four weeks vacation and medical insurance.

While Chris devoted increasing amounts of his time to his documentary and marine archaeology projects, Bill assumed all the airs of the international playboy he had always wanted to be. He used his money to become a total party animal. He bought boats, private planes, rented homes, hotel suits, drove sports cars, and indulged himself with fine art.

They had spent millions but it was clear that there were tens of millions more being held in reserve. The idea that the pair might continue living this good life indefinitely made Annunziata see red. He made his way to the office of the US Attorney in Seattle determined to reopen the case against the Shaffer brothers.

By then Peter Mueller had moved on to the civil division of the office and had handed over the baton in the Thai marijuana smuggling cases to a man who had provided him with solid assistance throughout the Daniels case, Mark Bartlett.

Then in his early thirties, Bartlett had become involved in the law to pursue the thrill of 'chasing bad guys and putting them away', a character trait that made him just the kind of prosecutor that DEA agents loved to work with. Instead of sitting back in his office and getting bogged down in paperwork, Bartlett liked to be there while the doors were kicked in and arrests were made.

When he first heard about the Shaffer brothers, he was cynical. 'I was being told that these guys were some of the biggest smugglers in the world, that they had made tens of millions of dollars and that not only had they never been caught but that they seemed to have retired from the business.

'With Daniels the case had been relatively straightforward because we had managed to get undercover agents right in the heart of the conspiracy and ultimately seized the dope that he had supplied. But with the Shaffers, there wasn't going to be any dope and no opportunity to introduce undercover officers. One of the biggest challenges as a prosecutor is taking on a murder case where there is no body. This was every bit as difficult – a dope case without any dope.'

The more Bartlett listened to Annunziata and heard about what the Shaffers were believed to have achieved in recent years, the more he agreed that not only were they a worthwhile target but that his department should devote considerable resources to their apprehension.

The Shaffers were marijuana traffickers working at the very highest echelons of the business. They were just the kind of men that President Regan had been talking about when he launched his multi-million-dollar programme. For that reason, Bartlett assigned the investigation OCDEF status, allowing him to bring in investigators from other parts of the judicial arena.

Key among them was Fran Dyer. A former counter-intelligence officer with the US air force during the Vietnam War, Dyer had spent five years as a detective in Seattle before joining the Internal Revenue Service Criminal Investigation Division.

An expert in financial matters and money-laundering investigations, his skills would prove invaluable in following the trail of money that the Shaffers had made during their smuggling days. With no chance of catching the brothers red handed, the law enforcement team had no choice but to build their case around testimony and whatever documentary evidence they could find. Millions of dollars flowing in and out of bank accounts would be amongst the most damning proof of illegal activity they would be able to find.

Dyer, Annunziata and Bartlett got together for the first time in November 1989. Using the information that Annunziata had already gathered about the Shaffer operation, they began to put together a list of names of all those who were involved in the case.

It soon emerged that the Shaffer brothers had made one crucial mistake in their last couple of operations. Instead of using only hardened, professional smugglers like Michael Carter and Gary Waldon, they had brought in a bunch of first-timers led by fisherman Tony Franulovich.

At the time it had given the gang a distinct advantage – none of those involved in the Anacortes fishing industry had any connection to the drug trade so the DEA had never had reason to watch them. With hindsight, however, the youngsters on the edge of the conspiracy would have little stomach for the long jail sentences they now faced. It became clear to Bartlett that if he and his team could begin to roll over the little guys, they would eventually find people willing to testify against the Shaffers themselves.

In early April 1990 Mark Bartlett was ready to go before a grand jury. That first indictment, case number CR90-0094C, issued in the United States District Court in the Western District of Washington at Seattle, listed twenty-seven names including both Shaffer brothers, Terry Restall, Brian O'Dea, Tony Franulovich, Michael Carter and Gary Waldon.

One of the few senior figures in the enterprise not mentioned in the indictment was Thai Tony – Thanong Siripreechapong – the man who had supplied the Shaffer brothers with their 1986 drug load. There had simply not been sufficient evidence to properly identify, let alone charge, him.

In keeping with standard law enforcement procedures, the indictment was initially kept secret in order to allow DEA agents to make as many arrests as possible before their targets had a chance to flee.

At 8 a.m. on the morning after the indictment had been issued, Brian O'Dea, the man who had been instrumental in helping the Shaffer brothers with the 1986 and 1987 loads, was woken by a knock at his door.

'My name is Gary Annunziata, I'm with the Drug Enforcement Agency,' he said, holding up a badge with one hand. 'Your name Brian O'Dea?'

'I wish it wasn't, but it is.'

'May we come in?'

'You've got the gun.'

Despite having made millions from the drug trade, the agents arrived to find O'Dea in a spartan apartment living on a diet of fruit juice and natural foods. He had sworn off drugs and alcohol having suffered a near fatal cocaine overdose which prompted a heart attack on the eve of his fortieth birthday, followed by his first sober day in almost twenty years. Almost all the money he had made had been spent on coke.

He awoke after a month in hospital to find that his wife had left him and his body was so fragile that doctors predicted he had at the most six months to live. Shocked into action, O'Dea turned to New Age and Far Eastern spirituality and began working as a volunteer at his local addiction recovery centre.

But Brian O'Dea was the exception rather than the rule. By the time the first round of arrests had been made and the indictment was unsealed, most of the fishing boat crews were in custody, though a dozen others involved in the smuggles were still at large and known to have millions of dollars at their disposal.

At the top of the list were the Shaffer brothers themselves. And now, for the first time in their lives, they were officially fugitives from justice.

27
NO QUARTER

The Shaffer brothers were not the only marijuana smugglers facing the might of an Organised Crime Drug Enforcement Task Force. During the spring of 1989, just as Mark Bartlett was issuing his first indictment, Ciro Mancuso, one of the original pioneers of the Thai marijuana trade, discovered that he himself was the target of a similar investigation, this time operating out of Reno.

Back in 1977, soon after his close call while smuggling drugs on the *Drifter*, Mancuso had assured his lawyer, Patrick Hallinan, that his dealing days were behind him and that he would instead concentrate on his construction business. Hallinan had taken his client at his word and, five years later, had called with the news that the statute of limitations on the *Drifter* case had expired. Even if Mancuso stood on the steps of the Halls of Justice and confessed to the crime, the Feds would no longer be able to charge him.

In the years that followed, believing Mancuso to be nothing more than an extremely successful businessman, he and Hallinan had gone on to become good friends, holidaying and partying together. Hallinan had even allowed Mancuso to use his personal bank account to wire $180,000 from Mexico when he was unable to complete the transaction himself. He had even employed him to build an extension to his home.

There was just one small problem. Mancuso had been lying. Not only had he carried on smuggling after 1977, he had done so in such quantities and with such success that his only real rivals had been the Shaffer brothers. Quietly and discreetly, Mancuso's organisation had brought in on average one shipment every year. He had been responsible for importing around 84 tons of Thai marijuana worth more than $200 million.

The *Drifter* operation had set the pattern for all future voyages. Over time Mancuso had linked up with other smugglers and expanded the scale of his operations. The boats became bigger and more expensive, the loads were heavier. In all, sixteen voyages are known to have been made between 1977 and 1989.

Planning for each smuggling season began a year in advance. Front money for the suppliers in Thailand was carried by couriers to Hong Kong, new vessels were purchased and outfitted, stash houses were bought or rented and unloading crews were organised.

The boat captains transferred their cargo off the California coast to smaller vessels that ran it up the San Joaquin-Sacramento River delta, where the load was trucked to a stash house in the quiet California town of Vacaville. There it was broken down, weighed, packaged and distributed. The smugglers often used the parking lot of the popular Nut Tree restaurant on Interstate 80 as a transfer point for shipments going to Nevada.

Once cash was collected from lower-level dealers, trusted subordinates turned it over to Mancuso and other principals at the Golden Gate Park, in the shadow of the famous bridge in San Francisco. Millions of dollars routinely changed hands this way.

By 1986 Mancuso was flush with success and it was hard to believe that anything could ever go wrong again. After bringing in three loads that year worth $34 million, Mancuso attempted two more in 1987.

This time, the landing site was Frankport Beach on the Oregon coast near the California border. The first arrived without incident on 17 May 1987. The second shipment landed on 21 June aboard the *California Sun*, a 51-foot shrimp boat. As darkness fell a resident on a nearby hillside above the beach noticed a ship coming close to shore without running lights. He picked up the phone and dialled 911.

The coastguard came in force sending ships, helicopters and patrol cars into the area. The *California Sun* turned tail, hit full power and tried to escape but ended up on the rocks, losing 19,800 pounds of Thai marijuana valued at $21.8 million. More than thirty people were arrested in connection with the *California Sun* incident but Mancuso had cleverly isolated himself from his smuggling organisation and once again, his name never even came up. Little wonder he was starting to believe that he was completely invincible.

By that time three separate grand juries had heard testimony against him and his confederates but none had felt there was sufficient evidence to hand up an indictment. But like Brian Daniels and the Shaffer brothers, the introduction of the Organised Crime Drug Enforcement Task Forces marked the beginning of the end.

The task force based in the Reno office of the US Attorney, led by a fearsome ex-marine prosecutor named Anthony White, took on the job of closing the net on Mancuso. This time, investigators had a powerful new weapon: the United States and Britain had forged an agreement ending the secrecy of offshore banks, whose records had been off-limits to US law enforcement agencies.

The team got a break early in 1988 when three couriers working for Mancuso left San Francisco carrying money that was to be laundered in Switzerland. Under their clothing, they wore custom-made Lycra money vests with Velcro fastenings that would not set off airport metal detectors.

Arriving in Frankfurt, they caught a train for the Swiss frontier, promptly violating a smuggling maxim: When you split up money to spread the risk, you do not then travel together.

Standing in line on a railroad platform, waiting to clear German customs at the border, one of them started haemorrhaging $100 bills from his trouser leg. In total $757,757 was seized.

Another break came later that same year when the coastguard seized the 65-foot racing ketch *Japy Hermes* at Shelter Cove in northern California. Abandoned in haste at the dockside, the ghostly vessel contained 33,000 pounds of top-quality Thai marijuana. Investigators traced the records of a pay phone on the pier and found that calls had been made to the Lake Tahoe area close to Ciro Mancuso's home, providing a vital link in the chain of evidence.

Hallinan and Mancuso first got wind of what was coming in March 1989 when Michael McCreary – the Half Moon Bay surf-shop owner who had taken a fall for Mancuso in 1974 over the possession of a small amount of cocaine – met with Hallinan in the attorney's office at Franklin Street in San Francisco. He was clutching a subpoena to testify before a grand jury in Reno four days later.

According to McCreary, Hallinan advised him to deny and lie about any criminal activity that occurred after 1974, to give vague answers to questions, to diminish the value and quantities of marijuana discussed and 'to disavow acquaintances' with as many people as possible. 'If they show you a photograph of somebody that you were with somewhere or sometime, and you recognise that person but you were never formally introduced, you don't really know that person, do you?' Hallinan told McCreary.

Even as the investigation reached a head, Mancuso continued to smuggle. In May 1989, a 17,600-pound load of Thai marijuana with a wholesale value of $19.4 million was landed at Cordova, Alaska. Meanwhile, Swiss authorities, acting in concert with American drug agents, froze Mancuso's bank account in that country and the grand jury hit him with multiple subpoenas for his records.

One day, Mancuso walked into the lead prosecutor's office in the Reno federal building where the OCDEF dealing with his case was based and dropped a bundle of requested documents on the attorney's desk. 'He just wanted to take a look,' she said later. 'He was an arrogant S.O.B. . . . and he really thought he was home free. I wanted to smack him right in the face.'

The task force finally struck in the early hours of 25 October 1989. More than 100 agents carrying search warrants and a 125-page indictment arrived at Squaw Summit, the copper-and-glass house that Mancuso had designed and built for himself which had been valued at more than $3 million.

Two agents drove him to Sacramento and deposited him in jail, leaving a copy of the indictment in his cell.

While the Shaffer brothers and their colleagues remained on the run and Ciro Mancuso stewed in jail awaiting his forthcoming court case, an event took place on the East Coast of America that would have profound implications for both sets of smugglers: the trial of William LaMorte.

As was the case with the Shaffer brothers, the prosecutors pursuing LaMorte did not have the luxury of having caught him red-handed with tons of marijuana. Instead they were running a 'no dope' case, relying on the testimony of others involved in LaMorte's division of The Ring to convince the jury of his involvement.

The big stumbling block of such an approach was that, as a result, the chief testimony in the case would be provided by convicted drug dealers who had agreed to speak purely because they hoped it would lead to more lenient treatment in their own cases.

It was an issue prosecutor Martin Klotz addressed as soon as the jury took its place in the court. He admitted there would be no tapes, photographs, videos or other physical evidence linking LaMorte to drug dealing, just testimony. 'You may not like them,' he said of the witnesses he was about to call, but added that he would not ask the jury to believe any one witness's testimony as each would be corroborated by others, including drug enforcement officials.

The case that Klotz presented was that LaMorte had been involved in smuggling marijuana and hashish from 1970 to 1985. Klotz said LaMorte withdrew from the drug business after two of his ring's boats were seized off the coasts of California and Nova Scotia in 1983 and 1985. LaMorte, he told the jury, was waiting for the five-year statute of limitations to expire on his drug crimes so he couldn't be prosecuted.

'And he almost got away with it, but he didn't quite,' Klotz said.

Six weeks of evidence followed. William LaMorte chose not to give evidence in his own defence, relying instead on numerous witnesses who testified that he had indeed carried out his last drug deal in 1984, meaning the statute of limitations had expired.

The jury deliberated for seven days and twice declared itself deadlocked before finally reaching a verdict of guilty on all counts.

Defence attorney Mark Summers argued that had LaMorte been arrested in the early 1980s, the typical sentence would have been less than ten years. He asked for a light sentence for his client, saying that he had voluntarily given up drug smuggling several years before his arrest and that during the seventies there was widespread public acceptance of marijuana and hashish use.

The judge decided to adopt a different approach, becoming particularly angry that a man born into such wealth and privilege should choose to pursue such a career.

He sentenced LaMorte to fifty years in prison and ordered him to pay more than $75 million in fines.

There could be no doubt – the world had changed. The days in which marijuana smugglers were not treated too harshly and were seen as a kind of fun throwback to the sixties were dead and gone.

Ciro Mancuso could only hope that his lawyer – the man who had kept him invincible for so long and whom he truly believed was one of the best lawyers on the planet – could strike him one hell of a deal. For the Shaffer brothers it was increasingly clear that coming in and trusting the judicial system was simply not an option. They had only one choice: keep on running.

28
ACROSS THE POND

There were just a few of them left. Each had access to millions of dollars, a selection of false passports, homes in several continents and a burning desire to stay hidden away for as long as possible.

Slowly but surely, everyone who had ever been involved in multi-ton marijuana smuggling out of Thailand was being indicted, rounded up and brought to justice but eight key fugitives remained: Chris and William Shaffer, Tom Sherrett, Michael Forwell, Michael Carter, Gary Waldon, Thai Tony and the character previously known only as 'Sonny', the wannabe actor who had collected millions of dollars-worth of marijuana from the Shaffers in New York.

As part of the round up of the Shaffer organisation, Sonny had finally been identified. Amongst those arrested in the sweep of junior members of the organisation was the cash courier who had had dinner with Sonny in New York and heard him relate how his real dream was to be an actor.

As it happened, a few weeks after the dinner, the courier had spotted Sonny in the background of a commercial for an artificial sweetener, dressed up like to look like an Amish farmer and performing a shuffling dance.

After his arrest the courier related his story to Internal Revenue Service agent Fran Dyer who was attached to the OCDEF unit investigating the Shaffers. He contacted the president of the sweetener company who in turn put him in touch with the advertising agency that had been hired to make the commercial.

'He was really upset,' Dyer recalled. 'He said, "You mean we've got a drug dealer advertising our product?"'

The agency records showed that Sonny was in fact Irwin Kletter, and listed him as living at two New York addresses, one in Manhattan, the other in Fire Island. The first was empty but when agents went to check out the second, they found signs that it had been recently occupied and that whoever lived there was likely to be returning soon.

The agents lay in wait until a man fitting Kletter's description showed up and then they pounced. 'Are you Irwin Kletter?' asked one.

'Kletter, yes,' came the reply. 'But not Irwin. I think you guys are looking for my brother.'

Their target had somehow found out about the first raid on his Manhattan apartment and gone to ground, along with the other seven fugitives. The hunt was on and the Seattle team settled in for the long haul.

'The mobility they have, their phoney IDs, their unlimited money and good contacts around the world make it more difficult to find these people,' said Bartlett. 'The money is probably the pivotal factor in their ability to avoid capture for long periods of time. We've got some fugitives who are ten to fifteen years on the books, and those we may never see.

'The truth is, once they became fugitives, their lifestyle is what helped us find them quicker. They were so flamboyant – it was like something out of *Lifestyles of the Rich and Famous* – and we got many leads. If they had just stayed in one place and cooled it, we would never have gotten a clue about where they were.'

As soon as the first inklings came that the Shaffer brothers might be hiding out in London, it suddenly seemed to be the most obvious place to look. Both brothers had spent many years there, knew the city well and had a great affection for all things European.

Part of the intelligence Bartlett's team had received was that the brothers had obtained at least three British passports in false names. One was the result of the classic *Day of the Jackal* technique where someone had gone to Somerset House and obtained a copy of a birth certificate of an individual that had passed away. Using this, they had applied for a genuine passport in a false name – one that would stand up to any level of scrutiny.

Another one of the passports being used by the brothers had been stolen, the photograph expertly removed and replaced with one showing Christopher Shaffer. Bill obtained his third passport with the help of the former offloaders from his smuggling crew, Gary Waldon and Michael Carter, who arranged for him to meet a former CIA operative at the Serpentine Restaurant in Hyde Park. The passport – this time German – was handed over in exchange for $50,000 in cash.

With the London connection firmly established Bartlett and Dyer knew they had to turn to Scotland Yard for help. After contacting the Justice Department Attaché at the US Embassy in Grosvenor Square, they were put through to the Metropolitan Police's International and Organised Crime branch, then headed up by Detective Sergeant Graham Saltmarsh.

The Seattle team could not have found a better ally.

Born and bred in and around South London's infamous Old Kent Road by parents who ran the local fish and chip shop, Saltmarsh attended the kind of school that ensured childhood games of cops and robbers would soon be played out for real.

While one of his classmates ended up doing life for murder and others went on to become notorious armed robbers, Saltmarsh chose the law.

He rose rapidly in the CID, investigating drug trafficking, terrorism and organised crime at a national and international level. He took part in dozens of undercover operations, including many in Northern Ireland during the height of the troubles. He was awarded a total of thirteen high commendations for his work including one for courage.

Interviewed about his work around the time of the Shaffer case, he echoed Mark Bartlett in his reason for coming to work each day: 'I really enjoy my job. I enjoy coming to work. The fact of the matter is that hunting down drug traffickers is actually very satisfying and very enjoyable because it's very hard. You're unravelling puzzles. I spoke to an American guy in the police force there and they've got helicopters, all this kind of equipment and they still can't curb their drug problem. They haven't sussed out that it's fun.'

Around the time that Saltmarsh and Reynolds started looking for him, William Shaffer was busy building a new life for himself.

He had spent time travelling around Europe, and threw parties on the boats in St Tropez and had a rented home in Geneva. Then he bought a million-pound town house in London's Alexander Square, off the Brompton Road.

It was while he was there that he got to know the noted television actress Cherie Lunghi, best known for her role in *The Manageress* and numerous Kenco coffee commercials.

She had just come out of an eight-year relationship with film director Roland Joffe which whom she had a young daughter. A whirlwind romance followed. 'Bill always told me he dived for treasure and that I was his latest find,' says Lunghi. 'We were extremely happy. We had a little adventure together. I am a hopeless romantic.'

During the time they were together Lunghi never had a clue that he had ever been involved in anything criminal or was a wanted man, even when they eventually began living together. She said later: 'I'm not good at twenty-four-hour-a-day relationships. I appreciate it if my partner's job or interests mean we do our own thing once in a while. I do tend to gravitate towards people who are similar to me in that respect; people who are adventurers, really.'

In March 1991, soon after Saltmarsh and Reynolds were assigned to the case, Bill Shaffer had checked into a suite at Dukes Hotel in the heart of Mayfair. Ever the big spender, he was flashing a lot of money around and making a general exhibition of himself. Not surprisingly, this lack of discretion soon attracted attention. That afternoon he asked the concierge of the hotel to put some roses in his suite – £500 worth of roses. That night he returned to the hotel with Cherie Lunghi on his arm.

Suspicious that their client might not be exactly who he said he was, someone in hotel security decided to make a discreet phone call to a friend at Scotland Yard, but the officer was on a stake-out for two days and did not return the call. By the time he did and Saltmarsh and Reynolds were on the case, Shaffer had already moved out.

For the British detectives, the enormity of the challenge facing them was obvious from the start. The Shaffer brothers, in common with many other international drug traffickers, had earned more than enough money to enable them to elude the authorities and stay on the run for ever.

The one weakness the Shaffers had was the fact that they liked to spend their money. By the start of the nineties a new breed of well-heeled traffickers had emerged who did their best to hide their wealth. They would live the good life but drive modest cars, live in nondescript houses and generally do their utmost to keep out of the limelight.

Authorities attribute the relatively low profile adopted by this new breed to the awareness of tougher federal laws that govern bail, money laundering and the seizure of assets obtained through drug sales. The laws have had an almost chilling effect, causing many drug smugglers to go out of their way to avoid drawing attention to their excessive wealth. Instead they try to keep it a secret and eliminate as many paper trails as possible.

The Shaffers were old-fashioned in that they didn't buy into that policy at all. They had made a lot of money and they wanted to spend it. Extravagance was the name of the game and the mere fact that they had become international fugitives seemed little reason for either brother to give up the lifestyle they had become accustomed to.

'The frustration was that they always seemed to be one step ahead,' says Graham Saltmarsh. 'We then found out that Bill Shaffer had a house in Alexander Square in South Kensington, but that too had been abandoned. One time we came within half an hour of tracking him down. We knew we were going to get him, we just needed a little help.'

By the summer of 1991 the Shaffers knew that both their time and their horizons were extremely limited. They were spending huge amounts of money on their living expenses and, although they had millions more stashed away, their inability to continue smuggling meant that for the first time there were no fresh injections of cash coming into the pot.

Both brothers made a number of business investments in the hope of growing their fortunes but it soon became clear that the only business they could ever have any real success in would be marijuana smuggling. All their investments turned out to be money losers.

Always at the back of their minds was the notion that, when they did eventually get caught, they wanted to be in a position to mitigate their sentences as far as possible. With this in mind they both began giving away substantial amounts of money to charity and became involved in good works.

Bill in particular spent a significant amount of time working with Médecins Sans Frontières, an international organisation that provides medical care to citizens of Third World countries. At one point Bill even considered working for the organisation full time: not only would it look good on his probation report but it also would have sent him to such remote parts of the world that it would have been almost impossible for anyone to track him down.

Once news of the initial indictments had emerged, Chris and Bill began contacting members of their team and encouraging them to give themselves up. In many cases they paid the cost of people returning to the States, the fees of their lawyers and other expenses. They even encouraged those they had worked with to offer to give evidence against them if that was what it took to get the best deal.

One mid-ranking member of the smuggling team recalled: 'Bill contacted me personally to let me know that I had been indicted on conspiracy charges. At that time he encouraged me to surrender and cooperate with the government in the hopes of minimising any sentence I would be facing. Confused and scared I foolishly ignored his good advice. I fled to Europe and became a fugitive. Several months passed before Bill was able to find me and make contact again. Finally we met on the island of Mallorca. It was then that Bill pointed out to me the pain and suffering that I was causing my family by selfishly remaining a fugitive. He shared with me his own tremendous guilt and pain for having been responsible for the same suffering in his own family. He convinced me to surrender to federal marshals and once again encouraged me to be frank and honest when confronted by the government.'

There was a method in this madness. If the Shaffer brothers could encourage all the major people from their crew to come in, each one saying how much the Shaffers had encouraged and supported them to do so, they would receive substantial credit for this when it came to their own sentencing. By contrast, if the Shaffers got caught and went before the judge too early, they would likely end up with the kind of sentences that had been handed out to Brian Daniels and William LaMorte.

But time was running out. Back in Seattle the phone link between the US Attorney's office and New Scotland Yard was in near constant use.

Bartlett and Dyer, along with Saltmarsh and Reynolds, were spending hours each day working their way through thick wads of paper containing lists of names of people who had stayed at hotels across London and beyond.

Bartlett recalls: 'We'd be looking through, come across a name that sounded as though it had been made up and turn to each other and say "Hey, you think this one sounds like it could be Bill Shaffer? Do you think Christopher would use a name like this one? Should we check it out?" It was completely crazy. We were clutching at straws.'

But the persistence paid off and with some of the names used by the pair finally identified, Bartlett and Dyer made the decision to seek the help of the public. In London, Graham Saltmarsh and Rick Reynolds knew just the place to turn to.

Phoning the BBC *Crimewatch* production office, Saltmarsh explained that he had something the programme might be interested in. The producer promised to take a look at it. Until then the show had concentrated exclusively on British criminals. On the evening of Thursday 12 September 1991, it broke new ground.

'The International and Organised Crime Branch at New Scotland Yard need your help to find William and Christopher Shaffer. They wish to discuss the importation of 90 tons of cannabis into the United States from South East Asia. We know the brothers enjoy the good life, staying in top class hotels when they visit England, Belgium and Holland. William Shaffer is forty-five, six feet tall and has been known to call himself Bill Raines. Christopher Shaffer is forty-two, also about six feet tall and uses the names Edward Knightly, Chris Roberts and Chris Kesner.'

Dozens of photographs of the pair were flashed up on screen during the short segment. They were shown dressed in dinner jackets, enjoying meals at fancy restaurants, scuba diving under a blazing hot sun from the decks of their yachts and racing their cars in the Monte Carlo rally. It was clear that whatever crimes the pair were involved in, they had become incredibly wealthy as a result.

Before the lines shut down, some seventy calls came into the studio. In ten of them, callers said they knew the Shaffers' whereabouts. Two of the ten came from the Continent and both of those callers reported that Bill Shaffer was living it up in Germany.

29
CONFIDENCE

Like the Shaffers, Gary Waldon and Michael Carter, the two men who headed up the brothers' offloading organisation and had introduced them to Brian Daniels, knew the odds were stacked against them but decided to stick with life on the run.

After so many years in the smuggling business they knew they faced conspiracy charges so serious that by the time they got out of prison they would be too old to enjoy whatever money they had managed to stash away.

But as the net closed around them it became obvious that they and their families would need professional help if they were going to stay one step ahead of the authorities, and when they asked for recommendations about who to turn to, one name kept cropping up above all the rest.

Paul LaVista was a fixer, the kind of man who helps make introductions, procures hard-to-find contraband, arranges safe passage out of the country for fugitives and organises the necessary bribes for evidence to be destroyed, all for payment of the appropriate fee.

A former CIA operative, LaVista had contacts deep within every major law enforcement agency in the world. During the Vietnam War he had been a member of an elite special forces squad specialising in the kind of black op work that is often essential to achieve military goals but is almost always denied by the authorities.

LaVista travelled frequently to the world's trouble spots, often disappearing for weeks at a time at a moment's notice. His wife, Kathy, would receive postcards from Central America, the Middle East and all over Europe. Once she received a fax saying that his plane was delayed on the island of Fiji. After LaVista had returned from one such trip, Kathy found a bullet hole in one of his shirts.

Having made enemies throughout his life, LaVista rarely went anywhere without his trusty .45, keeping it within easy reach throughout the night and even taking it into the shower each morning. Locals referred to his home as 'the compound'. The house in Olive Springs Road in Marietta was circled by a high black iron fence and topped with razor wire, while three large German shepherds patrolled the grounds night and day. In case these measures were not enough, a sign warned that the fence was electrified. 'I chose this lifestyle,' he would say by way of explanation. 'I'm a very private person.'

As a form of cover for his more shadowy activities, LaVista ran the Bullet Stop, an arms dealership and shooting gallery in Cobb County, Atlanta, where members of the public could rent a variety of machine guns and blaze away at targets of their choice.

His office at the Bullet Stop was decorated with dozens of pictures of haggard soldiers trekking through swamps, deserts and mountain ranges, prints of medieval knights and warriors, mounted antique firearms and dozens of photographs of his Siamese cat and young son.

Kathy LaVista recalls her husband telling her he was 'attached' to the Military Assistance Command special operations unit in Vietnam, and she had seen photos of soldiers in camouflage slogging through jungle terrain and others of well-known Saigon landmarks. However, her husband was in none of them. 'He said he stayed out of pictures because they could compromise his secrecy,' she said.

By the time Gary Waldon and Michael Carter made contact with LaVista, they were both desperate men. The net was closing in around them and, having seen the sentences handed out to Brian Daniels and William LaMorte, giving themselves up was something they were simply not willing to do. They needed help and they needed it fast.

Waldon and Carter initially paid LaVista $10,000 'to provide information on the current status of any investigation that might be focusing on them.'

Over the course of several months LaVista helped Waldon to obtain false East German passports and conceal his drug money, taking more than $600,000 of cash and placing it into his personal bank accounts. At one point LaVista even offered to shelter Waldon and his family, moving them into the 'Compound' for several weeks while he continued to dig up new sources of information on the case.

When other Shaffer fugitives found out about LaVista, they all wanted his help too. In fact, it had been LaVista who had provided Bill Shaffer with his German passport at a cost of $50,000. Within a matter of weeks he had been paid almost $1 million in return for gathering covert evidence and passing it on.

Finally, after months of living in the shadows, LaVista arranged – with help from friends who had formerly been in the CIA – for Waldon and his entire family to be smuggled out to Europe and set up with a brand-new identity. It seemed that Waldon at least would be safe.

A few months later, detectives on the trail of Waldon made the connection with LaVista and arrested him, charging that he had aided and abetted a fugitive. It was to be the start of a deadly new chapter in LaVista's life.

It had started out as just another Wednesday morning at the suburban Mercedes dealership, RBM of Atlanta, in Dunwoody.

For mechanic Jim Williams the first major job of the day was an S-Class Mercedes that had been towed in after the owner, Paul LaVista, reported that it would not start. Williams turned the key in the ignition and the lack of response told him immediately that something was wrong with the starter motor.

He popped the hood and started to inspect the engine, but

then he saw some wires that he didn't recognise and began tracing them. One wire led directly from the ignition to the starter motor. The other led from the battery to a metal disc sitting on a block of clay-like material that in turn was attached to the engine frame. Williams called over a colleague, an army veteran with experience of explosives, and soon his worst fears were confirmed. The disc was a blasting cap and the clay-like substance was 2 pounds of C4 plastic explosive. Someone had planted a bomb in the car.

The explosives, combined with the fuel in the tank, would have, had it been wired up correctly, destroyed the car and left a huge crater in the ground. Anyone sitting inside would have been killed instantly. 'Evidently whoever did it wired it up wrong,' said Fulton County Police Lt. David Guy. 'Instead of fixing the car so it would blow up, he fixed it so it wouldn't start.'

The following day LaVista's luck went from bad to worse and left no one in any doubt that someone was after him.

He was sitting in his wife's Mercedes in the parking lot of a shopping centre, waiting for a prescription to be filled. He opened the door of the car in order to stub out a cigarette on the ground when he felt a gun up against his ear. 'I grabbed his arm, and pulled him toward the car,' LaVista said later. 'That's when he fired.'

The first bullet tore into LaVista's right shoulder. LaVista tried to get his own gun out of its holster but it fell to the ground. The man fired twice more but in the struggle both shots missed. LaVista reached for the keys and started his engine, driving off at speed, blood pouring from his wound.

In his rear view mirror he could see the man who had shot him in hot pursuit in a white car. The chase ended when LaVista called the police on his car phone and pulled up outside his store.

For Bill and Christopher Shaffer, still on the lam in Europe, the attacks on LaVista were a terrifying development. Although no one could be 100 per cent certain, the most obvious motivation behind the attack was that someone was trying to get to the members of their gang.

LaVista knew where many of the Shaffers' top operatives were hiding, he knew where hundreds of thousands of dollars worth of their assets were being hidden. If he could be intimidated into giving up the information, they could all be in grave danger.

Thanks to the nature of his work, narrowing down a list of suspects who might want to kill LaVista was a formidable task. It was made all the more difficult by the fact that LaVista himself seemed particularly unwilling to help out.

That may have been why LaVista failed to respond the way police expected him to when he was first informed about the bomb. Detectives noted he was only 'somewhat surprised' by the news. Agent Joe Gordon of the Federal Bureau of Alcohol, Tobacco and Firearms said Mr. LaVista's reaction to the news was 'not really what you'd expect. He took three hours to respond. We notified him at four thirty and he didn't show up until eight.'

Agents from the ATF were keen to speak to LaVista, not just because of the explosives incident. At the time the bomb was discovered, LaVista himself had been under investigation by the agency for more than a year. He was being scrutinised after the ATF had their suspicions that he had been violating federal firearms laws including the possession, manufacture and receipt of unregistered weapons such as machine guns, machine-gun parts and silencers.

A few days later the police received an unusual tip-off. Instead of calling them directly, the anonymous source had called RBM, the dealership where the bomb had been discovered in the Mercedes.

'I used to work at the Bullet Stop,' the man said. 'I used to work with Paul LaVista. While I was there he asked me to rent a lock-up garage in my name but to give him the keys. It's at Attic Self Storage, 155 Heatherset Drive in Marietta. You might want to check it out.' Early in January 1992 they did just that.

Explosives were found similar to those used in the car bomb. And suddenly the finger of suspicion was pointing squarely at LaVista himself.

More startling revelations continued to emerge as local reporters dug deeper into the story. LaVista never served in the military, according to the Military Personnel Records Centre in St. Louis. And even though the CIA, true to form, would not comment, off the record an anonymous spokesman said LaVista had no connection with the organisation.

Mark Bartlett, hot on the trail of his remaining fugitives, soon chose to indict LaVista as well. The document he produced left little doubt about what had really happened. 'LaVista's entire relationship with Waldon was based on lies and deceit. LaVista portrayed himself as a CIA operative with inside information . . . but all indications are that this information was fabricated whole cloth or was merely a restatement of newspaper articles available to anyone.'

'LaVista preyed upon Carter and Waldon,' adds Bartlett. 'He basically stole their money. He gave them horrible advice about why they should remain fugitives, in truth telling them at the time that he was arranging things with the CIA and the United States Government to make these problems go away when in fact what Mr LaVista was doing was ripping off all their money.'

Waldon and Carter were captured soon afterwards – (Waldon was in Amsterdam, Carter in Africa) – and returned to Seattle to await their fate, but by then the ordeal that LaVista had put them through had done the seemingly impossible; generated an element of sympathy towards the two hardened traffickers. Carter received eleven years.

The revelations were as much of a shock to LaVista's wife as anyone else. Her attorney, Tom Browning, told the *Seattle Times* that his client's life was like 'being married to Cary Grant and then, one day, somebody leaves a note on the pillow saying he wasn't Cary Grant, he was a Martian.'

30
OUT OF TIME

On the morning of 15 January 1992 Mark Bartlett was just about to deliver his closing speech at a courthouse in Tacoma, where he had been prosecuting a methamphetamine gang, when the doors swung open and his young assistant started walking towards him, a certain urgency in her step.

She came over to where he was sitting and bent down to whisper in his ear. 'They just arrested William Shaffer in Germany.'

It had been four months since Shaffer's case had been featured on *Crimewatch*. During that time, all too well aware that he was being sought by police from several different countries, he had moved constantly, rarely being seen in public. He would later claim it was a terrible, miserable experience but when arrested by officers from the Bavarian State Police, his old arrogance came flooding back. When they grabbed him he shrugged and said: 'Congratulations. Today is your lucky day. You've won the big one.'

Mark Bartlett hoped he would be able to bring Bill Shaffer back to Seattle within a week but Shaffer had immediately hired a local lawyer to fight his case.

Shaffer applied for bail at once, but was refused. Instead the German court sent him to a notorious antiquated high security prison in Frankfurt named Justizvollzugsanstalt. Home to terrorists such as the members of the Baader-Meinhoff gang, murderers and others accused of crimes of violence, conditions in the facility were so appalling it had been due to be torn down.

Built to house 520 inmates, the place was hopeless, over-crowded and was usually home to at least 850 prisoners. With up to 75 per cent of the inmates from outside Germany, tensions between different ethnic groups ran high. There were regular gang battles, stabbings and suicides. For Bill Shaffer, used to his designer suits, fine wines and life without violence, it was all something of a shock.

For his own protection Shaffer was kept in solitary confinement, staying in his cell for twenty-three hours each day. His recreation was limited to one hour per week in a rubbish-strewn courtyard below the cells, where other prisoners would often dump their own excrement. With no glass in the windows his cell became near freezing during the winter and, because it faced north and received no sunlight, it was little better in the summer. Day and night, a single 25-watt bulb burned in the ceiling.

Despite the appalling conditions, Shaffer chose to stay and fight extradition rather than return to the States to face the music. He lasted a full eight months before giving up his fight and allowing himself to be flown back to Seattle.

One brother had been captured but Chris Shaffer was still at large. Graham Saltmarsh and Rick Reynolds redoubled their efforts to find him and eventually tracked him down to Ireland. They tipped off the Garda but Shaffer barely managed to give them the slip and escaped to France in the back of a rented van. It became clear that he was not working alone; someone was helping him.

It was around the same time that Mark Bartlett received word that two other fugitives from the case, Edwin and Summer Brown, were now living in Paris near the Jardin de Luxembourg. Convinced that they were in touch with Chris and offering him regular assistance, Bartlett asked the local police to arrest them.

At 9am one morning in November 1992 a police officer disguised as a workman knocked on the Browns' front door. Summer answered but her French wasn't good enough for her to work out what the man wanted, so she called out to her husband, who was on the phone.

No one knew it at the time but Chris was on the other end of the line. He had been hiding out at a small hotel five blocks away. Ed said, 'I'll call you back Chris' and went to open the door. As he did so, several armed officers stormed inside.

The Browns were handcuffed and police began to search their apartment. Chris had grown impatient waiting for Ed to call him back so he had dialled the flat. The police chose to let the phone ring, hoping to collect incriminating evidence on the answering machine but Chris never left a message.

Knowing that Ed had just gone to answer the door and was now unable to pick up the phone, left Chris totally unnerved. He immediately checked out of his hotel. The tension of months of being on the run was taking its toll. Stressed beyond breaking point, Chris began changing hotel rooms every night, afraid even of his own shadow. His wife had returned to the United States a year earlier with the couple's two children. He was alone and worn out. When he could bear it no more he called a lawyer friend back in America and asked him to help negotiate the terms of his surrender.

He returned to America and registered in the Hotel Vintage Park in Seattle under his real name. Now on the very edge of a nervous breakdown, it marked the end of a world of lies and deception, where false names, phoney passports and a fast lifestyle supported by millions in drug proceeds had been the name of the game.

He would later describe this time as 'a horrible nightmare, living with constant fear and the threat of apprehension.'

He handed back the form and the receptionist smiled and welcomed him to the hotel, reading his name off the card. Shaffer's face went deathly pale. 'He just freaked out,' says Bartlett. 'He was very, very shocked that someone had used his real name. He hadn't heard it for more than two years because of all the aliases he had been using. It kind of brought the reality of his situation home for him.'

With so many of the negotiations already completed by William, the Shaffer brothers were ready to be sentenced by the summer of 1993.

On 1 July, eight days before he was due to appear before Judge Coughenour, William Shaffer wrote to him: essentially a last-ditch attempt to evoke as much sympathy as possible.

'I have just come from another meeting with Mark Bartlett, Fran Dyer and my attorney. This meeting concerned fugitives and their possible location and surrender and the illegal activities of the Los Angeles attorney responsible for banking. I also found out that 9 July will be the sentencing date. There is so much paperwork involved in my case I can't believe it. Your Honour, I have written you over a dozen long letters since my arrest and incarceration eighteen months ago in Germany. Some of them were over thirty pages long. In this final letter I promise to be brief.

'I recognise the corrupting influence that my involvement in marijuana smuggling has had on society, even though at the time I was actively involved I was operating under the naïve and misguided belief that dealing in marijuana, avoiding guns and violence, was not all that bad. I was wrong, Your Honour, and will pay for it.

'As I say goodbye to my kids, I realise nothing can justify the damage I inflicted on my family, my friends and myself. As I come before you about to be sentenced, all I can do is make a commitment to you and myself that I will do whatever is humanly possible to make up for the past mistakes in the future.

'I've already started travelling down that path by trying to work with the government by this joint resolution of all remaining cases, by my assistance to the government, and my collecting of all assets and cash. Your Honour, I am a proud father and an honest person. I have practised meditation for years and I listen well. I heard you in court when you talked to us. I no longer own a car, a house, a boat. No "Armani" suits or fancy shoes. That ridiculous life is over! Your Honour, most of us, particularly the older people you have sentenced, were involved in a variety of legal and illegal activities. Ironic as it might seem to the outside world, without exception our lives, as a result of our arrest, are better than before.

'Our families no longer life in fear and terror of the unknown. We know what we must face. We know what we must do. Reality has returned. This new reality, difficult as it might seem, is something we can and will build on. Our previous fantasy had the instability of a castle built on sand. I thank God this period of my life is over.

'Your Honour, I started out as a teacher. I was a good teacher. "What goes around comes around" is a jailhouse saying. Karma! I am happy to serve and teach once again, albeit in very difficult circumstances. Now I teach remedial reading to prisoners in Kent City jail. I also teach meditation to manic depressives, drug addicts, bank robbers and wife beaters. I promise you I have made a positive difference to both my German and American fellow inmates and I will continue to make this court and my family proud of me during my incarceration.

'Until I came to King County jail, I had never personally witnessed a casualty from marijuana. Now, sir, I have, particularly among the disenfranchised. It shook me on a fundamental level. I now recognise a reality I had never believed before. That marijuana can lead to harder drugs and social problems. And it's not just the marijuana, it's a combination of the marijuana and the breaking of laws that builds contempt and disrespect for the law, and sets in motion an attitude that does cause society problems. Serious problems. It is clear to me now that I participated in a negative way. I was a part of society's problems, not its solutions. I will make up for this, I promise.

'Your Honour, in closing, I am, as I know I must be for the

court and myself a camel going through "the eye of a needle". And this camel would like to say a poem, a haiku, to the court that illustrates my state of mind.

> *Last night my barn burned down!*
> *I survived.*
> *Aah. And now I can see the moon.*

'I will continue to look up and by moonlight, sunlight, starlight or neon prison light, I will educate myself and all others who will listen about how to avoid the tragic outcome one inevitably encounters when you break the law. Respectfully. William W Shaffer.'

Christopher took a different approach. His own letter to the judge played down his own involvement, particularly in the later smuggles that made the brothers so notorious.

'Another major concern is that I have been characterised and am being viewed simply as "one of the Shaffer brothers",' he wrote. 'I love my brother and will do anything I can to support him, but I hope it is evident that we are two very different people.'

'The major focus of my part of the smuggling operation has always been in the role of providing transportation because of my abilities as a sailor. By the mid-eighties when Brian Daniels came in and the shipments became so large, my involvement actually decreased. I wanted to get out. I had become involved with Penny Ciarlo and she was pregnant with our first child. My role at that time became basically a coordinator for shipping and communications. Terry Restall became Bill's right-hand man in the operation . . . I was not a manager or an overall director.'

On 9 July 1993 the sentence was handed down. Due to a combination of many things; the Shaffers' guilty pleas, their personal appeals to the judge for mercy, the encouragement they had given others to come in and their work to help track down the remaining fugitives, their sentences were comparatively lenient.

Bill was ordered to serve thirteen years, Christopher twelve. As for the money, the Shaffers claimed that they had handed over every last penny that they had ever made. Many found this hard to swallow.

Despite four years of work, 550 interviews, 15,000 man hours and the cooperation of law enforcement agencies in eight countries the task force managed to confiscate only around $12 million of the estimated $60 million the brothers made during their smuggling careers.

As he was handed his term by Judge Coughenour, Bill Shaffer, slick and greasy to the last, could not resist allowing a little of the charm that had served him so well throughout the years to shine through.

'Your honour, could I say one word? My brother and I were not the professionals in this. I think that the professionals were your staff, Mr Bartlett and Mr Dyer, and I just wanted to recognise that those are the real professionals.'

Five months later, in December 1993, another leading member of The Ring fell.

Immigration officials at Amsterdam airport were checking the passports of passengers arriving off a flight from Geneva when they noticed that a German man appeared to be using false passports.

Told there seemed to be a problem with his German passport, the man told officials that he actually had dual nationality and that he had a British passport locked up in a bank safe-deposit box back in Switzerland.

Happy to allow the man to become someone else's problem, the Dutch authorities put him on the first plane back to Switzerland. The moment he arrived, the man told immigration officials that he was a British citizen and demanded to be allowed to leave the airport. When they refused, he demanded to be allowed to call the US consulate.

Within hours the man had been identified as Thomas Sherrett.

He had managed to stay on the run for five years but now he too was behind bars and set to be returned to America to face the music, this time in his native Oregon.

The members of The Ring had scattered far and wide but, one by one, they were all being tracked down, either through their own stupidity, through first-class detective work or, more often, a combination of both.

'He had claimed to be a British citizen. But then when he was under pressure, he asked to talk to the American consulate,' noted one of the officials on duty that day, 'which kind of gave him away. He had nowhere left to go.'

31
TURNCOAT

For more than two decades, Ciro Mancuso had stayed one step ahead of the authorities, relying on Patrick Hallinan to fight his corner and keep him out of whatever trouble threatened to get in his way.

'I thought we had not only a trusting attorney-client relationship, but a friendship guided by respect, honour and trust,' Mancuso wrote Hallinan from his jail cell a few months after his arrest. 'I am a person that you can count on if you ever need to, and I think that you know that I am counting on you now.'

Hallinan was the type of lawyer who always managed to give his clients hope, who slapped them on the back and told them that everything was going to be OK. As the federal case against him mounted, Mancuso kept waiting for the slap on the back, but it never came.

'Ciro thought he [Hallinan] would take care of it,' said a friend. 'But Ciro was in too deep even for Hallinan to save him. He just wasn't dealing with reality.'

That job was left to Hallinan. 'In preparing the case, it became very evident to me that they were going to convict him,' says the lawyer. 'And when that became evident, I said to him: "Ciro, you know, they're going to convict you, and the punishment's going to be awful. We have to make some deal for you." And so he said, "Go ahead and make it." He never did admit to me that he really did the things that he was charged with, but he said, "Go ahead and make the deal."'

Because Mancuso was at the top of the heap, he had no one above him to give up. His only salvation lay in betraying his old friend Brian Degen and a handful of other suspected smugglers. As soon as Mancuso got an inkling that this might be part of the deal, he objected in the strongest possible terms. 'Dear Patrick,' he wrote, 'I have given some serious thought to the situation and have made some decisions. First and foremost I will not even consider turning in or in any way whatsoever cooperating with the government against ANY of my friends or acquaintances, so that possibility can be completely eliminated from any negotiations.'

But the government prosecutors desperately needed Mancuso's testimony to convict others whose cases were weaker. So the government turned up the screws. Mancuso's wife, Andrea, was indicted and threatened with prison for being part of his drug operation.

'I was put under tremendous pressure to cooperate with the government, including having a direct threat made – and threats followed up on – to indict my wife,' says Mancuso. 'We had two small children. She could very easily get a long prison term, and my children wouldn't have anybody to raise them.'

As negotiations progressed late into the spring of 1990, Hallinan fell off a ladder in his home while hanging one of his archaeological treasures. He underwent surgery for a fractured heel and then contracted pneumonia. During his long recuperation, he assigned the Mancuso case to one of his junior associates, Katherine Alfieri.

When Hallinan returned he finally managed to convince Mancuso that there was no other way forward. He negotiated a plea agreement assuring Mancuso's 'full and complete cooperation and truthful testimony'. In exchange, the government dropped charges against Andrea Mancuso and allowed the couple to keep more than $1 million cash in Swiss and Austrian bank accounts and property worth up to $3 million.

It was a sweet deal. Mancuso had been facing a life sentence but, under the terms of the agreement, the government agreed to seek only ten years in prison. Hallinan was elated with the results of his negotiations and had every reason to believe his client would be too.

On 27 September 1990, Mancuso was due to plead guilty in

federal court to charges of operating a continuing criminal enter-prise and evading taxes. Minutes before the hearing was due to begin, Hallinan met with his client in his holding cell. Exactly what was discussed is not clear but the conversation ended with a furious Mancuso sacking his lawyer, claiming he showed little or no compassion for his client's situation.

Mancuso not only fired Hallinan but he also hired Kate Alfieri, the woman who had taken over the case in Hallinan's absence, to whom he had grown close. Alfieri promptly quit Hallinan's firm and set up her own practice.

And that was when the worm began to turn. Mancuso worked out that there was someone above him in the conspiracy that he could testify about after all.

'Kate comes in to my office and she says, "I'm leaving, and I'm taking Ciro with me." And I said, "You can't do that, Kate,"' said Hallinan. 'And she says, "I'm doing it, and I'll tell you what. I will keep Ciro quiet about you. I won't testify against you." I said, "Bullshit, Kate, you've got nothing to testify about."'

A few weeks later, Mancuso was released on bail. He had begun informing and found that once he started talking, he could not stop. Credible, believable and articulate with detailed information, he enabled the government to indict a further twenty-five defendants and seize a further $15 million in assets. And then Patrick Hallinan received a curious phone call from his former client.

'I made millions of dollars in the drug business, and the only one that has any of the money left is you,' screamed Mancuso. 'I'll guarantee you that I'll cause you to go through the same kind of shit that I've come through. And I don't care what I have to say, and I'm gonna get up there, and I'm gonna tell the truth, and I've been protecting you, and if you can't see that for yourself by now . . . then you're gonna have some big trouble and you're gonna be sorry, Patrick.'

Hallinan was stunned. 'You're – you're – that's just blackmail, Ciro,' he replied.

*　　*　　*

Another phone call between the men followed a few weeks later.

'I feel like I'm sitting here covering for you because I think you're involved in the conspiracy,' Mancuso said to Hallinan. 'And I think that if I go to them and tell them about all the shit you did with the Mexico property and all that, I think you'd be in deep shit.'

'Ciro, this is just blackmail,' Hallinan shot back. 'You're gonna blackmail me? Ciro, look here, this is bullshit.'

'Well if you think it's bullshit, fine,' said Mancuso. 'If you think it's all bullshit, I'll just go tell the Feds about it and you can deal with them . . . cause I think they'll make your life miserable.'

Thanks to Mancuso's testimony, the DEA had made dozens of extra raids and arrests in connection with his operation. But they had saved the biggest one until last.

Hallinan recalls: 'I was working in my library, and I saw these two figures come out of the kitchen and up the stairs. And they had machine guns. And they ordered me on the floor, and I thought, "My God, they're going to rob the house." And then they stood up, and I saw across their chest "DEA", and I realised that these were the cops, and I had this feeling of relief. And then it dawned on me that they weren't there by accident.'

At the heart of Mancuso's testimony was the allegation that it was Hallinan, not he, who was in charge of the marijuana smuggling operation. Hallinan had spent thousands of hours in court over the course of his career but never before had faced such a battle. The stakes were high. If he lost he would spend the rest of his life behind bars. Most sickeningly of all, he would be in prison while Mancuso would be free.

In his 1963 autobiography, *A Lion in Court*, the legendary San Francisco lawyer Vincent Hallinan warned: 'When you go into a law case, you must remember that difficulties do not come from your opponent. Often the greatest danger is your own client.'

As Patrick 'Butch' Hallinan made his way to the Reno court

house on the morning of 26 January 1995 for the first day of his trial on charges of conspiracy to smuggle marijuana, money laundering and running a criminal enterprise, his father's prophetic words were ringing in his ears.

'One minute I was doing my job to the best of my ability, the next I was quite literally fighting for my life. They wanted my house, my law office and $20 million. Everything I had ever worked for was on the line.'

By then more than seventy people had been arrested and charged in connection with Ciro Mancuso's smuggling operation during an investigation that had lasted almost fifteen years, but Hallinan himself was the first to actually face a jury.

The others had simply pleaded guilty or struck up deals with the prosecution, but for Hallinan there was never even the merest shadow of a doubt that he would go to trial. For his defence he hired John Keker, one of the few San Francisco lawyers with a reputation equal to his own.

Keker would require every ounce of his skill to win the case. Hallinan was just as much a product of the hippy counter-culture as the parade of drug dealers that would be lining up to give evidence against him. In ultra-liberal California, where possession of a small amount of marijuana is a misdemeanour, this had always played in his favour. In Nevada with its older, far more conservative population, where possession of even a small amount of marijuana is a felony, it was a distinct disadvantage.

And here was a case involving 84 tons of the stuff.

Hallinan was revered and respected throughout San Francisco but a virtual unknown in Reno. The jury would therefore be far more willing to believe anything bad they might hear about him from the prosecution.

In order to properly gauge just how much of a problem this was going to be, Keker arranged to hold a couple of mock trials. He wanted to see exactly how the evidence would play out among a jury chosen from a typical cross-section of Reno's elderly and blue-collar workers.

The result was disappointing to say the least. Although the prosecution case rested almost entirely on the testimony of self-confessed drug dealers, each of whom had been promised leniency in return for their cooperation, the attitude of the jurors was that they assumed the government would not have gone to all the trouble of cutting the deals unless the man in the dock was a bigger target than all of them combined. The conclusion made flesh of Hallinan's worst fears: he would be seen as a guilty man from the moment he stepped into the courtroom.

The prosecution case was simple: in essence, it was Hallinan, not Ciro Mancuso, who had been at the head of the smuggling organisation.

By the time of the trial the original indictment had been superseded five times, the charges against Hallinan becoming ever more serious with each new revision. He was ultimately accused of, amongst other things, helping to launder drug proceeds, coaching members on the gang on how to lie to the grand jury, helping members of the gang to flee to countries with no extradition treaties.

By far the most serious charge was that Hallinan had conspired to smuggle and distribute marijuana, an allegation which, if proved, would enable the prosecution to state that Hallinan had been part of every single drug venture the gang was involved in since 1977.

'Each one got worse and worse and worse, so that in the first one I was really accused as being the *consiglieri* of this marijuana-smuggling ring. In the last indictment, I was charged under RICO with a racketeering – a racketeering charge, which would have put me in prison for the rest of my life. And when you read that indictment, it sounded like I was the *capo* who was doing the smuggling and planning the operations and marketing the goods. It was ludicrous, but deadly. It was very dangerous.'

The indictment also alleged that Hallinan shielded Mancuso through phony fee deals and the acceptance of cash for fees.

Mancuso told federal agents that he paid around $1.2 million to Hallinan during the course of their relationship, often in cash. About half the money went to Hallinan's fees and the rest to pay other prominent Bay Area criminal lawyers to represent other members of the Mancuso ring. Under White's obstruction theory, Hallinan told these lawyers to stop their clients from cooperating.

Two members of Mancuso's gang claimed that Hallinan had advised them to lie to the grand jury while others said he told them to flee the country. One said Hallinan told him to bury his money in the ground. Finally, while Hallinan was pressuring Mancuso to strike a deal, Hallinan warned him not to mention the fact that his lawyers were involved.

Anthony White was used to fighting uphill battles and had never lost a case, no matter how great the odds. In 1988 he had prosecuted a Nevada-based amphetamine ring in one of the longest federal trials in US history. During the sixteen months in court, White was the sole prosecutor up against a team of fifteen defenders. All were convicted.

But White still knew that his entire case rested on the credibility of Mancuso and the other members of his drugs gang, all of whom had been promised greatly reduced sentences in return for their testimony. It was an issue he addressed with his very first words to the jury.

'When the play is cast in hell,' he said as he paced back and forth across the courtroom floor, 'don't expect angels for actors. That's an adage used in law enforcement. Unfortunately, we don't write the script.'

He went on to describe Mancuso's massive drug conspiracy and the role of the accused. 'Mr Hallinan was house counsel of this enterprise, willing to do anything to protect it as long as he was handsomely paid. And he was handsomely paid. This enterprise represented a cash cow from Mr Hallinan's perspective. Greed and a personal sense of immunity drove him over the line.

And he didn't just cross the line once; he repeatedly took quantum leaps into the criminal underworld.'

Keker countered with an equally robust opening of his own. 'There is something deeply wrong with the case. The men on whose testimony most of the government's case is based have a motive to trade false testimony, any testimony, against Mr Hallinan for lenient treatment. Watch their eyes. They are desperate men. They are facing life sentences. They haven't been sentenced yet . . . One of the appropriate things you want to consider is, are they telling a story here?

'The prosecution is relying on the accusations of felons who, when they sought bail just a few short months ago, this same prosecutor argued to the judge that they were a danger to the community and should not be out amongst decent people. Others have even been allowed to keep some of their ill-gotten gains. In exchange for their testimony, half a dozen drug smugglers hope to receive lenient sentences and will be permitted to keep millions of dollars in drug profits. In some cases, the government has agreed to forgive taxes owed on millions of dollars in drug proceeds and has even helped some of the dealers to obtain money seized in overseas banks.'

He turned to face his client. 'This is one of the best-loved, most respected people in the San Francisco Bay Area. Patrick is one of the best criminal lawyers in the United States, willing to stand up for his clients and take on the government if necessary.'

Hallinan's defence was straightforward. Anything he did was simply in the performance of his duty as Mancuso's lawyer. Any financial transactions involved money that he genuinely believed had been earned through the real estate business. So far as he was concerned, Mancuso had given up drug smuggling in 1977.

Keker continued: 'The evidence will show that Mancuso, the architect of this case, lied to everybody. He's going to lie to you. He is a master manipulator of people and now that they've let him out, he's doing the same thing right now.'

Keker warned the jury that they could expect to find some of the smugglers 'quite charming.'

The first major government witness was Michael McCreary, a former owner of a surf shop in Half Moon Bay, a skateboard manufacturer and the man whose small package of cocaine had led to Mancuso's first major arrest, the same arrest that led him to appoint Hallinan in the first place.

McCreary had been arrested with several tons of marijuana and was facing a life sentence but had agreed to cooperate with the agents and testify against Hallinan.

He had been convicted four times of drug-related charges but the sentencing in the most recent conviction had been postponed until the end of Hallinan's trial.

Choosing his words carefully, he related how, the moment he received a subpoena to appear before a federal grand jury in Reno in 1988, he immediately sought the advice of Hallinan who told him to lie about the people he had met while carrying out criminal activities and to tell investigators that his heavy drug use over the years had impaired his memory.

'My testimony was totally untruthful,' he explained. 'Patrick told me to deny any involvement in drug smuggling after 1974. He told me that he would get me through the grand jury.'

Like each of the thirteen former drug dealers scheduled to give evidence, McCreary had spent long hours going over his testimony with federal agents. From the few details of this process disclosed to the defence, Keker had begun to see that many of the accounts started out poles apart but over time became not only more cohesive but also far more incriminating.

It seemed that, as the plea agreements had become more favourable, so the information they recalled about Patrick Hallinan became more sinister.

During his cross-examination by Keker, McCreary admitted he had told the same lie to a different lawyer, one he had hired to represent him long before his discussion with Hallinan. And he also admitted that he never had any intention of testifying honestly before the grand jury.

Not only that, Keker pointed out to the jury that in a previous case White himself described McCreary as someone with: 'a lengthy history of lying to the courts, of manipulating the system and whose word is meaningless.'

But Keker's biggest success came after McCreary detailed some of his personal involvement in Mancuso's marijuana smuggles using such stilted language that at times it almost seemed as though he was quoting direct from the indictment or at the very least repeating testimony that had been heavily rehearsed.

At one point Keker stood in front of McCreary and folded his arms. 'You're a surfer and dope smoker, right?'

'Yeah, so?'

'So when did words like "facilitate" and "utilise" enter your vocabulary?'

If the jury weren't already convinced that McCreary had been coached and told to stick to a pre-arranged script, they became so as the cross-examination went on.

Struggling to recall what he was supposed to say, McCreary turned to the judge at one point and pleaded: 'Your honour, am I allowed to answer in my own words?'

At the end of the first week even the presiding judge, Howard McKibben, was describing White's conspiracy theory as 'amorphous, at best'. Despite its solid foundations, the first cracks in the prosecution case were starting to appear.

When Mancuso himself took the stand, Keker chipped away at his credibility by confronting him with inconsistencies in his testimony.

Keker accused Mancuso of lying to federal investigators, to the Internal Revenue Service, to the court in his recent divorce proceedings, and to his lawyers, including Hallinan and his current attorney, Katherine Alfieri.

After denying that he had lied to conceal assets, evade taxes and minimise his involvement in smuggling ventures during the late eighties, Mancuso attributed some inconsistent statements to 'misunderstandings' and gradually acknowledged that he some-times withheld information.

'At some point, I did not tell exactly the truth about everything,' he said. 'I didn't practise lying to my lawyers very much. What's true,' he said, referring to his divorce battle with his wife over the division of property, 'changes as you gain knowledge. Most of the time it was just omissions.'

By the end Keker managed to get Mancuso to admit that he lied habitually to his lawyers. 'Tell the jury your practice when it came to lying to your lawyers,' Keker asked.

'Sometimes,' Mancuso replied, 'when a question was asked, I didn't answer. Sometimes I didn't tell them everything the way it was.'

As the trial wore on Judge McKibben grew so frustrated with Mancuso's constant obfuscation that he issued repeated warnings for him to answer the questions directly instead of going all around the houses.

The theory was that Hallinan had been motivated by greed, but even that allegation fell down under closer examination. The evidence showed that Hallinan made around $400,000 for repre-senting Mancuso over a ten-year period, a reasonable sum for a top-of-the-line defence lawyer. As further proof of this, the defence introduced a letter from another well-known San Francisco lawyer who had offered to handle Mancuso's drug smuggling case through trial for between $500,000 and $650,000. The lawyer was never taken on but the price tag made an impression with the jury.

It didn't make any sense. The smugglers were earning millions of dollars but, by comparison, Hallinan was getting only peanuts.

By 21 February the judge had thrown out racketeering charges against Patrick Hallinan but allowed the trial of the San Francisco defence attorney to move forward with a welter of other charges carrying potentially severe penalties.

The judge agreed with Keker that the government had failed to prove the existence of a Racketeer Influenced Corrupt Organisation (RICO), as defined by the law. No such entity served the loose confederation of smugglers as a front to conceal their activities, he concluded.

The purpose of the RICO statute, he said, 'is to prevent infiltration of organised crime into legitimate business enterprises.'

In pressing the judge to preserve the obstruction of justice charges, prosecutor Anthony White labelled as 'absolute falsehood' statements that Hallinan had made on behalf of Mancuso at the smuggler's bail hearing on 31 October 1989, a week after his arrest.

During bail hearings, defence attorneys cast their clients in the most positive light to win their release from custody. It is a ritual of legal representation, but White attacked Hallinan, saying he deliberately covered up Mancuso's activities and then stood before a judge and knowingly 'lied to him'.

Keker fired back that the government had taken Hallinan's statements from the bail hearing out of context to use against him. 'Lawyer argument is not evidence but opinion,' Keker said.

The defence case opened with a parade of notable lawyers from around the country, all of whom spoke about Hallinan's great honesty and character.

Four weeks into the trial Patrick Hallinan himself took the witness stand. Frequently addressing the jurors as 'ladies and gentlemen', he described how his relationship with his former client deteriorated after he discovered that the smuggler had repeatedly lied to him and manipulated people.

When Hallinan testified, he said he first helped Mancuso in 1974. After that, he heard from him three years later when two people were arrested trying to bring in a shipment of marijuana from Thailand. Following that, Hallinan told the court that Mancuso insisted his drug dealing days were over: 'He said to me, "I've learned my lesson. I don't need this any more". By then Mancuso had a successful construction business.'

By the time Hallinan urged Mancuso to plead guilty to spare his family from more grief, he had learned from other smugglers that his client was far more involved in the conspiracy than he had acknowledged. 'My attitude and my view of Mancuso had clearly degenerated because I had come to the conclusion that Ciro Mancuso was one of the most exploitative psychopaths that I had ever met.'

Hallinan claimed that Mancuso had underhandedly impregnated his wife to gain sympathy from the court and had enticed his carpenters to carry drug money to Hong Kong, when they could ill afford to defend themselves.

'He used and exploited people and he was a singular liar,' Hallinan said. 'He was a liar with no remorse. It was like falling into a pit of mud. You could never grab hold of it to pull yourself up.'

He paused for a moment then scratched his nose and smiled. 'Maybe the best bit of lawyering I ever did for Ciro Mancuso was to provide him a way to get out of jail,' he said, drawing a laugh from jurors and spectators alike.

Hallinan told the jury that his nearly twenty-year relationship with Mancuso was, with a few exceptions, 'always an attorney-client relationship.' But as law enforcement agents tightened their net on Mancuso in the late eighties, Hallinan said that he began developing 'lots and lots of scepticism about the things Ciro Mancuso was telling me.'

Nevertheless, he had an obligation to 'fight like the dickens for my client and get him out of jail. That's my duty.'

Hallinan did acknowledge receiving large cash payments, including one payment delivered to his office in a cardboard box, but said there was nothing wrong with receiving his fees in cash.

In 1982, Hallinan said, he and his wife travelled to Mexico to help Mancuso sell some property near Guadalajara. Hallinan said the trip 'was more of a lark than anything else' and said he had been convinced the sale was a legitimate transaction.

At the last minute, Mancuso claimed to have forgotten his bank account numbers. Hallinan said he had agreed to permit $180,000 in proceeds from the sale to be wired to his personal bank account in San Francisco. The prosecution said that the land sale was bogus and designed to launder drug proceeds. And they insisted Hallinan was a willing partner in the deal.

'This was something I thought was rock solid,' Hallinan said of the supposed property sale. 'I would never have transferred the money to my personal checking account if I thought it was a phoney deal, because it could be traced and would have put me in the soup.'

He had even hired Mancuso in 1981 to build an addition to his Marin County house 'because he was the only developer I knew, and he did really fine work. I, in very good faith, believed in my client. I may have been a fool to do so.'

At one point, the prosecutor White asked Hallinan to explain the phrase 'fronting for someone' as used by drug dealers.

'Mr White, I'm not in the drug world,' he responded. 'I don't deal dope, and I don't conspire with people to import dope, and I don't have anything to do with the distribution or sale of dope.'

Later Hallinan admitted that a lot of clients, such as convicted drug smuggler Ciro Mancuso, told him about their crimes during his long career as a defence attorney, but says that knowledge doesn't make him a crook, too.

'I'm a lawyer who represents people who get into trouble and get arrested. If people didn't get into trouble and get arrested, I'd go broke. In my entire lifetime, I have never conspired with anyone, anywhere to import, distribute or do anything else with marijuana,' Hallinan told the jury.

White tried a different tack. 'Isn't it fair to say you ignored the warning signs that Ciro Mancuso continued to be involved in marijuana smuggling?'

'Mr White,' Hallinan replied, 'if I were a DEA agent I would have looked for these warning signs. But I do the best I can for my client. I don't make those kind of presumptions.'

By the end of March the judge had thrown out even more charges, leaving just a handful of the original eleven remaining.

The closing arguments were every bit as robust as the opening remarks had been. With White busy with other duties, Assistant US Attorney William Welch took the honours. 'Documents do not lie and do not have a memory problem,' he said. 'The defence team is trying to smear the witnesses and hope the smear sticks. It is like the way an octopus shoots out a cloud of ink to escape danger, hoping the attacker will lose his way. Every time the defence gets desperate to disprove something, they put out a new cloud.

'This is a case about a lawyer who crossed the line between legal and illegal. This is not a case about Ciro Mancuso versus Patrick Hallinan.'

But Keker countered by arguing that the case was indeed just that: 'This is not a war on drugs. This is a war against defence lawyers. More importantly, a war against Patrick Hallinan.

'When you look at the world through dirty windows too long, everything becomes sinister. But the government cannot change the evidence in a case by clever argument; they can not turn liars into truth tellers by massaging their testimony for thousands of hours.'

Keker reminded the jury that seven of the thirteen felons called to testify against Hallinan had yet to be sentenced and had been promised leniency. 'Who wouldn't tell the government whatever they wanted to hear for rewards like this? The word gets around that crime does pay, if you work for the DEA and the IRS.'

The closing arguments did not conclude until after 8 p.m. so the jury did not begin their deliberations until the following morning. Four hours in, the foreman sent the judge a note saying they were ready to return to court.

It had been such a short time that Anthony White was convinced that they could not possibly have reached a verdict so quickly. Instead, he assumed they wanted to clarify a point of law or perhaps have a portion of testimony repeated to them. He was wrong. The jury had decided the case and found Patrick Hallinan not guilty on all counts.

'Wanna know how I feel?' Hallinan beamed at reporters as he left the courthouse-building a free man. 'Once the great sense of relief of having the angel of death floating over me wears off, then I can express my anger at what was a vicious and concentrated attack on the right of the defence bar to stand up and vigorously defend people against accusations by the government. That's what this case is all about. Vindicated? No, I don't feel vindicated, because I never felt guilty.'

Hallinan later spoke to the jury foreman, thanking him for the decision. 'He told me that while they were in the jury room, someone had said 'surely the government wouldn't have brought this case unless there was some truth in it.' In reply the foreman said: 'I used to be in the marines and I was fighting in Cambodia at a time when the government was going on the record and insisting that no American troops were there. Of course they lie.'

White's prosecution team were beginning to realise that they had made exactly the same mistake as Patrick Hallinan: they had stuck with Ciro Mancuso for too long.

As one courtroom observer put it, the government's case could be neatly summed up with an old Nevada saying: big hat, no cattle.

In June 1995 Mancuso returned to court to be sentenced for his crimes.

Despite glowing testimonials that Mancuso had devoted most of the last five years to helping government agents dismantle the organisation he had helped create in the seventies and eighties, he received a nine-year sentence.

His attorney, Katherine Alfieri, argued eloquently for probation and some form of community service. 'Justice does not require the incarceration of a rehabilitated man,' she said.

In his own impassioned statement to the judge, Mancuso said:

'I felt it was essential to destroy the organisation that I had helped to build . . . and the organisation became extinct . . . I'm appalled with myself. I'm going to have to live with that for the rest of my life.'

But the judge, noting that the importation of 66,900 pounds of Thai marijuana equates to more than 59 million joints, said zealous cooperation alone is 'not enough to zero things out.'

In the absence of his assistance, Mancuso would have faced a term of around sixty years, but although he kept his composure in court, inside he was furious.

'I can't think of anything possibly that I could have done for them [the government] that I didn't do. It was implied that if my cooperation went well, that that was my part of it, and then that their part of it was to go to the judge and to make sure that I was fairly treated – in other words, that vast, tremendous consideration would be given to what I had done at time of sentencing.

'The prosecution lost. And being on their team, the blame for that, I believe, was shifted as much as possible to me. And at that point, the betrayal set in. I believe that had the prosecution won the case and gotten a conviction against Hallinan that I would not have come back to prison at all.'

32
A CHANCE ENCOUNTER

Michael Forwell always hoped he would be the one to get away with it.

Almost five years after the capture of the *Encounter Bay* he was still at liberty, still in possession of tens of millions of dollars and enjoying his new, quiet life to the full.

Over the years he had seen and heard snippets of information about how the other members of The Ring had been faring. The Shaffer brothers had been caught, as had most of the people who ever worked for them. Brian Daniels was behind bars, as were his one-time partners the Colflesh brothers.

Even David Ortiz – the man who had helped found the market for Thai marijuana by importing small loads by military mail during the mid-seventies and then graduated to become one of the leading offloading organisations on the West Coast had been jailed, caught red handed as he tried to offload several tons of marijuana onto a beach at Santa Barbara. However, Forwell believed that the fate of the other conspirators would not happen to him. He was too well prepared, too smart and loved his freedom too much.

Anxious he might be traced, Forwell, along with his Asian-born wife May and their three young children, fled Singapore within days of the *Encounter Bay* being seized and started moving from country to country under a succession of false names and bogus identities that soon saw their trail go completely cold.

Mark Bartlett and Fran Dyer busied themselves searching for the other fugitives from The Ring but at the start of 1993 the investigators received evidence that pointed to Forwell now living in England.

The evidence had come from an unlikely source – Forwell's mother in Australia. Unbeknownst to her, police had been monitoring her mail and soon found evidence that her son had applied for a false passport in the name of Charles Michael Young and was living somewhere in north-west London.

The collaboration with Scotland Yard had produced excellent results last time around when it came to tracking down the Shaffer brothers so Bartlett asked Fran Dyer to get back on the phone to the International Organised Crime Unit. By then Saltmarsh had moved on and instead Dyer found himself speaking to a soft-voiced Welshman, Detective Sergeant David Jones. An enthusiastic sportsman who had been forced to retire from rugby after cracking his skull, Jones was a twenty-year veteran of the murder squad and an expert at tracking fugitives. DS Jones decided to start his investigation at the UK Passport Office headquarters in south London.

Although the team had a likely address for Forwell, Jones didn't want to spook his target by making even a casual approach. 'You only get one chance with fugitives. If you mess it up, then you lose them for good,' he explains.

He spent the next few days at the Passport Office, searching records issued in 1988. It was a daunting task. Back then the records were not computerised and were listed only by date of birth. DS Jones had no choice but to get through each and every paper application by hand and examine the accompanying photograph. When that first search failed to produce any results, Jones went back to 1987. Again nothing, so he tried 1986.

Incredibly, it paid off. He found himself staring at a photograph of Michael Forwell from an application for a passport in the name of Michael Charles Young. By then the application was almost six years old so Jones was not at all surprised when the address listed – Manchester Street – turned out to be empty.

Jones ran a credit card check and found one in Young's name matching the birthdate used on the passport form. A recent transaction was for petrol in a north London garage. DS Jones went there and demanded to see the CCTV footage. The car concerned was a dark-coloured Volvo driven by a young woman.

A check of the Volvo's registration with the relevant authorities produced a new address: 351 West End Lane, London, NW6. The net was closing in.

The address belonged to a shop. 'Dream Street Designs Arts and Antiques' was written in large gold letters on the pane of green glass that faced the street.

Jones decided to set up a surveillance operation and drafted in a couple of plain-clothes officers to help him to watch the property. The following morning the front door opened and three small children trooped out. The woman shepherding them towards the car was Asian, in her thirties. Jones immediately recognised her from the video in the garage forecourt. By now a rough image had been sent to Seattle and Dyer had identified the woman as May Forwell, Michael's wife.

DS Jones picked up his radio and spoke to his colleagues. 'I'm going to go after her. You guys stay here and watch the house.'

For the next twenty minutes Jones carefully followed the Volvo at a discreet distance as it navigated its way north and east through rush hour traffic. At 9 a.m. they were approaching Hampstead Heath when the Volvo indicated right and pulled into a narrow, gravel-filled driveway. Jones made a note of the address and soon learned it was the King Alfred School. A discreet call to the headmaster confirmed that the Young children had been attending since September 1992.

Jones could feel he was getting close. Forwell had always been portrayed as a man who absolutely doted on his children and was unable to go more than a few days without seeing them. He stepped up his surveillance and within a day he and six colleagues watched 351 West End Lane, twenty-four hours a day, seven days a week. But nothing happened. They took turns to shadow May Forwell. Most days after dropping the children she went into the West End, giving her pursuers a guided tour of some of the best clothes shops and restaurants the capital has to offer, but no sign of her husband.

After nearly two weeks Jones was getting frustrated. What on earth was going on? As with police forces around the world, Jones had to keep one eye on his budget and could not continue such intense surveillance indefinitely, especially when there was no sign of any progress and even less guarantee of getting any kind of a satisfactory result.

On the twentieth day a large white Transit van parked outside number 351. A tall, well-built man in faded jeans and a pale green sweatshirt jumped down from the cab. Jones quickly swung his binoculars into position but could not get a full view of his face. The height and build were spot on. So was the man's hair colour. Could it be Forwell at last?

The man went into the shop. Now the van stood between Jones and a clear sighting. A few minutes later the man came back out but Jones again could not see exactly who he was. He had to make a split-second decision. Should he follow him or not? Should he make the arrest? He told his men to stay where they were. The van drove away. Jones couldn't help wonder whether he had just missed his one and only chance to catch his fugitive.

Two days later the van was back. This time the driver was an Asian man in his thirties. As it left number 351 Jones made a decision to go after it. It pulled up outside a large detached house just north of Finchley Road, halfway between the house and the school, the kind of well-heeled suburb Jones had imagined Forwell living in.

But instead of going inside the house the driver made off down an alleyway. Jones could feel the adrenaline rising in his body. The property at 351 West End Lane had never seemed quite plush enough for Forwell to be living in. He had long suspected that there was another address, perhaps nearby, which was also in use. Now it seemed as thought the driver of the van was going to lead him right to it.

Leaving two officers to watch the house, Jones hurried after the Asian man on foot. For ten minutes he pursued him through a maze of suburban streets. Jones moved quickly, keeping to the shadows wherever he could, anxious not to allow himself to be seen. The man crossed the street several times and sometimes changed direction at the last minute. It was almost as if he was aware he was being watched and was trying to lose his pursuer. None of the man's tricks caused Jones any problems and he continued the pursuit.

And then Jones found himself back in a road that he recognised: West End Lane. The Asian man went through the door of 351 and vanished. 'My hopes had risen. I really thought I had him, but the whole thing just turned out to be some kind of security precaution,' says Jones. By the end of another week Jones felt completely and utterly deflated. Trying to catch Michael Forwell was like trying to catch the wind.

The following day Jones was back on the phone with Fran Dyer in Seattle who had a new suggestion. Dyer had learned that Forwell had often laundered his money by buying and selling antiques. It was possible that, with cash being hard to come by, he might have taken to selling some of his rarer specimens.

Jones sent a female detective posing as a shopper into Dream Street Designs. Inside, instead of porcelain she found a wide selection of English oak and stripped pine furniture for sale.

Acting on a hunch one Sunday, Jones decided to check out Camden Lock, the London market that includes old converted warehouses stuffed with antique furniture, just the kind of place a shop owner would go to source material for his business. Jones shouldered his way slowly through the crowds, sometimes going in and out of the shops. After an hour he spotted an arch on which The Stables was emblazoned in gold capital letters and walked under it into a cul-de-sac of Victorian warehouses. A large sign on the wall read 'restored oak furniture'. On the far side he saw a tall man with a mop of hair and DS Jones knew he was looking at Michael Forwell.

After waiting for back up, Jones moved in to make his arrest. In the seconds it took him to close the distance between them, the detective had already decided to make the arrest under a ruse. He didn't want to alert Forwell to the fact that he knew exactly who he was. He didn't want Forwell warning anyone back at West End Lane or any other property about what was happening.

Jones stood in front of Forwell and waited for him to meet his gaze. 'Michael Charles Young.'

'Yes,' said the man with a puzzled smile.

'Detective Sergeant David Jones, Scotland Yard. I am arresting you for possession of a forged passport.'

Forwell seemed unconcerned. He shrugged and went with Jones out of the market.

Jones had radioed Scotland Yard for three uniformed officers and a WPC to meet him at Forwell's house and once they arrived they found May and the children and another Asian couple waiting for them in the living room.

If May was concerned when Jones told her that he was about to search the house and the shop, she managed to hide it well. A team of detectives arrived and began to go through the place with a fine-tooth comb but it was quickly obvious that nothing incriminating was being uncovered. During the search Forwell leaned against the wall, smoked cigarettes and looked bored.

Jones moved downstairs to the basement, a makeshift office containing a large desk heaped with papers and files. As the detective sergeant scanned the bookcase a badly folded map jammed between two dusty volumes caught his eye. When he reached for it he saw Forwell staring hard at him, concern showing on his face for the first time since he had been arrested. And Jones knew he had stumbled across something crucial.

Jones pulled it out. It was a map of Queensland's Gold Coast where Forwell had been brought up. It felt strangely heavy. Jones unfolded it carefully. Inside were eleven variously shaped passport stamps. Brilliant forgeries, they were well inked and had been used frequently.

With a half smile on his face Jones looked up and stared at the fugitive. 'Michael, I know exactly who you are. I'm arresting you for drug trafficking.'

Forwell's shoulders slumped and his face fell briefly but within a second or two, he had recovered enough to put on one last-ditch display of arrogance. 'I've got nothing to hide, Jones, so I've nothing to say,' Forwell told him. 'You have just made a very big mistake.'

It was only the beginning. Like Daniels and Bill Shaffer before him, Forwell decided not to come quietly. He quickly announced his intention to fight tooth and nail against his extradition and swore that he would never end up back in the US.

As Jones gathered more information on behalf of Dyer and Bartlett, he soon found himself working on another, related case. Increasingly he became convinced that May Forwell was not the innocent housewife she had continually claimed to be. In fact, the evidence pointed to May having taken over many of her husband's business affairs since he had gone on the run. Furthermore, bank statements showed that it had been May, not Michael, who had been shifting millions through numerous bank accounts all around the world in order to disguise the couple's cash and assets.

On the day of Forwell's first court appearance for his extradition case, May did not come to court. Jones thought this was strange and, acting on another of his hunches, made a few calls to the airport authorities. He quickly learned that May had booked herself onto a flight to Singapore that evening. He had to act fast.

On her way to the airport May Forwell was arrested and charged with money laundering.

Although the suspicion was there, Jones lacked hard evidence of the crime, or at least evidence that he could understand. Dozens of thick files of lists and numbers had been uncovered at Forwell's house but even Scotland Yard's top money-laundering experts were having trouble deciphering exactly what they meant.

If they wanted to resolve the case, they needed some help. And they got it from another unlikely source. Samuel Colflesh, the man who had piloted the *Encounter Bay*, was a few months into his ten-year sentence when Bartlett and Dyer made him an offer he chose not to refuse. In return for becoming an informant in the case, Colflesh would get early release from his own sentence.

Soon Colflesh was sitting down opposite DS Jones and explaining the relevance of the lists of figures. 'These were the profit and loss accounts I prepared for our 1987 project, shipping the product into San Francisco. The code names referred to dealers on the West and East Coasts who distributed the marijuana and to crew members on *Encounter Bay*.'

Even better was to come. Colflesh had been at the Forwell's house in Singapore when crates of cash had arrived. He had seen May counting it. She had knowingly paid it into bank accounts. 'May was Michael's downfall. She knew exactly what Michael did. Her only concern was getting her hands on enough of his money to buy jewellery, property, anything to safeguard her future. If it wasn't for May bleeding Michael, he could have retired years ago a rich man.'

Jones interviewed May again in the light of the new knowledge. 'I am just an innocent housewife,' she told him repeatedly. 'I had no knowledge of my husband's business dealings. I just did what he told me to do.'

But Jones discovered that May had instructed her sister to transfer 390,000 Hong Kong dollars from a bank account in Hong Kong to one in Singapore. He also learned that May had attempted, without success, to obtain fake documents to show that the house in West End Lane had been bought with inheritance money from Michael's Scottish grandfather.

In April 1994 May went on trial at Southwark Crown Court in south London. Fran Dyer flew over to give evidence, as did Sam Colflesh and Larry Brant. She was found guilty and sentenced to three years in prison and made to forfeit assets of £750,000.

Judge Mota Singh told her: 'It is not disputed that your husband was involved in trafficking on a massive scale. Your defence was that you had no knowledge of his activities. The jury verdict shows you knew and you helped him to launder the profits.'

On the same day May Forwell was sentenced, Michael Forwell had his latest appeal against extradition to the United States turned down in the High Court. For the next year he tried to postpone the inevitable for as long as possible but then all of a sudden, he simply gave up. And that was when things became a good deal more sinister.

In the late spring of 1995, shortly before Michael Forwell suddenly gave up his extradition battle, Scotland Yard had received two credible pieces of information about him.

The first was that while he had been held at Belmarsh maximum security prison in south London, Forwell had struck up a friendship with a man known to have worked as a professional hitman. Forwell had offered the man, who was due to be released from Belmarsh in the very near future, a substantial sum of money to execute several officers linked to Forwell's case. Top of the list was Detective Sergeant David Jones.

The second piece of information was that Forwell had used his substantial resources to fund a plan to have him sprung from court during his final appearance.

'This was all happening around the time that Forwell threw in the towel over the extradition thing,' says Jones. 'It made everyone very nervous and suspicious. His mood changed and he seemed very calm and calculated. He was looking at twenty-five years but he had the money to buy himself out of pretty much any situation! We all knew he must have had his reasons and we couldn't help but think that the threats we had heard about were a big part of it.'

The revelations added a new level of complexity to the task of getting Forwell out of the country.

'We wanted to use a route which would be easy to protect and that we could vary at the last minute. In the end we made up three separate plans along with a couple of dummy convoys so that no one – not even those on the team – would know exactly where he was at what time.'

The initial plan had been to fly Forwell to New York. There Jones would have handed him over to the US Marshals. The plan was just about to be put into action when a lawyer from Bartlett's office phoned in a panic and told them to cancel it.

Because Forwell had been caught outside the States and the indictment had been issued in Seattle, he had to be returned to that state for the extradition to be valid. If Forwell had entered America anywhere else, the Marshals would have had no authority to hold him and he could have walked away scot-free.

'We had to take him straight to Seattle but there was only one direct flight per day from the UK, run by British Airways. That meant it would be obvious to anyone trying to spring him exactly what flight he would be going on, what airport he would be leaving from and his time of arrival and departure. Any attempt to disguise how we were going to be taking him would be impossible,' says Jones.

There were two choices. Jones could either make the trip high profile, lights flashing, motorcycle outriders and marked cars, or do things as quietly as possible.

'We decided to go for the latter. We had a team of unmarked cars, each one bristling with armed officers carrying machine guns and sidearms, hidden from public view of course but on hand at the first sign of trouble.

'We had drawn up a whole load of contingency plans for how we were going to do it but as is always the case with these things, the whole lot of them went to shit. We had three convoys, each made up of four unmarked cars, heading out at the same time. One went west, one went east and the one he was actually in went north.

'After a couple of miles one of the middle cars in the northbound convoy breaks down in the middle of the road, just grinds to a halt. All the marksmen grabbed their guns and took out defensive positions. They were convinced they were under some kind of attack. Everyone was as jumpy as hell because they'd all been briefed about the fact that a rescue attempt was such a strong possibility.'

'But then it turned out that the clutch cable had snapped. For a while no one was quite sure what to do but it turned out that the car had broken down right next to a garage used by the Metropolitan Police for some of its fleet. They grabbed Forwell and took him out of the car, surrounded by armed officers, and rushed him into the office of the garage. The poor guys who ran it must have wondered what was going on when they found themselves descended on by a dozen guys with guns. The mechanics managed to fix the car in a few minutes and Forwell was taken back so the convoy could continue on its way.'

By now the division commander at Heathrow had been informed about the dangerous prisoner who was arriving at the airport that day. Unaware of DS Jones's request for a low profile entrance, he made his own arrangements.

'As we got close to Heathrow we realised that all the approach roads had been closed off. They had brought the entire airport to a standstill and had two uniformed armed officers at the entrance to every junction. As we drove through, everyone was looking at us, a sea of noses pressed up against the glass. No one was in any doubt about what was going on.

'We made it through the terminal and there were constant sirens going off, motorcycle escorts, helicopters flying overhead. It was awful. The complete opposite of what I had wanted. It had been raining and as we made our way out on the tarmac all of the gunmen had to dive down into the puddles to take up their defensive positions. By the time we got on the plane – escorted by more uniformed armed guards – the captain was getting a bit flustered by the whole thing, wondering just what on earth the guy we were putting on his plane had done.'

'By then I was getting pissed off too. I said to the captain, "Listen, this is getting completely out of hand. If you want us to get off this plane right now that will be OK. You'll get no argument from me."'

The captain waved them through. He soon regretted it. The only seats available were in first class and a curious little boy soon began running up and down the aisles telling other passengers what was going on at the front of the plane. The passengers threatened to mutiny if Forwell wasn't taken off immediately, but the captain finally managed to calm them down and the flight got underway.

'For the first few hours, Forwell didn't say a single word. In fact the only time I heard him speak at all was when they asked if he wanted tea or coffee with his meal. He didn't even go to the toilet.'

Eventually Jones's curiosity got the better of him and he leaned over and whispered in his prisoner's ear. 'Just out of interest, just between you and me. It goes no further. How much money did you make from all this?'

Forwell's head turned slowly like a tanker taking up a new heading.

'Me personally or the whole team?'

'Both.'

'Personally, I guess $200 million. The team? Gotta be $900 million.'

He said nothing more for the rest of the journey.

There was one more scare in store for Jones. As the plane landed and taxied on the tarmac a door on the adjacent terminal flew open and a man came running out towards the plane. A split second later two more men followed, both brandishing machine guns. Jones, along with the plane's captain, thought that this was it, the attack they had all feared. In fact it was an illegal immigrant who had attempted to jump the airport's barriers and flee the authorities.

Although the rest of the exchange went without a hitch, Jones believes to this day that Forwell had set up an escape scheme and somehow, his plans had not come to fruition.

'At the end of the day, I think he had something in mind. I don't know why he suddenly gave up the fight for extradition. The record is seven years and he was nowhere near that. Even if the Home Secretary says you have to go back, you still have the right to a further appeal so you can make it go on a long time.

'We lost a lot of things that we should have been able to track down. We traced assets worth more than £10 million but we know there was a lot more where that came from. Forwell had a collection of antiques worth hundreds of thousands of pounds that we never managed to find. We didn't get to the Cook Islands where he had several bank accounts and we know he had assets spread out all across the world.

'We know he wasn't sleeping at 351 West End Lane either. Somewhere out there was another property. Whatever assets we failed to find, I have a feeling he has probably managed to hold on to. When he finally gets out, it may well all be there waiting for him.'

33
THE TAKE

The arrest and imprisonment of Brian Daniels, the Shaffer brothers, Ciro Mancuso, Michael Forwell and the rest of The Ring had seemingly all but crippled the entire global trade in Thai marijuana.

Within two years of the *Encounter Bay* seizure, virtually all of the leading American smugglers who had once rubbed shoulders at the Superstar bar and made millions through their domination of the multi-ton load business had been indicted or arrested. Within five years the vast majority were in custody.

Daniels' domination of the supply end of the chain had depended largely upon his ability to deal with growers and corrupt government officials, as well as his personal relationship with the Chinese drug lords who dominate the northern region of that country.

The drug lords, who included former military commanders and criminals who fled China during the communist revolution, controlled fiefdoms in northern Thailand and parts of Burma and Laos. Having seen the potential profits that could be made from the drug market they began to demand payoffs for allowing their territory to be used for marijuana, hashish and heroin cultivation.

With Daniels out of the picture, only one other man could come close to exerting that kind of influence and therefore be in a position to step in and fill the vacuum: Thanong Siripreechapong, better known as Thai Tony.

One of the few people to benefit directly from the collapse of the Brian Daniels' ring and the failure of all the major smugglers to successfully land any shipments during the whole of 1988, Thai Tony had swiftly stepped up his own level of production to meet demand.

In late 1988, soon after the debacle of the *Encounter Bay*, Tony supplied an 8,000-pound load that was brought into Shelter Cove, California, by sailboat. The drugs were sold for $10.5 million of which Tony received just under $2 million. It was the first successful major importation of Thai marijuana that year.*

An unsuccessful boatload followed so Thai Tony switched tactics and began concealing his drugs in 40-foot containers which were then loaded onto commercial ships in Bangkok. He was paid more for a container-load than a boatload because he had to pay off more people for using containers and because containers held more product that boats.

He also tried to launch a smuggle using a DC6 plane which would be flown from a military airport in Vietnam or Laos to Alaska, and then into Washington State. Hundreds of thousands of dollars were invested in the scheme but Tony fell out with the pilots and the plan was ultimately abandoned.

By now Tony was working with distributors based in California, Idaho, New York and Mexico and the trade had started to move away from the 'idealistic hippy' era that Daniels and the Shaffer brothers had presided over. Thai marijuana was now profitable enough to attract investors from organised crime proper. In New York, Tony's main contact at the docks where his containers arrived was connected to the Genovese family, one of New York's five Mafia mobs.

Unfortunately for Tony, the quality-control problems that had affected his past dealings with the likes of the Shaffers were still apparent. Arriving in Los Angeles to collect payment

---

* Ciro Mancuso had put three loads on the water in 1988. The first had
 been seized in Australia, the second was jettisoned on approach to
 California after the crew learned that their companion vessel had been
 seized down under. The third was found on the abandoned Japy Hermes.

from one group of smugglers, Tony was told that he would receive only half of what he had been promised because the marijuana had been substandard and was selling for a much lower price.

Thai Tony had always been something of a hothead and had earned himself a reputation for having a fearsome temper. Following a huge argument in Beverly Hills over a $3 million down payment for a future shipment with one of his long-term contacts, Tony allegedly pulled out a gun and began shooting at his smuggling partners.

'He shot at us point blank range in Beverly Hills,' the man recalled. 'Seven shots. I dove over a Cadillac, the adrenalin going. I mean, fuck. When they start shooting, especially a partner you've been with since day fucking one, you know it's been a tough road, man.'

None of the bullets found their target and Tony escaped from the scene before the police arrived, but he was becoming increasingly isolated. Believing he was safe just so long as he spent most of his time in Thailand, Tony had no idea that his days were in fact numbered.

The Pacific North-west may have been the scene of many of the largest importations of Thai marijuana, and the Seattle office of the US Attorney may have been responsible for the majority of the indictments of members of The Ring, but it was far from the only authority involved.

William LaMorte had been tried in the Eastern District of New York, Tom Sherrett had been taken down by prosecutors based in Oregon, a team operating out of Reno, Nevada, had led the case against both Ciro Mancuso and the $7 million seized in a casino laundering sting.

Mark Bartlett and Fran Dyer watched all these cases with particular interest, but Thai Tony had remained a source of some frustration for them. He had been the source of supply for at least two shipments organised by the Shaffer brothers, yet despite reams of testimony from the brothers, themselves as well as the likes of Terry Restall, the Seattle office had not managed to gather sufficient evidence to launch a full investigation into the man's activities.

When news began to circulate in confidential law enforcement circles that Thai Tony was finally being looked at, Bartlett and Dyer could not help but feel a tiny thrill. With the exception of Irwin 'Sonny' Kletter, Tony was the last remaining person connected to The Ring who had not yet been brought to justice.

This time around the investigation was being run out of San Francisco, the Northern District of California, and the lead agency was the US Customs service.

At a time when, thanks to the infiltration of the Brian Daniels organisation by the likes of Larry Brant and the two fake Mafia men, criminals and drug smugglers were becoming increasingly wary and adept at spotting undercover law enforcement agents, the San Francisco office of the Customs Service had an ace up their sleeve. His name was Frank Gervacio.

While almost all the other agents came from the same narrow range of ethnic backgrounds and spoke and acted in the same manner, Gervacio was in a league of his own.

Both his parents hailed from the Pacific Islands and he had inherited their dark skin and hair and brooding good looks that made his exact background hard to pin down. He could just as easily pass for a native of Hawaii or Samoa as someone from Vietnam or the Philippines. As one of the few ethnic minorities serving with the US Customs at that time, Gervacio's superiors quickly realised that he was a unique asset – a man who no one would ever suspect of batting for the other side.

Gervacio joined customs in 1983 and went on his first undercover mission soon after completing basic training, even though he had not received any specialised instruction in how to carry out such work.

He enjoyed the challenge and quickly chalked up a number of

successes against low-level drug gangs, but at the same time the stress of living a double life quickly began to exact a heavy toll. Gervacio began drinking heavily and he would suffer huge bouts of depression and guilt. His once strong marriage began to come under increasing strain.

Part of the problem was that, because of his lack of training, Gervacio often found himself drawn to the people he was meeting in his undercover work and would then feel guilty about having to turn them in. He had not been taught how to deal with such conflicts.

In 1987 Gervacio was introduced to Michael Woods, a small-time dealer who had been caught with a small amount of cocaine and had agreed to become an informant rather than go to jail. Woods offered to provide information about a ring of dealers operating out of San Francisco and Gervacio was assigned to be his handler.

The two men hit it off right away and what started out as a formal arrangement soon became an informal friendship. The pair began hanging out, partying and drinking together regularly, spending far more time together than was appropriate for an agent/informant relationship, though no one at customs felt it was worth broaching the subject. When Michael Woods got married, Frank Gervacio was his best man.

Woods didn't only sign up as an informant to keep himself out of jail – there were other benefits too. By way of acknowledging that the information provided by informants can often save hundreds of thousands of man hours of investigation and resolve cases that would otherwise go stale, US Customs, in keeping with other law enforcement agencies, pay cash rewards for information, many of them substantial.

One of Woods's first tips involved a Thai marijuana-smuggling ring based in California and run by the same man that Thai Tony had shot at during the dispute over the missing $3 million. Following on from the information that he had received, Gervacio tracked down a 40-foot container that had been shipped to

Washington State from Thailand with nearly nine tons of marijuana inside.

In September 1989, police officers in San Francisco spotted a car being driven erratically in the early hours of the morning and pulled it over. Frank Gervacio was behind the wheel and Michael Woods was beside him. The pair had been out drinking heavily to celebrate Woods's reward pay cheque, which Gervacio had secured for him for the tip about the marijuana container. It had totalled more than $15,000.

The police officer waited until Gervacio rolled down his window. The smell of alcohol on the man's breath hit him instantly.

'Licence and registration please.'

'Sure,' said Gervacio. 'Let me give you this too.' He handed over a small black folder. Inside was a badge identifying him as a special agent of the US Customs Service.

'I'm on duty,' Gervacio continued, his words slurred and his eyes glassy. 'I'm here with my CI. I'm working.'

'Where you going?'

Gervacio paused for a moment then giggled. 'We're on our way to buy a truck.'

The officer glanced at his watch. 'At 1 a.m.?'

Gervacio had no reply.

Gervacio was charged with DUI but was never disciplined for the incident by his bosses at customs. As for his relationship with Woods, if anything the pair grew closer.

'Everyone knew that Frank had a drinking problem,' says one former colleague. 'But there were too few non-Americans to go around to work the undercover cases. He was still delivering the goods so everyone just turned a blind eye.'

Back at work Gervacio continued to investigate the source of the marijuana in the container. As he did so, the name of 'Thai Tony' had kept cropping up as the driving force behind the shipment. All that Gervacio knew in those early days was that Tony was a Thai citizen, fabulously wealthy and one of the biggest suppliers of marijuana to the American market.

The sources he had cultivated suggested that Thai Tony had been involved in supplying drugs since the early seventies, but it was here that Gervacio made his first mistake. With no proper way of identifying exactly who Thai Tony was, some of his informants got confused between the original Thai Tony who had supplied Ciro Mancuso and the Coronado Company, and Thanong Siripreechapong who began using the same title following the death of the original Thai Tony.

Unaware of his confusion, Thai Tony seemed to be a lead worth pursuing, the kind of case that could make an agent's career. Little did Gervacio know that the investigation would mark the beginning of his own demise.

By May 1991, Frank Gervacio's life was going from bad to worse.

Although he had only just finished his last high-risk undercover assignment, he was told to report to the docks for a new mission to infiltrate a massive drug ring led by a notorious Canadian smuggler planning to bring a load of hashish into the States.

Confidential informants within his organisation had tipped off customs that a vast and highly sophisticated importation was being planned and the undercover officers had managed to get the smugglers to agree to use their boat as the offload vessel. The team negotiated a payment of $3.25 million for the job and had already received $400,000 in advance.

The target was a boat called the *Lucky Star* and was carrying up to 100 tons of hashish. It was one of the biggest operations that the San Francisco office of US Customs had ever undertaken and the agents involved were under intense pressure to ensure the whole thing went off without a hitch.

It was not to be.

The undercover vessel met up with the *Lucky Star* in the middle of the ocean and came alongside in order to allow the smugglers to transfer the drugs. Without them, the government would have no evidence against the smugglers.

The weather had been appalling by the time the customs officers spotted the *Lucky Star* and got steadily worse the closer they got to their target. By now it was the middle of the night – the preferred time for such transfers as there is less chance of being spotted by surveillance aircraft or other vessels. But the darkness also made it near impossible to judge the sea conditions. As Gervacio and the others attempted to tie up along side, huge swells appeared out of nowhere, smashing two boats against one another with enormous force.

The *Lucky Star*, by far the bigger of the two, was in little danger from these encounters but it was clear that the undercover vessel could easily be sunk. Conditions were grim and, though the crew had lifejackets, they did not have enough survival suits to go around. If they ended up in the water, some of them were going to die.

The customs officer in charge of the operation sent a message back to headquarters telling his superiors that conditions were simply too bad and the transfer could not take place. He received a stark message in reply: 'Don't even think about coming back here without those drugs!'

The crew were forced to try to make the transfer again and again over the next four days. Several times the huge waves threatened to engulf the undercover vessel; the sound of metal smashing against metal seemed to signal a hole being torn in the hull of the small ship that would send them down to the bottom of the ocean. Time and time again Gervacio and his colleagues were convinced they were all about to die. By the end of the four days they had managed to take on board just 2.4 tons out of the 100 tons the *Lucky Star* was carrying. Each and every member of the undercover team, but Gervacio in particular, had been pushed to the edge of trauma.

The battered ship finally received permission to return to San Francisco while other customs and coastguard vessels went after the *Lucky Star*. The job had been a success but only just. In the days, weeks and months that followed, Frank Gervacio's condition began to deteriorate rapidly. Although he continued to work, no one realised that he was on the verge of a massive nervous breakdown.

In November 1991, a grand jury was convened in San Francisco, under the jurisdiction of the Northern District of California, to hear evidence about an alleged kingpin involved in the supply of marijuana to the United States.

The case was a relatively simple one by grand jury standards. There was only one witness: Special Agent Frank Gervacio.

The members of the jury listened in silence as Gervacio explained that Thanong Siripreechapong was involved in smuggling, conspiracy to smuggle and had operated a continuing criminal enterprise since 1973.

These were serious charges. Should the grand jury choose to indict, each charge would have been punishable by ten years to life in prison along with a fine of up to $4 million. But Thanong was a major player in the drug world, operating at the very highest level.

Gervacio explained that Thanong had been responsible for smuggling around 45 tons of marijuana into the United States over a fourteen-year period. The money he had earned had been used to buy property including a $1 million home in Beverly Hills and a Mercedes Benz.

Gervacio made it clear that, while his information had come from two drug dealers who had decided to cooperate with the government, one of them had been jailed in Oregon while the other was in prison in California.

A grand juror asked, 'In other words, they didn't have an opportunity – is this true, Agent Gervacio – to talk to each other and to make up a story together?'

'That's right,' Gervacio replied. 'There would have been no opportunity for them to collaborate over the evidence.'

Gervacio further testified that Thanong had been responsible for pioneering a method of smuggling using commercial containers, that he had gathered many of his facts from first-hand interviews with witnesses and that similar conclusions had been drawn by other agents involved in parallel investigations.

The evidence was powerful and compelling. In fact, the only shortcoming of Gervacio's testimony was that none of it was true. A borderline alcoholic with a failing marriage and a continuing improper relationship with his informant, Gervacio was not fit to be making a presentation to the grand jury at all.

There was, of course, clear evidence that Thanong had been involved in supplying marijuana that was smuggled to the United States, but Gervacio had drawn the conclusion that he had been supplying his informants since 1973 out of the air.

And while one of the dealers he had spoken to was indeed in Oregon while the other was in California, Gervacio was only too well aware that both men had shared a cell in Washington for several weeks before being transferred out.

Furthermore, one of the dealers would later claim that he never implicated Thanong while talking to Gervacio and the other would deny knowing anything about the container method that Thanong was supposed to have pioneered. At the time they were questioned, both dealers could have been rewarded with significant reductions in their jail time for giving up Thanong as a source but neither had done so.

As for the reports from other agents that reached similar conclusions, there simply weren't any. However, other agents had conducted a series of interview with witnesses – the same witnesses Gervacio claimed to have spoken to first-hand when all he really did was read the other agents' reports.

Everything he knew about Thanong, Gervacio had learned second-or third-hand from his informants. Although he was the case agent and specialised in undercover work, he had not participated in any covert activity in connection with the Thanong investigation.

Unaware of these facts and with no reason to doubt the evidence they had heard, the grand jury came back with an indictment on all the charges. For the San Francisco Attorney's office, the first obstacle in the battle to bring Thanong to justice had been overcome.

For US officials, the snag was bringing Thanong to San Francisco to stand trial. An internal US Customs report, written in late 1995, cited State Department memos outlining the Thai government's 'adamant refusals to consider' extradition because it was viewed 'as an affront to the sovereignty and national pride of Thailand.'

Federal agents first moved on Thanong in 1992 by seizing a Beverly Hills mansion he owned, as well as a Mercedes-Benz. But the case did not become public until 1994, when the sealed indictment was revealed to the Thai press at a time when the Thai government was in a constitutional crisis.

Thanong was then a member of the opposition party, under attack for its links to voter fraud and drug trafficking. When the United States moved to extradite Thanong, political opponents seized on the issue. He became the target of a probe in parliament, according to court records and Thai press accounts.

He resigned shortly after the drug case against him became public. From the start, he depicted himself as a victim of political foes and a pawn in US efforts to use economic pressure to win Thai cooperation with its drug war.

'His visibility was important,' said Herbert Phillips, a leading Thai expert and retired University of California-Berkeley professor. 'The whole business of Tony being extradited had to do with political machinations in Thailand. Tony was viewed as somebody expendable.'

Thanong maintained his riches came from a flourishing real estate business that included one of Thailand's major hotel chains. But US officials insist the wealth was connected largely to the drug trade. In January 1996, after losing appeals in the Thai courts, Thanong was placed on a Northwest Airlines flight to San Francisco to face the federal indictment.

The Bangkok government had never before extradited one of its citizens to the US and even the then Attorney General Janet Reno made a point of praising the country for its cooperation in the capture of the flamboyant peasant turned politician.

By the following spring, Thanong appeared ready to concede defeat and enter a plea deal with prosecutors. The deal: plead guilty in exchange for a prison term ranging from thirteen to twenty years.

At the time, Assistant US Attorney John Lyons, the lead prosecutor in the case, issued a warning letter to Thanong's lawyers. 'Let me make myself clear,' he wrote. 'If this matter does go to trial, I intend to seek mandatory life imprisonment of Thanong after conviction.'

The case looked headed for a satisfactory conclusion for the government. But Lyons, when he wrote the warning letter, had been keeping a secret throughout plea negotiations: the Gervacio investigation.

Gervacio had come forward to his bosses in the US Customs Service in September 1996 and disclosed that he accepted $4,000 from his informant Michael Woods in 1992. Woods had also given the agent a $100 pair of running shoes.

Gervacio, full of despair and worried the $4,000 he eventually spent on clothes for his daughter would jeopardise the Thanong case, confessed to former San Francisco Customs chief Rollin Klink.

'What I received from Mr. Woods was of an innocent nature and not a bribe,' Gervacio said in a letter to Klink. 'I have been carrying this misjudgement and guilt with me for five years where I am now at the point of having to reach out for help. I am greatly ashamed and embarrassed to have done something like this.'

But as the lead agent in the Thanong case, credibility was crucial. He was the only government witness to testify before the federal grand jury that indicted Thanong and the Thai government had relied heavily on his testimony when deciding whether or not to extradite Thanong.

Lyons was told in September 1996 about Gervacio's admission but did not disclose it to the judge in the case until June 1997. During that time, the veteran prosecutor was not only negotiating the plea deal but also defending Gervacio's credibility against defence claims the agent had misrepresented facts in the extradition.

Gervacio's admission may have remained secret, but Thanong had second thoughts about his plea deal. After firing his original defence team in June 1997, he decided to go to trial. At that point, Lyons came forward and told all he knew about Gervacio to Judge Walker, who then made the information public.

But Gervacio's predicament looked set to produce a result impossible to foresee when the case began years earlier: that the law enforcement agent goes to jail while the accused smuggler goes free.

In June 1999 Thanong pleaded guilty to one single count of conspiring to smuggle marijuana into the United States. All the remaining charges against him were dropped and after three and a half years in prison, he was allowed to go home. Gervacio was jailed for a year and lost his job.

The case that should have been the crowning achievement in the US government's fight against the Thai marijuana trade had ended with the chief suspect being cleared of virtually all the charges against him. Not only that, but the agent who had been responsible for bringing the case to court had ended up in prison.

What had started out as the greatest triumph in the battle against The Ring had ended up as the greatest disaster instead.

EPILOGUE

By the summer of 2001, thirteen years after the *Encounter Bay* was captured and the Shaffer Brothers were identified as major players in the Thai marijuana smuggling business, the Seattle office of the US Attorney had overseen more than seventy-five arrests and sixty convictions.

Mark Bartlett, now elevated to the number two position, had gained the respect of his colleagues throughout Washington State and beyond for his hard work and dedication in pursuing all those involved. The cases he had helped to put together had been so solid that almost all the fugitives had chosen to give up life on the run and ultimately hand themselves in.

Fran Dyer, Graham Saltmarsh and Peter Mueller – members of the original law enforcement team that had helped bring down Daniels and the others – had all retired from active service, safe in the knowledge that all the fugitives and suspects they had indicted had been brought to justice.

All but one.

Irwin 'Sonny' Kletter had been identified thanks to his small role in a commercial for an artificial sweetener and had been indicted in Seattle shortly afterwards, though the authorities were unable to track him down. In 1995 he picked up another indictment in Denver, Colorado where local investigators discovered he had set up a money laundering and drug distribution network. They too failed to make an arrest.

DEA agents reported sightings of Kletter everywhere from Canada to the Caribbean but when it came to solid information about an actual address or location, Kletter seemed to have vanished off the face of the earth.

In reality, he had simply switched products. Although marijuana supplies from Thailand had long dried up, for the past thirteen years this affable, slightly rotund man had been the main vein in the drug supply chain to New York City, arranging and facilitating the trafficking of tons of high-grade Mexican cannabis into the area.

The drugs were smuggled into the US across the Mexican border using specially converted pick-up trucks loaded with new furniture and fresh vegetables. Occasionally, in an effort to frustrate law enforcement surveillance teams, the couriers would switch techniques and load the drugs onto the backs of donkeys. The animals would then be led out to remote parts of the desert, and come across the border that way.

Once inside the US, the drugs were taken to warehouses in Texas, Arizona and Southern California that were equipped with special machines to compact the drugs into vacuum-sealed brick-sized blocks. The smugglers even used a system of sophisticated bar codes that were stamped on the packaging to ensure shipments were always sent out while they were fresh.

'Every few weeks I would fly down to Texas or Southern California and shop through multi-ton loads of high quality cannabis, hand-picking the stuff I wanted to purchase. It was just like buying meat in a supermarket,' says Sonny. 'The buys would then be delivered to my network of warehouses in Brooklyn and Long Island and I'd take care of the distribution to street dealers from there.'

Kletter had been buying in bulk from a major supplier and doing most of the work himself, but when things got too hot for him he decided to move underground. He got in touch with an up-and-coming smuggler named Gary Winkel and swiftly reached an agreement that suited them both.

Kletter would give Winkel access to his contacts and supply

network to enable him to move large amounts of marijuana. In return, Winkel would pay Kletter $25 for every pound of marijuana that he handled, thus allowing Kletter to continue living a well-financed lifestyle while maintaining the lowest possible profile.

The pair would meet on a regular basis so that they could establish new lines of covert communication, or so that Winkel could hand over the cash payments that Kletter hoped would enable him to stay on the run indefinitely.

But the net began to close in during the late nineties when authorities in New York launched a task force aimed specifically at multi-ton marijuana and hashish smugglers and distributors bringing in the drugs from Thailand, Pakistan and Mexico.

The task force consisted of agents from the DEA, US Customs, US Marshals, the Internal Revenue Service and members of the Nassau and Suffolk County Police Departments, all coordinated by the Nassau and Suffolk County District Attorney's office. Within three years more than one hundred men and women fitting this profile had been identified or arrested and tens of millions of dollars worth of property and drug money had been confiscated.

US Attorney Burton Ryan, the man in charge of many of the prosecutions, fixed a huge chart to his wall showing all the people under investigation, the countries where they were based, where they sourced their drugs from and their role in the business. Some of the names were new to law enforcement, others – including the likes of Thanong Siripreechapong – were familiar to investigators on the West Coast.

As the months went by more and more evidence was gathered, more indictments were issued and more and more names were crossed off the chart. But Irwin Kletter remained at large.

Then an informant linked to the task force told his handler about the connection between Kletter and Winkel – already a target for the investigators – and at last the authorities believed they had a way to track Kletter down.

In early August a secret indictment was issued against Kletter and, three days later, a check of the phone records of some of his former associates revealed a series of calls to a condominium in Pompano Beach, Florida.

He had been living there for less than a month under a false name, and was grabbed by a dozen agents just as he was leaving home. 'You guys almost gave me a heart attack,' he said as they took him into custody.

Kletter, who had once handed over suitcases containing millions of dollars, claimed to have fallen on hard times but was still in possession of gems worth more than $50,000, artwork valued at $170,000 and stock certificates worth $75,000.

Kletter's arrest marked the final chapter of Assistant US Attorney Mark Bartlett's 15-year investigation into the pot-smuggling activities of Brian Daniels, the Shaffer brothers and the rest of The Ring.

In total the members of The Ring had collectively smuggled marijuana worth more than $1 billion and made tens of millions of dollars of profits. But like Kletter, in the end, few of them had much left to show for it.

On 26 January 2007 at the main courthouse in Islip, Long Island, the final piece of the fifteen-year-old jigsaw puzzle was put in place.

Having pleaded guilty at an earlier hearing, Irwin 'Sonny' Kletter appeared before Judge Thomas Stahl in order to be sentenced on charges of conspiracy to import cannabis and money laundering.

'I want to say how sorry I am for all the pain and suffering I have caused my family over the years,' Kletter told the court. He explained that, although he had been a fugitive from justice for many years, his involvement in smuggling had ended several years earlier as new, younger and more violent gangs made an appearance on the criminal scene and any influence he might once have had faded away to nothing.

'I'm an old man. I just want to go and do my time quietly so that I can come out and start my life over again.'

WHERE THEY ARE NOW

MARK BARTLETT
Now the number two in the Washington US Attorney's office.

BRIAN DANIELS
Incarcerated in California. Still serving his sentence, having exhausted a lengthy series of appeals. His projected release date is 5 May 2010.

BRIAN DEGEN
Long-time friend of Ciro Mancuso and his partner in crime during the early days of the smuggling empire. Degen, who holds joint Swiss/US nationality, fled to Switzerland shortly after being indicted. As the Swiss will not extradite their own citizens to the US, he has remained there ever since. In his absence, the US government seized his assets, which amounted to more than $3 million worth of property and other goods.

MICHAEL FORWELL
Released from federal prison in 1999 under the international prisoner exchange programme. Current whereabouts unknown.

PATRICK HALLINAN
Has returned to running a thriving practice in San Francisco. Despite turning seventy in 2006, he shows no sign of planning to retire.

WILLIAM LaMORTE
Remains incarcerated in a Federal Correctional Institution in New Jersey. LaMorte had the last in a long series of appeals against his conviction and sentence refused in 2005. His projected release date is 25 March 2019.

DENNIS INGHAM
Recaptured a few weeks after his dramatic prison escape, Ingham was subsequently convicted on numerous drug charges stemming from at least three states. Ingham served 78 months and managed to remain out of trouble until 2003 when investigators discovered he was leading a new plot to import marijuana from Canada. He planned to use the profits from the job to set up a larger operation bringing in tons of the drug from war-torn Iraq. Now 64, he was convicted again in 2005 and is currently incarcerated in federal prison with a projected release date of May 2012.

CIRO MANCUSO
Was released in 2000 and has since returned to the Squaw Valley area. He maintains a particularly close relationship with his middle daughter, Julia, who took out her anger and frustration at his arrest by spending increasing amounts of time on the ski slopes.

At the 2006 Winter Olympics in Torino, Italy, Julia won the gold medal in the Giant Slalom. Her father was in the crowd cheering her to victory waving a 'Super Jules' flag.

BRIAN O'DEA
Released from prison in 2001. Now a highly successful television producer in Toronto, Canada. Wrote a biography *High: Confessions of a Pot Smuggler*, which was published in Canada in April 2006. A film adaptation is said to be in the works.

EDWARD OTERO
Sells air-conditioning units in Nevada.

GRAHAM SALTMARSH
Now an art-theft consultant.

WILLIAM AND CHRISTOPHER SHAFFER
Released from prison in 1998, the brothers are now working together once more, having launched their own entertainment

company in Santa Monica. In 1999 they allegedly sold the film rights to their story for $1 million. Brad Pitt was lined up to play Bill Shaffer and the project, provisionally titled *Smugglers Moon*, was due to begin filming immediately after *Ocean's Eleven*. The film has, however, stalled at the development stage and no progress has been made since the original announcement.

HANK SHEPPARD
Went to ground immediately after the ill-fated DEA operation against the Shaffer brothers, and broke all contact with members of The Ring. Now believed to be living under a new identity with the help of the federal Witness Protection Programme.

THANONG 'THAI TONY' SIRIPREECHAPONG
Returned to Thailand after his release and attempted to re-enter politics. On 15 December 2003 Thanong met with three men on the outskirts of Bangkok to settle a debt problem. The meeting did not go well and two of the men began beating Thanong. Upset, the former MP fetched a pistol from his car and fired at one of the men, fifty-five-year-old Wallop Supapornpasuphat, hitting him four times. Thanong then drove off.

Wallop sustained gunshot wounds to his right shoulder, two in his right upper chest and one in his left arm, and was rushed to hospital. Four days later, Thanong presented himself to police, driving to the station in his brand new BMW. He was charged with attempted murder but released on bail. He was ordered to surrender his licensed .38 pistol.

STEPHEN SWANSON
The crooked former DEA agent who had first assisted Dennis Ingham in remaining one step ahead of the authorities, and later proved crucial in allowing the Shaffer brothers to avoid the DEA while importing their last marijuana load. Swanson's double-dealings finally caught up with him in 1997 when authorities in Florida charged him with racketeering and money laundering in

connection with a ring that smuggled hashish and marijuana into the United States. Swanson claimed that he was working for the government at the time and had done nothing wrong. He went on trial in April 2000. At the end of the closing arguments Swanson, who was on bail, borrowed a car from his lawyer, drove out to the nearest interstate, parked on the roadside and then walked into the path of an oncoming lorry. He was 56.